ON FREUD'S
"FORMULATIONS ON THE TWO PRINCIPLES OF MENTAL FUNCTIONING"

CONTEMPORARY FREUD
Turning Points and Critical Issues

Series Editor: Gennaro Saragnano

IPA Publications Committee

Gennaro Saragnano (Rome), Chair; Leticia Glocer Fiorini (Buenos Aires), Consultant; Samuel Arbiser (Buenos Aires); Paulo Cesar Sandler (São Paulo); Christian Seulin (Lyon); Mary Kay O'Neil (Montreal); Gail S Reed (New York); Catalina Bronstein (London); Rhoda Bawdekar (London), ex-officio as Publications Officer; Paul Crake (London), IPA Executive Director (ex officio)

On Freud's "Group Psychology and the Analysis of the Ego"
   edited by Ethel Spector Person

On Freud's "Mourning and Melancholia"
   edited by Leticia Glocer Fiorini, Thierry Bokanowski, Sergio Lewkowicz

On Freud's "The Future of an Illusion"
   edited by Mary Kay O'Neil and Salman Akhtar

On Freud's "Splitting of the Ego in the Process of Defence"
   edited by Thierry Bokanowski and Sergio Lewkowicz

On Freud's "Femininity"
   edited by Leticia Glocer Fiorini and Graciela Abelin-Sas

On Freud's "Constructions in Analysis"
   edited by Thierry Bokanowski and Sergio Lewkowicz

On Freud's "Beyond the Pleasure Principle"
   edited by Salman Akhtar and Mary Kay O'Neil

On Freud's "Negation"
   edited by Mary Kay O'Neil and Salman Akhtar

On Freud's "On Beginning the Treatment"
   edited by Christian Seulin and Gennaro Saragnano

On Freud's "On Narcissism: An Introduction"
   edited by Joseph Sandler, Ethel Spector Person, Peter Fonagy

On Freud's "Inhibitions, Symptoms and Anxiety"
   edited by Samuel Arbiser and Jorge Schneider

On Freud's "Observations on Transference-Love"
   edited by Ethel Spector Person, Aiban Hagelin, Peter Fonagy

On Freud's "Creative Writers and Day-Dreaming"
   edited by Ethel Spector Person, Peter Fonagy, Sérvulo Augusto Figueira

On Freud's "A Child Is Being Beaten"
   edited by Ethel Spector Person

On Freud's "Analysis Terminable and Interminable"
   edited by Joseph Sandler

On Freud's "The Unconscious"
   edited by Salman Akhtar and Mary Kay O'Neil

On Freud's "Screen Memories"
   edited by Gail S. Reed and Howard B. Levine

ON FREUD'S "FORMULATIONS ON THE TWO PRINCIPLES OF MENTAL FUNCTIONING"

Edited by
Gabriela Legorreta and Lawrence J. Brown

Series Editor
Gennaro Saragnano

CONTEMPORARY FREUD
Turning Points and Critical Issues

KARNAC

First published in 2016 by
Karnac Books Ltd
118 Finchley Road
London NW3 5HT

Copyright © 2016 to Gabriela Legoretta and Lawrence J. Brown for the edited collection, and to the individual authors for their contributions.

The rights of the contributors to be identified as the authors of this work have been asserted in accordance with §77 and 78 of the Copyright Design and Patents Act 1988.

All rights reserved. No part of this publication may be reproduced, stored in a retrieval system, or transmitted, in any form or by any means, electronic, mechanical, photocopying, recording, or otherwise, without the prior written permission of the publisher.

British Library Cataloguing in Publication Data

A C.I.P. for this book is available from the British Library

ISBN 978-1-78220-302-5

Edited, designed and produced by The Studio Publishing Services Ltd
www.publishingservicesuk.co.uk
e-mail: studio@publishingservicesuk.co.uk

Printed in Great Britain by TJ International Ltd, Padstow, Cornwall

www.karnacbooks.com

CONTENTS

CONTEMPORARY FREUD
    IPA Publications Committee   viii

ACKNOWLEDGEMENTS   x

EDITORS AND CONTRIBUTORS   xi

PART I
"Formulations on the two principles of mental functioning" (1911b)
    Sigmund Freud   1

PART II
Discussion of
"Formulations on the two principles of mental functioning"   15

Editors' introduction to Chapter One   17

1   Filling in Freud and Klein's maps of psychotic states of mind: Wilfred Bion's reading of Freud's "Formulations regarding two principles in mental functioning"
    Joseph Aguayo   19

Editors' introduction to Chapter Two 36

2   The world as it is *vs*. the world as I would like it to be: contemporary reflections on Freud's "Formulations on the two principles of mental functioning"
    David Bell 39

Editors' introduction to Chapter Three 65

3   Second thoughts on Freud's "Two principles"
    Fred Busch 67

Editors' introduction to Chapter Four 83

4   Dreaming the analytical session: between pleasure principle and reality principle
    Roosevelt M. S. Cassorla 85

Editors' introduction to Chapter Five 105

5   Where does the reality principle begin? The work of margins in Freud's "Formulations on the two principles of mental functioning"
    Giuseppe Civitarese 107

Editors' introduction to Chapter Six 126

6   Freud's "Formulations on the two principles of mental functioning": its roots and development
    Antonino Ferro 129

Editors' introduction to Chapter Seven 148

7   Two principles and the possibility of emotional growth
    Howard B. Levine 151

Editors' introduction to Chapter Eight 165

8   Time is short
    Jacques Mauger 168

Editors' introduction to Chapter Nine	182
9 The quest for the real *Juan Tubert-Oklander*	185
Editors' introduction to Chapter Ten	201
10 Mental functioning and free thinking *Susann Heenen-Wolff*	204
11 Concluding thoughts *Lawrence J. Brown and Gabriela Legorreta*	221
REFERENCES	239
INDEX	255

CONTEMPORARY FREUD

IPA Publications Committee

This significant series was founded by Robert Wallerstein and subsequently edited by Joseph Sandler, Ethel Spector Person, Peter Fonagy, and lately by Leticia Glocer Fiorini. Its important contributions have always greatly interested psychoanalysts of different latitudes. It is therefore my great honour, as the new Chair of the Publications Committee of the International Psychoanalytical Association, to continue the tradition of this most successful series.

The objective of this series is to approach Freud's work from a present and contemporary point of view. On the one hand, this means highlighting the fundamental contributions of his work that constitute the axes of psychoanalytic theory and practice. On the other, it implies the possibility of getting to know and spreading the ideas of present psychoanalysts about Freud's *oeuvre*, both where they coincide and where they differ.

This series considers at least two lines of development: a contemporary reading of Freud that reclaims his contributions and a clarification of the logical and epistemic perspectives from which he is read today.

Freud's theory has branched out, and this has led to a theoretical, technical, and clinical pluralism that has to be worked through. It has therefore become necessary to avoid a snug and uncritical coexistence of concepts in order to consider systems of increasing complexities that take into account both the convergences and the divergences of the categories at play.

Consequently, this project has involved an additional task—that is, gathering psychoanalysts from different geographical regions representing, in addition, different theoretical stances, in order to be able to show their polyphony. This also means an extra effort for the reader that has to do with distinguishing and discriminating, establishing relations or contradictions that each reader will have to eventually work through.

Being able to listen to other theoretical viewpoints is also a way of exercising our listening capacities in the clinical field. This means that the listening should support a space of freedom that would allow us to hear what is new and original.

In this spirit we have brought together authors deeply rooted in the Freudian tradition and others who have developed theories that had not been explicitly taken into account in Freud's work.

"Formulations on the two principles of mental functioning", written in 1911, is one of Freud's most important theoretical writings. As brief as rich of contents, it describes the fundamental difference between primary and secondary processes, and between pleasure and reality principles, as well as the difficulties in the passage from the former to the latter. A number of basic theoretical implications come from this conceptualisation: the development of attention and memory, the origin of fantasy and reality testing, the role of education and art, a widening of the theory of neurosis and of unconscious functioning, and many others.

Gabriela Legorreta and Lawrence J. Brown have brilliantly edited this new volume which enriches the "Contemporary Freud. Turning points and critical issues" series. They have asked ten eminent and well distinguished colleagues to discuss and put Freud's ideas in the light of contemporary psychoanalytic thinking. The result is this important book, which will surely encounter the favour of every psychoanalytic student as well as of general people interested in the complexity of mental life. So many thanks to the editors and contributors of this brand-new volume that continues the tradition of this successful IPA book series.

Gennaro Saragnano
Series Editor
Chair, IPA Publications Committee

ACKNOWLEDGEMENTS

The editors wish to thank our ten contributors for their thoughtful and creative contributions, the members of the IPA Publications Committee and, lastly, Sigmund Freud for bestowing on us this wonderful paper. "Two principles" offers a timeless reflection of the nature of human psyche that is still very relevant to contemporary psychoanalytic theory and practice.

EDITORS AND CONTRIBUTORS

Joseph Aguayo is a training and supervising analyst at Psychoanalytic Center of California in private practice in West Los Angeles. He is also a Guest Member of the British Psychoanalytical Society in London. He holds UCLA doctorates in both Clinical Psychology and European History. He has been awarded a number of research fellowships from the IPA's Research Advisory Board and has merged his clinical and research interests by numerous publications in the *International Journal of Psychoanalysis* on the clinical history of Kleinian and Bionian psychoanalysis. His current book is a co-edited project with Barnet Malin: *Bion's Los Angeles Seminars and Supervision* (Karnac, 2013). His most recent publication: "Bion's notes on memory and desire—its initial clinical reception in the United States: a note on archival material" (*International Journal of Psychoanalysis*, 95(5): 889–910, 2014).

David Bell is a training and supervising psychoanalyst of the British Psychoanalytic Society of which he is a past President. He is a consultant psychiatrist in the Adult Dept. of the Tavistock where he directs a specialist unit for serious/complex psychological disorders. In 2012–2013 he was Visiting Professorial Fellow at Birkbeck College

London. His writing and lecturing interests include the development of psychoanalytic concepts, psychosis, personality disorder, suicide, and trauma. Throughout his professional career he has been deeply involved in the relation between psychoanalysis and other disciplines: literature, philosophy, culture, and socio-political issues and has published in these areas. He is one of the UK's leading psychiatric experts in asylum and human rights. Publications include *Paranoia*, *Psychoanalysis and Culture*, *Reason and Passion*, and *Living on the Border*.

Lawrence J. Brown, co-editor of this book, is a graduate of the Boston Psychoanalytic Institute (BPSI) in both child and adult psychoanalysis and is a supervising child analyst there. He is also on the faculty of BPSI and the Massachusetts Institute for Psychoanalysis. He has served on the Editorial Boards of the *International Journal of Psychoanalysis* and the *Psychoanalytic Quarterly*. Dr Brown is President of the Boston Group for Psychoanalytic Studies and was co-chair (with Howard Levine) of the Bion in Boston International Conference held in July, 2009. His book, *Intersubjective Processes and the Unconscious: An Integration of Freudian, Kleinian and Bionian Perspectives*, was published by Routledge Press in early 2011 and another book, co-edited with Dr Howard Levine, *Growth and Turbulence in the Container/Contained*, was published by Routledge in 2013. He is currently writing a book, *Contemporary Psychoanalysis: The Theory and Technique of Transformations*, to be published by IPA Publications/Karnac. He is also the author of many papers covering such topics as countertransference, trauma, the Oedipus complex, and dreaming.

Fred Busch is a training and supervising analyst at the Boston Psychoanalytic Society and Institute, a geographical supervising analyst of the Minnesota Psychoanalytic Institute, and a visiting supervisor at the Vermont Psychoanalytic Institute. His third book, *Creating a Psychoanalytic Mind: A Method and Theory of Psychoanalysis*, was published by Routledge in 2013.

Roosevelt M. S. Cassorla, MD, PhD is psychoanalyst in private practice in Campinas, Brazil and titular member and training analyst of the Campinas Psychoanalytic Study Group and Brazilian Psychoanalytic Society of São Paulo. He has worked as full professor at the Psychiatry and Psychological Medicine Department, State University of Campinas and the Postgraduation Course of Mental Health. He is member of the Editorial Board of the *International Journal of Psychoanalysis*. He has edited three books on suicide and death and is author of a number of book chapters and papers on psychoanalysis and medical psychology. His recent papers refer to analytical technique and borderline configurations.

Giuseppe Civitarese is a training and supervising analyst in the Italian Psychoanalytic Society (SPI), and a member of the American Psychoanalytic Association (APsaA) and of the International Psychoanalytical Association (IPA). He lives, and is in private practice, in Pavia, Italy. Currently he is the editor of the *Rivista di Psicoanalisi*, the official journal of the Italian Psychoanalytic Society. He has published several books, which include: *The Intimate Room: Theory and Technique of the Analytic Field*, Routledge, 2010; *The Violence of Emotions: Bion and Post-Bionian Psychoanalysis*, Routledge, 2012; *The Necessary Dream: New Theories and Techniques of Interpretation in Psychoanalysis*, Karnac, 2014; *Losing your Head: Abjection, Aesthetic Conflict and Psychoanalytic Criticism*, London, 2015; *The Analytic Field and its Transformations* (with A. Ferro), Karnac, 2015; *Truth and the Unconscious in Psychoanalysis*, Routledge, 2016. He has also co-edited (with V. Egidi) *L'ipocondria e il dubbio: L'approccio psicoanalitico* [Hypochondria and Doubt: the Psychoanalytic Approach], FrancoAngeli, 2011; (with G. De Giorgio) *Le parole e i sogni* [The Words and the Dreams], Alpes, 2015, and (with H. Levine) *The Bion Tradition*, Karnac, 2015.

Antonino Ferro is President of the Italian Psychoanalytic Society and also Consultant Associate Editor of the *International Journal of Psychoanalysis*. He is a training and supervising analyst in the Italian Psychoanalytic Society, the American Psychoanalytic Association, and the International Psychoanalytical Association. He has been a visiting professor of psychoanalysis in various institutions in Europe, North America, South America, and Australia. He received the Sigourney Award in 2007.

Susann Heenen-Wolff, is a training analyst at the Belgian Society of Psychoanalysis (Brussels) and Professor of Clinical Psychology at the University of Louvain (UCL), Belgium. She conducted a research project on the long term effects of trauma in former hidden Jewish children and got in 2009 the Hayman Prize of the IPA for one of the respective papers. She has published many articles and books in German, French, and English. Presently she works on epistemological problems in psychoanalysis.

Gabriela Legorreta, co-editor of this book, is a training and supervising analyst at the Montreal Psychoanalytic Society (French section of the Canadian Psychoanalytic Society) and is in private practice in Montreal. She is a teacher and supervisor at the Argyle Institute of Human Relationships and is the Chair of the Psychoanalytic Bridges with Latin America study group. She is also in charge of the Spanish section of the Advisory Committee on Foreign Language Book reviews of the *Journal of the American Psychoanalytic Association*. She is a member of the Group of Study for the Psychoanalytic Process, the consultant for the Montreal Fertility Centre and a member of the Publication's Committee of the IPA.

Howard B. Levine is on the faculty at the Psychoanalytic Institute of New England East (PINE), on the Editorial Board of the *IJP* and *Psychoanalytic Inquiry*, on the Board of Directors of the International Psychoanalytical Association and in private practice in Brookline, Massachusetts, He is a founding member of the Group for the Study of Psychoanalytic Process (GSPP) and The Boston Group for Psychoanalytic Studies, Inc. (BGPS), has authored numerous articles, book chapters, and reviews on psychoanalytic process and technique, intersubjectivity, the treatment of primitive personality disorders, and the consequences and treatment of early trauma and childhood sexual abuse. He is the editor of *Adult Analysis and Childhood Sexual Abuse* (Analytic Press, 1990), co-editor (with Lawrence Brown) of *Growth and Turbulence in the Container/Contained* (Routledge, 2013), (with Gail Reed and Dominique Scarfone) of *Unrepresented States and the Construction of Meaning* (Karnac, 2013), (with Gail Reed) *Responses to Freud's Screen Memories Paper* (Karnac, 2014), (with Giuseppe Civitarese) *The W. R. Bion Tradition* (Karnac, 2015), and (with Jose Junqueira de Mattos and Gisele Brito) *Bion in Brazil* (forthcoming).

Editors and contributors

Jacques Mauger is a French-speaking psychoanalyst member of the Montreal Psychoanalytic Society (French section of the Canadian Psychoanalytic Society) and of the Montreal Psychoanalytic Institute. He is a training and supervising analyst. He has published many articles in different psychoanalytic journals.

Juan Tubert-Oklander, MD, PhD was born, studied medicine, and trained as a group therapist in Buenos Aires, Argentina. He lives and works in private practice in Mexico City since 1976, where he trained as a psychoanalyst, being now a Mexican citizen. Author of numerous papers and book chapters, published in Spanish, English, Italian, French, Portuguese, Czech, and Hebrew. Co-author, with Reyna Hernández-Tubert, of *Operative Groups: The Latin-American Approach to Group Analysis* (Jessica Kingsley, 2004), author of *Theory of Psychoanalytical Practice: A Relational Process Approach* (IPA/Karnac, 2013), and *The One and the Many: Relational Psychoanalysis and Group Analysis* (Karnac, 2014). He is a full member of the Mexican Psychoanalytic Association, the Argentine Psychoanalytic Association, and the Group-Analytic Society International and a training and supervising analyst at the Institute of the Mexican Psychoanalytic Association.

PART I

"Formulations on the two principles of mental functioning" (1911b)

Sigmund Freud

EDITOR'S NOTE

FORMULIERUNGEN ÜBER DIE ZWEI PRINZIPIEN DES PSYCHISCHEN GESCHEHENS

(*a*) German Editions:

1911   *Jb. psychoan. psychopath. Forsch.*, **3** (1), 1–8.
1913   *S.K.S.N.*, **3**, 271–9.
1924   *G.S.*, **5**, 409–17.
1931   *Theoretische Schriften*, 5–14.
1943   *G.W.*, **8**, 230–8.

(*b*) English Translation:
'Formulations Regarding the Two Principles in Mental Functioning'
1925   *C.P.*, **4**, 13–21. (Tr. M. N. Searl.)

The present translation, with a modified title, is based on the one published in 1925, but has been largely re-written.

We learn from Dr. Ernest Jones that Freud began planning this paper in June, 1910, and was working at it simultaneously with the Schreber case history (1911*c*). His progress at it was slow, but on October 26 he spoke on the subject before the Vienna Psycho-Analytical Society, but found the audience unresponsive, and was himself dissatisfied with his presentation. It was not until December that he actually began writing the paper. It was finished at the end of January, 1911, but was not published till late in the spring, when it appeared in the same issue of the *Jahrbuch* as the Schreber case.

With this well-known paper, which is one of the classics of psycho-analysis, and with the almost contemporary third section of the Schreber case history, Freud, for the first time after an interval of more than ten years, took up once again a discussion of the general theoretical hypotheses which were implied by his clinical findings. His first extensive attempt at such a discussion

216   TWO PRINCIPLES OF MENTAL FUNCTIONING

had been in quasi-neurological terminology in his 'Project for a Scientific Psychology' of 1895, which, however, was not published in his lifetime (Freud, 1950*a*). Chapter VII of *The Interpretation of Dreams* (1900*a*) was an exposition of a very similar set of hypotheses, but this time in purely psychological terms. Much of the material in the present paper (and especially in its earlier part) is derived directly from these two sources. The work gives the impression of being in the nature of a stock-taking. It is as though Freud were bringing up for his own inspection, as it were, the fundamental hypotheses of an earlier period, and preparing them to serve as a basis for the major theoretical discussions which lay ahead in the immediate future—the paper on narcissism, for instance, and the great series of metapsychological papers.

The present exposition of his views is exceedingly condensed and is not easy to assimilate even to-day. Although we know now that Freud was saying very little in it that had not long been present in his mind, at the time of its publication it must have struck its readers as bewilderingly full of novelties. The paragraphs marked (1), for instance, on p. 219 ff., would be obscure indeed to those who could have no acquaintance either with the 'Project' or with the metapsychological papers and who would have to derive what light they could from a number of almost equally condensed and quite unsystematized passages in *The Interpretation of Dreams*. It is scarcely surprising that Freud's first audience was unresponsive.

The main theme of the work is the distinction between the regulating principles (the pleasure principle and the reality principle) which respectively dominate the primary and secondary mental processes. The thesis had in fact already been stated in Section 1 of Part I of the 'Project' and elaborated in Sections 15 and 16 of Part I and in the later portions of Section 1 of Part III. It was again discussed in Chapter VII of *The Interpretation of Dreams* (*Standard Ed.*, **5**, 565–7 and 598 ff.). But the fullest treatment was reserved for the paper on the metapsychology of dreams (1917*d* [1915]), written some three years after this one. A more detailed account of the development of Freud's views on the subject of our mental attitude towards reality will be found in the Editor's Note to that paper (*Standard Ed.*, **14**, 219 ff.).

Towards the end of the work a number of other related

topics are opened up, the further development of which (like that of the main theme) is left over for later investigation. The whole paper was, in fact (as Freud himself remarks), of a preparatory and exploratory nature, but it is not on that account of any less interest.

The greater part of this paper, in the 1925 version, was included in Rickman's *General Selection from the Works of Sigmund Freud* (1937, 45–53).

FORMULATIONS ON THE TWO PRINCIPLES OF MENTAL FUNCTIONING

WE have long observed that every neurosis has as its result, and probably therefore as its purpose, a forcing of the patient out of real life, an alienating of him from reality.[1] Nor could a fact such as this escape the observation of Pierre Janet; he spoke of a loss of '*la fonction du réel*' ['the function of reality'] as being a special characteristic of neurotics, but without discovering the connection of this disturbance with the fundamental determinants of neurosis.[2] By introducing the process of repression into the genesis of the neuroses we have been able to gain some insight into this connection. Neurotics turn away from reality because they find it unbearable—either the whole or parts of it. The most extreme type of this turning away from reality is shown by certain cases of hallucinatory psychosis which seek to deny the particular event that occasioned the outbreak of their insanity (Griesinger).[3] But in fact every neurotic does the same with some fragment of reality.[4] And we are now confronted with the task of investigating the development of the relation of neurotics and of mankind in general to reality, and in this way of bringing the psychological significance of the real external world into the structure of our theories.

In the psychology which is founded on psycho-analysis we

---

[1] [The idea, with the phrase 'flight into psychosis', is already to be found in Section III of Freud's first paper on 'The Neuro-Psychoses of Defence' (1894*a*). The actual phrase 'flight into illness' occurs in Section B of his paper on hysterical attacks (1909*a*).]

[2] Janet, 1909.

[3] [W. Griesinger (1817–1868) was a well-known Berlin psychiatrist of an earlier generation, much admired by Freud's teacher, Meynert. The passage alluded to in the text is no doubt the one mentioned by Freud three times in *The Interpretation of Dreams* (1900*a*), *Standard Ed.*, **4**, 91, 134 and 230 *n*., and again in Chapter VI of the book on jokes (1905*c*). In this passage Griesinger (1845, 89) drew attention to the wish-fulfilling character of both psychoses and dreams.]

[4] Otto Rank (1910) has recently drawn attention to a remarkably clear prevision of this causation shown in Schopenhauer's *The World as Will and Idea* [Part II (Supplements), Chapter 32].

have become accustomed to taking as our starting-point the unconscious mental processes, with the peculiarities of which we have become acquainted through analysis. We consider these to be the older, primary processes, the residues of a phase of development in which they were the only kind of mental process. The governing purpose obeyed by these primary processes is easy to recognize; it is described as the pleasure-unpleasure [*Lust-Unlust*] principle, or more shortly the pleasure principle.[1] These processes strive towards gaining pleasure; psychical activity draws back from any event which might arouse unpleasure. (Here we have repression.) Our dreams at night and our waking tendency to tear ourselves away from distressing impressions are remnants of the dominance of this principle and proofs of its power.

I shall be returning to lines of thought which I have developed elsewhere[2] when I suggest that the state of psychical rest was originally disturbed by the peremptory demands of internal needs. When this happened, whatever was thought of (wished for) was simply presented in a hallucinatory manner, just as still happens to-day with our dream-thoughts every night.[3] It was only the non-occurrence of the expected satisfaction, the disappointment experienced, that led to the abandonment of this attempt at satisfaction by means of hallucination. Instead of it, the psychical apparatus had to decide to form a conception of the real circumstances in the external world and to endeavour to make a real alteration in them. A new principle of mental functioning was thus introduced; what was presented in the mind was no longer what was agreeable but what was real, even if it happened to be disagreeable.[4] This setting-up of the *reality principle* proved to be a momentous step.

(1) In the first place, the new demands made a succession of

[1] [This seems to be the first appearance of the actual term 'pleasure principle'. In *The Interpretation of Dreams* it is always named the 'unpleasure principle' (e.g. *Standard Ed.*, 5, 600).]

[2] In the General Section of *The Interpretation of Dreams*. [I.e. in Chapter VII. See in particular *Standard Ed.*, 5, 565–7 and 598 ff. But what follows is for the most part also foreshadowed in the 'Project' of 1895. Cf., for instance, the end of Section 11 and Section 15 of Part I.]

[3] The state of sleep is able to re-establish the likeness of mental life as it was before the recognition of reality, because a prerequisite of sleep is a deliberate rejection of reality (the wish to sleep).

[4] I will try to amplify the above schematic account with some further

220 TWO PRINCIPLES OF MENTAL FUNCTIONING

adaptations necessary in the psychical apparatus, which, owing to our insufficient or uncertain knowledge, we can only retail very cursorily.

The increased significance of external reality heightened the importance, too, of the sense-organs that are directed towards that external world, and of the *consciousness* attached to them. Consciousness now learned to comprehend sensory qualities in addition to the qualities of pleasure and unpleasure which hitherto had alone been of interest to it. A special function was instituted which had periodically to search the external world, in order that its data might be familiar already if an urgent internal need should arise—the function of *attention*.[1] Its activity meets the sense-impressions half way, instead of awaiting their appearance. At the same time, probably, a system of *notation* was introduced, whose task it was to lay down the results of this

---

details. It will rightly be objected that an organization which was a slave to the pleasure principle and neglected the reality of the external world could not maintain itself alive for the shortest time, so that it could not have come into existence at all. The employment of a fiction like this is, however, justified when one considers that the infant—provided one includes with it the care it receives from its mother—does almost realize a psychical system of this kind. It probably hallucinates the fulfilment of its internal needs; it betrays its unpleasure, when there is an increase of stimulus and an absence of satisfaction, by the motor discharge of screaming and beating about with its arms and legs, and it then experiences the satisfaction it has hallucinated. Later, as an older child, it learns to employ these manifestations of discharge intentionally as methods of expressing its feelings. Since the later care of children is modelled on the care of infants, the dominance of the pleasure principle can really come to an end only when a child has achieved complete psychical detachment from its parents.—A neat example of a psychical system shut off from the stimuli of the external world, and able to satisfy even its nutritional requirements autistically (to use Bleuler's term [1912]), is afforded by a bird's egg with its food supply enclosed in its shell; for it, the care provided by its mother is limited to the provision of warmth.—I shall not regard it as a correction, but as an amplification of the schematic picture under discussion, if it is insisted that a system living according to the pleasure principle must have devices to enable it to withdraw from the stimuli of reality. Such devices are merely the correlative of 'repression', which treats internal unpleasurable stimuli as if they were external—that is to say, pushes them into the external world.

[1] [Some remarks on Freud's views about attention will be found in an Editor's footnote to the metapsychological paper on 'The Unconscious' (*Standard Ed.*, **14**, 192).]

periodical activity of consciousness—a part of what we call *memory*.

The place of repression, which excluded from cathexis as productive of unpleasure some of the emerging ideas, was taken by an *impartial passing of judgement*,[1] which had to decide whether a given idea was true or false—that is, whether it was in agreement with reality or not—the decision being determined by making a comparison with the memory-traces of reality.

A new function was now allotted to motor discharge, which, under the dominance of the pleasure principle, had served as a means of unburdening the mental apparatus of accretions of stimuli, and which had carried out this task by sending innervations into the interior of the body (leading to expressive movements and the play of features and to manifestations of affect). Motor discharge was now employed in the appropriate alteration of reality; it was converted into *action*.[2]

Restraint upon motor discharge (upon action), which then became necessary, was provided by means of the process of *thinking*, which was developed from the presentation of ideas. Thinking was endowed with characteristics which made it possible for the mental apparatus to tolerate an increased tension of stimulus while the process of discharge was postponed. It is essentially an experimental kind of acting, accompanied by displacement of relatively small quantities of cathexis together with less expenditure (discharge) of them.[3] For this purpose the conversion of freely displaceable cathexes into 'bound' cathexes was necessary, and this was brought about by means of raising the level of the whole cathectic process. It is probable that thinking was originally unconscious, in so far as it went beyond mere ideational presentations and was directed to the relations between impressions of objects, and that it did not acquire further qualities, perceptible to consciousness, until it became connected with verbal residues.[4]

[1] [This notion, often repeated by Freud, appears as early as in the first edition of his book on jokes (1905c, towards the end of Chapter VI) and is examined more deeply in his late paper on 'Negation' (1925h).]

[2] [Cf. 'Project', Part I, Section 11.]

[3] [Cf. 'Project', Part I, Section 18, and *The Interpretation of Dreams*, Standard Ed., 5, 599–600.]

[4] [Cf. 'Project', Part III, Section 1, and *The Interpretation of Dreams*, Standard Ed., 5, 574 and 617. This is developed further in Section VII of 'The Unconscious' (1915e).]

222   TWO PRINCIPLES OF MENTAL FUNCTIONING

(2) A general tendency of our mental apparatus, which can be traced back to the economic principle of saving expenditure [of energy], seems to find expression in the tenacity with which we hold on to the sources of pleasure at our disposal, and in the difficulty with which we renounce them. With the introduction of the reality principle one species of thought-activity was split off; it was kept free from reality-testing and remained subordinated to the pleasure principle alone.[1] This activity is *phantasying*, which begins already in children's play, and later, continued as *day-dreaming*, abandons dependence on real objects.

(3) The supersession of the pleasure principle by the reality principle, with all the psychical consequences involved, which is here schematically condensed into a single sentence, is not in fact accomplished all at once; nor does it take place simultaneously all along the line. For while this development is going on in the ego-instincts, the sexual instincts become detached from them in a very significant way. The sexual instincts behave auto-erotically at first; they obtain their satisfaction in the subject's own body and therefore do not find themselves in the situation of frustration which was what necessitated the institution of the reality principle; and when, later on, the process of finding an object begins, it is soon interrupted by the long period of latency, which delays sexual development until puberty. These two factors—auto-erotism and the latency period—have as their result that the sexual instinct is held up in its psychical development and remains far longer under the dominance of the pleasure principle, from which in many people it is never able to withdraw.

In consequence of these conditions, a closer connection arises, on the one hand, between the sexual instinct and phantasy and, on the other hand, between the ego-instincts and the activities of consciousness. Both in healthy and in neurotic people this connection strikes us as very intimate, although the considera-

---

[1] In the same way, a nation whose wealth rests on the exploitation of the produce of its soil will yet set aside certain areas for reservation in their original state and for protection from the changes brought about by civilization. (E.g. Yellowstone Park.) [Cf. the discussions of phantasies in 'Creative Writers and Day-Dreaming' (1908*e*) and in 'Hysterical Phantasies and their Relation to Bisexuality' (1908*a*). The term '*Realitätsprüfung*' seems to make its first appearance in this sentence.]

tions of genetic psychology which have just been put forward lead us to recognize it as a *secondary* one. The continuance of auto-erotism is what makes it possible to retain for so long the easier momentary and imaginary satisfaction in relation to the sexual object in place of real satisfaction, which calls for effort and postponement. In the realm of phantasy, repression remains all-powerful; it brings about the inhibition of ideas *in statu nascendi* before they can be noticed by consciousness, if their cathexis is likely to occasion a release of unpleasure. This is the weak spot in our psychical organization; and it can be employed to bring back under the dominance of the pleasure principle thought-processes which had already become rational. An essential part of the psychical disposition to neurosis thus lies in the delay in educating the sexual instincts to pay regard to reality and, as a corollary, in the conditions which make this delay possible.

(4) Just as the pleasure-ego can do nothing but *wish*, work for a yield of pleasure, and avoid unpleasure, so the reality-ego need do nothing but strive for what is *useful* and guard itself against damage.[1] Actually the substitution of the reality principle for the pleasure principle implies no deposing of the pleasure principle, but only a safeguarding of it. A momentary pleasure, uncertain in its results, is given up, but only in order to gain along the new path an assured pleasure at a later time. But the endopsychic impression made by this substitution has been so powerful that it is reflected in a special religious myth. The doctrine of reward in the after-life for the—voluntary or enforced—renunciation of earthly pleasures is nothing other than a mythical projection of this revolution in the mind. Following consistently along these lines, *religions* have been able to effect absolute renunciation of pleasure in this life by means of the promise of compensation in a future existence; but they have not by this means achieved a conquest of the pleasure principle. It is *science* which comes nearest to succeeding in that conquest;

[1] The superiority of the reality-ego over the pleasure-ego has been aptly expressed by Bernard Shaw in these words: 'To be able to choose the line of greatest advantage instead of yielding in the direction of least resistance.' (*Man and Superman.*) [A remark made by Don Juan towards the end of the Mozartean interlude in Act III.—A much more elaborate account of the relations between the 'pleasure-ego' and the 'reality-ego' is given in 'Instincts and their Vicissitudes' (1915c), *Standard Ed.*, **14**, 134–6.]

224   TWO PRINCIPLES OF MENTAL FUNCTIONING

science too, however, offers intellectual pleasure during its work and promises practical gain in the end.

(5) *Education* can be described without more ado as an incitement to the conquest of the pleasure principle, and to its replacement by the reality principle; it seeks, that is, to lend its help to the developmental process which affects the ego. To this end it makes use of an offer of love as a reward from the educators; and it therefore fails if a spoilt child thinks that it possesses that love in any case and cannot lose it whatever happens.

(6) *Art* brings about a reconciliation between the two principles in a peculiar way. An artist is originally a man who turns away from reality because he cannot come to terms with the renunciation of instinctual satisfaction which it at first demands, and who allows his erotic and ambitious wishes full play in the life of phantasy. He finds the way back to reality, however, from this world of phantasy by making use of special gifts to mould his phantasies into truths of a new kind, which are valued by men as precious reflections of reality. Thus in a certain fashion he actually becomes the hero, the king, the creator, or the favourite he desired to be, without following the long roundabout path of making real alterations in the external world. But he can only achieve this because other men feel the same dissatisfaction as he does with the renunciation demanded by reality, and because that dissatisfaction, which results from the replacement of the pleasure principle by the reality principle, is itself a part of reality.[1]

(7) While the ego goes through its transformation from a *pleasure-ego* into a *reality-ego*, the sexual instincts undergo the changes that lead them from their original auto-erotism through various intermediate phases to object-love in the service of procreation. If we are right in thinking that each step in these two courses of development may become the site of a disposition to later neurotic illness, it is plausible to suppose that the form taken by the subsequent illness (the *choice of neurosis*) will depend on the particular phase of the development of the ego and of the libido in which the dispositional inhibition of de-

[1] Cf. the similar position taken by Otto Rank (1907). [See also 'Creative Writers and Day-Dreaming' (1908*e*), as well as the closing paragraph of Lecture XXIII of the *Introductory Lectures* (1916–1917).]

TWO PRINCIPLES OF MENTAL FUNCTIONING 225

velopment has occurred. Thus unexpected significance attaches to the chronological features of the two developments (which have not yet been studied), and to possible variations in their synchronization.[1]

(8) The strangest characteristic of unconscious (repressed) processes, to which no investigator can become accustomed without the exercise of great self-discipline, is due to their entire disregard of reality-testing; they equate reality of thought with external actuality, and wishes with their fulfilment—with the event—just as happens automatically under the dominance of the ancient pleasure principle. Hence also the difficulty of distinguishing unconscious phantasies from memories which have become unconscious.[2] But one must never allow oneself to be misled into applying the standards of reality to repressed psychical structures, and on that account, perhaps, into undervaluing the importance of phantasies in the formation of symptoms on the ground that they are not actualities, or into tracing a neurotic sense of guilt back to some other source because there is no evidence that any actual crime has been committed. One is bound to employ the currency that is in use in the country one is exploring—in our case a neurotic currency. Suppose, for instance, that one is trying to solve a dream such as this. A man who had once nursed his father through a long and painful mortal illness, told me that in the months following his father's death he had repeatedly dreamt that *his father was alive once more and that he was talking to him in his usual way. But he felt it exceedingly painful that his father had really died, only without knowing it.* The only way of understanding this apparently nonsensical dream is by adding 'as the dreamer wished' or 'in consequence of his wish' after the words 'that his father had really died', and by further adding 'that he [the dreamer] wished it' to the last words. The dream-thought then runs: it was a painful memory for him that he had been obliged to wish for his father's death (as a release) while he was still alive, and how terrible it would have been if his father had had any suspicion of it! What we have here is thus the familiar case of self-reproaches after the loss of someone loved, and in this instance the self-reproach

---

[1] [This theme is developed in 'The Disposition to Obsessional Neurosis' (1913*i*), p. 324 ff. below.]

[2] [This difficulty is discussed at length in the later part of Lecture XXIII of the *Introductory Lectures*.]

went back to the infantile significance of death-wishes against the father.[1]

The deficiencies of this short paper, which is preparatory rather than expository, will perhaps be excused only in small part if I plead that they are unavoidable. In these few remarks on the psychical consequences of adaptation to the reality principle I have been obliged to adumbrate views which I should have preferred for the present to withhold and whose justification will certainly require no small effort. But I hope it will not escape the notice of the benevolent reader how in these pages too the dominance of the reality principle is beginning.

[1] [This dream was added to the 1911 edition of *The Interpretation of Dreams* (1900a), *Standard Ed.*, 5, 430–1, soon after the publication of the present paper.]

PART II

Discussion of "Formulations on the two principles of mental functioning"

Editors' introduction to Chapter One

In this introductory chapter, Dr Aguayo begins by contextualising the "Two principles" paper within the framework of Freud's concurrent writings. Aguayo tells us that "Two principles" was written simultaneously with his work on the Schreber case and that each of these important papers addressed the relationship to reality in both the neurotic and psychotic mind. Ever reworking and expanding on his theories, Freud elaborated his ideas about primary process thinking by introducing the concepts of the *pleasure* and *reality principles*. In this brief and compact paper, Freud examined other factors such as consciousness, memory, and mature levels of thinking associated with the development of the reality principle. With regard to thinking, Freud in "Two principles" wrote about thinking as *experimental action*, thereby drawing a link between action and thinking that continues to be an important topic in current psychoanalytic theories. Aguayo also underscores Freud's idea that the reality principle does not replace the pleasure principle; indeed, quoting Freud, Aguayo notes that the reality principle actually "safeguards" the pleasure principle.

Aguayo, both an historian and a psychoanalyst, also considers the place of "Two principles" in the relationship between Freud and

Jung and their respective views on the nature of psychosis. Although they had enjoyed a remarkably successful visit to Clark University in 1909, their relationship began to falter on Freud's insistence on the importance of the sexual instincts in psychosis with which Jung disagreed. Consequently, though Freud (1911c) wrote about the psychotic's relationship to reality in *Psycho-analytic Notes on an Autobiographical Account of a Case of Paranoia* and "Two principles", Aguayo tells us that "Thus, the two collaborators became adversaries—and mutually repelled from one another's work after 1911." Aguayo notes that even though Freud's attention was drawn away from the study of psychotic processes, this lapsed interest was later taken up by Karl Abraham and his analytic descendants: Melanie Klein, Bion, and other analysts in the British Society. Aguayo also discusses how Klein and Bion henceforth became the "heir" to Freud's unfinished work on the nature of psychosis.

Aguayo's Introduction discusses in important detail the ways in which Klein and Bion expanded on our understanding of the reality principle through their work on the *epistemophilic instinct* (Klein) and studies on the nature of the *apparatus for thinking* (Bion). Aguayo thus informs us of the important place this short paper holds in Freud's oeuvre; describing how the "Two principles" paper seeded the start of a vital, on-going discussion about the nature of contact with reality, its relationship with the pleasure principle, the notion of thinking as necessary for dealing with reality, and other lines of thinking hatched by this essential paper.

1

Filling in Freud and Klein's maps of psychotic states of mind: Wilfred Bion's reading of Freud's "Formulations regarding two principles in mental functioning"

Joseph Aguayo

During the last months of 1910, Freud found himself tacking back and forth between the writing of "Formulations regarding two principles in mental functioning" (hereafter "Two principles") and his longer paper on the Schreber case (1911c). Since both papers appeared in the same volume of the *Jahrbuch für psychanalyse und pathologische Forshungen*, (1911, 3(1): 1–8) it is noteworthy that these efforts on Freud's part were, among others, attempts to persuade the journal's editor, Carl Jung, of the viability of a psychoanalytic understanding of psychotic disorders. In his letters to Jung during this time, Freud repeatedly mentioned the various drafts of "Two principles", all of which received no response from his Swiss colleague (Freud & Jung, 1974, 19 June 1910, p. 332; 10 August 1910, p. 343; 18 August 1910, p. 349, n. 6; 18 December 1910, p. 379; and 22 January 1911, p. 387).

Had Jung concerned himself with reading "Two principles', he would have read a rather compact paper that represented Freud's re-thinking of earlier hypotheses, but with a more general audience of readers in mind. Freud's argument: the neurotic's "flight into illness" forces the patient out of his real life, and alienates him from reality. Reality is experienced as unbearable, so in neurotics, it leads to repression; in the severely disturbed, the tendency towards "hallucinatory psychosis", an extreme turning away from reality that is often tied to a particular event that occasioned the outbreak of their insanity. The neurotic affects a less exaggerated version of what psychotics do with some fragment of reality (Freud, 1911b). Contrasting these developmental derailments with the psychic processes occurring at the outset of early mental life, the primary processes are governed by the pleasure–unpleasure principle (*Lust–Unlust*), which Freud now called the "pleasure principle". These processes strive towards pleasure and retreat from unpleasure. The infant's instinctual wishes appear gratified in some hallucinatory way, just as they do in the nightly dreams of adults. Yet the disappointment that ensues leads to the abandonment of this attempt at satisfaction by means of hallucination. The psychical apparatus then decides on a different method when it forms a different conception of the real, external circumstances—and makes a suitable adjustment. A new principle of mental functioning emerges, one now referred to as the reality principle.

The increasing importance of external reality heightens the importance of the ". . . sense-organs that are directed towards the external world, and of the *consciousness* attached to them" (Freud, 1911b, p. 220). Attention is developed to scan the external world to see how one's needs might be brought into alignment with it; "notation" is developed, ". . . whose task it was to lay down the results of this periodic activity of consciousness—a part of what we call *memory*" (pp. 220–221). One compares experiences based on memory to see if some impartial passing of judgment can occur, one that supersedes judgments made previously on the basis of the repression of unpleasurable ideas. Formerly, under the domination of the primary processes, hallucinatory wish-fulfilment occurs in the form of motoric discharge of "accretions of stimuli" by action. Now under the sway of the secondary process–reality principle, there is restraint instigated by the process of thinking. Thinking simultaneously allows the tolerance of increased tension while postponing the process of discharge. Freud wrote: "It is essentially an experimental kind of acting, accompanied by displacement of relatively small quantities of cathexis together with less expenditure (discharge) of them" (p. 221).

Freud also addressed admixtures of the reality and pleasure principles, noting that older sources of pleasure are sometimes tenaciously held on to, so that split-off pockets could exist and remain immune to the reality principle. Once the reality principle becomes ascendant, it does not therefore imply the complete eclipse of the pleasure-principle, ". . . but only a safeguarding of it" (p. 223). In sum, the reality principle never completely supersedes the pleasure principle—and to make this point, Freud also pointed out how the "ego-instincts" deal with the "sexual instincts", and described their evolution from auto-erotic to object directed love (as well as their regressive aspects).

So what about those instances where there is an entire disregard for the reality principle? More disturbed patients can evince a tendency to equate their thoughts with reality; and their wishes with fulfilment. Freud concluded his short paper with these brief thoughts about the severely disturbed by acknowledging that it was "preparatory rather than expository . . .", insofar as he had been looking at the ". . . psychical consequences of adaptation to the reality principle" and how it came into being (p. 226).

Aside from Freud's brief paper, these were also heady times insofar as Freud in 1909 had just given the successful Clark University Lectures in the US—and along with Jung was regarded as a leading proponent of the new psychological approaches to the treatment of nervous disorders. But beneath the apparent affinity of interests lay a deeper fissure between the two men: despite the Zürich school's long-standing interest in the treatment of psychotic disorders, Freud's international acclaim now led to an intensification of his need to have psychoanalytic adherents subscribe more completely to his sexual theory of libido—at least this is Makari's (2008, pp. 181–292) argument—and it rings true (Aguayo, 2013). In the years before Freud received international acclaim, he had allowed his Viennese adherents, men like Wilhelm Stekel and Alfred Adler, some leeway in respectful but nonetheless different views from those of the Professor. It was the recognition by Eugen Bleuler and C. G. Jung of the Burghölzli Clinic that changed this situation. Between 1907 and 1911, C. G. Jung emerged as a muscular advocate for Freud's psychoanalysis—and this in turn made some of the Viennese less useful adherents.

Jung was then elevated as Freud's "crown prince" to eminent positions, such as President of the new International Psychoanalytical Association, conference organiser, and journal editor. These were the years when Jung gladly accepted the role of mentee to Freud as mentor. Freud in the interim accepted both Jung and Bleuler's standing reservations about the libido theory since having the support of the renowned Zurich school meant so much during an earlier and less steady time for the movement. But with increased acclaim after 1909 came new adherents—and Freud now insisted on more full-bodied allegiance to his analytic theories; and this all unfortunately clashed with Jung's increasing need to individuate and pursue his own clinical and research aims. Thus, the two collaborators became adversaries—and mutually repelled from one another's work after 1911.

The project on psychotic disorders also fell to the side. Among the legacies of this fall-out, very few analysts expressed interest in taking up the arduous task of explicating the psychoses in a thoroughly systematic and psychoanalytic manner. Of the few that did, gifted analysts, such as Karl Abraham, died at an early age in 1925 and thus was unable to complete work he had done on psychotic states such as manic-depression. Of his own students and analysands, Melanie Klein had long thought that at some point in her career, she would realise her analyst's belief that the psychoanalytic understanding of the psychoses was possible, but her London group was not able to carry out any thorough research until after the Second World War (at the time when the British Society concluded the Controversial Discussions and the three-track training system was realised in London). In Klein's (1946) programmatic statement set out in "Notes on some schizoid mechanisms", she asked if there might be sufficient interest among psychoanalytically informed psychiatrists to tackle the problem of the psychoses. All three of her analysands, Herbert Rosenfeld, Hanna Segal, and Wilfred Bion, took up her call—and in a series of groundbreaking papers from 1947 to 1959, this publishing cohort of London Kleinians explicated and elaborated upon Klein's notion of the treatment of psychotic patients by means of five-times-a-week psychoanalysis (Aguayo, 2009).

Klein's ideas about psychoses were purely psychological and focused on the nature of the patient's internal subjective experience—with an emphasis of instinct over nurture, destructive impulses rather than the failure of maternal provision. In one form or another, each of her trio of analysts also took up Klein's crucial idea of projective identification as not only a prototype of aggressive object relations, but implicated it as a central mechanism in psychotic states of mind. It was a structuring presence in Klein's new formulation of the "paranoid–schizoid position", now deemed the earliest stage of the infant's mental life, which also became a point of experiential fixation for the psychotic. In terms of his contribution, Bion (between 1954 and 1959) took up the psychotic's disordered thinking, specifically their misuse of language as a mode of action. Where thought was required, the psychotic took action; where action was necessary, the psychotic remained hopelessly trapped in an internal mental web in which he attacked his own mind. In his *Los Angeles Seminars* of 1967, Bion (2013) gave a riveting example: a psychotic analysand was riding on a train to his session when he saw that he had gone past his station stop; so he merely tried to get off the moving train, only to suffer the inevitable contusions and injuries—there was a stiff price to be paid for treating external reality as if it were a dream, where such actions are always possible.

Bion also extended the conceptual reach of analysts treating psychotic patients by taking up the objectively and highly disturbing nature of their disordered thinking on the mind of the analyst. When the patient forcefully intruded his delusions and misperceptions *into* the analyst's mind, how did the analyst maintain his neutrality, let alone remain able to interpret the meaning of the patient's most peculiar communications? Taking up Heimann's (1950) idea of countertransference as an "instrument of research", Bion regarded what he came to understand as the psychotic patient's "ideo-motor activities" as a total communicational and organising field of experience. When these activities were forcefully intruded by the patient into the mind of the analyst, it led to a consideration of how the analyst was to extricate himself from such an imprisoning literality. Bion came to regard the patient's projective identification as potentially illuminating his countertransference—as he was projectively put in the patient's shoes. Yet the analyst also carried the ego discriminating activity of being the bearer of sanity, which often also aroused envious attacks on the patient's part. Bion wrote about how the analyst survived these bits of psychic shrapnel, especially when the psychotic attacked both his own mind as well as that of the analyst. The analyst had to be mindful of how the psychotic was gripped by omnipotent destructive phantasies, which he often treated as concrete "facts". Massive projective identification attacks left the psychotic with "bizarre objects", as he attacked the links to his mind and to others. The analyst attempted to digest the psychotic's experience, so that metabolised understanding might indeed result (Aguayo, 2009).

Interspersed in his writings on psychosis between 1954 and 1959, Bion returned to Freud's earlier formulations on the nature of psychosis and revised them. It was not just that the psychotic hated reality, he despised his *awareness* of reality. I maintain that Bion continued the analytic dialogue with Freud's writings on psychosis that had been somewhat broken off when Jung left the movement; and it was through his following up on Klein's leads in the "Schizoid mechanisms" paper that Bion returned in the 1950s to think through Freud's nascent thoughts on the nature of psychotic thinking. My aim here is to trace Bion's conceptual evolution in his lesser known dialogue with the work of Freud.

While at the outset of "Notes on the theory of schizophrenia", Bion (1954) gave Klein's work primacy of place in his understanding of schizophrenic thinking, he merely adduced some clinical material from Freud's (1915e) paper on "The unconscious", where a patient with an obsessive preoccupation with blackheads was regarded by Freud as working out his castration complex. Bion (1954, p. 115; 1967a, p. 29) implied that a symbolic equation was at work: it seemed to be that when the patient picked the blackheads off his face, he imagined that he had created a deep cavity that he feared was noticed by others; Freud in turn tied this to the patient's castration complex that was mediated by guilt feelings about masturbation; feminisation thus became an internal punishment. Bion's implication here also seemed to suggest a psychotic pocket underlying a neurotic symptom.

In "Development of schizophrenic thought", Bion (1956, p. 344; 1967a, p. 36) again cited Freud's work *en passant* when he appeared to refer to "Two principles" without a specific citation ("Freud's description . . . of the mental apparatus called into activity by the demands of the reality principle and in particular by that part of it which is concerned with the conscious awareness of sense impressions"). On the other hand, Bion did cite Freud's *Civilization and Its Discontents* (1930a), claiming that it was left to Klein and her students to follow up on the importance of the conflict between the life and death instincts, crucially implicated in the understanding of schizophrenia.

It was only with "Differentiation of psychotic from non-psychotic" that Bion (1957) substantively began to grapple with aligning Freud's views on psychoses with both Klein's and his own. Very much in the spirit of Klein's work, which had filled in Freud's detailed map of the neurotic disorders in adults when she extended the range of analytic understanding into the actual analysis of young, pre-latency aged children, Bion now attempted to reconcile Kleinian and Freudian's views of psychotic states of mind. First and foremost, he accomplished this by a creative mis-reading of Freud's "Two principles" paper. Bion effected what J. Fisher (2009) termed a "conceptual leap" in his discussion of Freud's reality principle when he extended Freud's analysis of the capacity to acknowledge the reality of the external world to the patient's capacity to acknowledge emotional/internal reality. I agree with Fisher here that Bion now became Freud and Klein's heir in the development of the psychoanalytic understanding of psychosis.

Bion (1957) here began to define a process of thinking by means of which it became possible to incorporate emotions. So in taking up Freud's descriptions of the "ego functions" (attention, memory, judgment, thought, and action), those aspects that were so crucial to Freud's view of adhering to the reality principle, Bion adduced clinical examples from his work with psychotic patients in order to demonstrate how this adherence to the reality principle went awry. Yet the failure to adhere to the reality principle was only one aspect of the psychotic's profound dilemma: Bion also added that what was attacked was the psychotic's *awareness* of reality. So at the heart of Bion's deployment of Freud's "Two principles" paper was a profound rethinking of some fundamental psychoanalytic assumptions about the relationship between the pleasure and reality principles. Bion reasoned that if analysts could understand the capacity leading to the awareness and acknowledgement of both external and internal reality, then we could examine how psychotic states of mind resulted from a disruption of that process.

In "Language and the schizophrenic", Bion (1955, p. 221) described how the psychotic attacks his own mind by in effect attacking the ego functions associated with it. In effect, in his most regressed states, the psychotic patient attacks his ego functions in the form of ". . . destructive attacks on all those aspects of his personality, his ego, that are concerned with establishing external contact and internal contact". Bion's phenomenological approach was in turn augmented in his "Differentiation" paper when he proposed a different model for the psychotic's destructive attacks. Here Bion drew upon Klein's notion of the "splitting of the self or ego" and the projective evacuation of the ensuing fragments. Not only could the psychotic split off despised affective states, but more importantly, he could attack, split off, and project the mental functions Freud associated with the institution of the reality principle. It was clear in Bion's thinking that projective identification was the defining signature driving the psychotic's attacks on his own mind—and he had said so earlier in 1954:

> It is therefore to projective identification that I now turn, *but my examination of it is restricted to its deployment by the schizophrenic against all that apparatus of awareness that Freud described as being called into activity by the demands of the reality principle*. (Bion, 1956, p. 345, italics in the original)

Going against his general inclination to present clinical illustrations in his publications, Bion (1957, p. 270f.; 1967a, p. 52f.) presented some of his work with a psychotic patient with the ironic introduction that the illustration was ". . . based on these theories rather than the description of an experience on which the theories are based". (I think Bion was here putting some order to what might have otherwise been an overly chaotic presentation.) A long-term analysand began the session by communicating in a fragmented way—first about "not being able to do anything", then about ringing up his mother, and finally about ". . . nothing but filthy things and smells". Had he lost his sight? The analyst also thought about the patient's odd-looking physical movements on the couch—and was left to wonder about what other associative material might be linked. Was the totality of the fragmented speech and odd physical movements meaningful but, as yet, indecipherable? The analyst finally concluded that he was watching a ". . . conglomeration of bits out of a number of such <dramatic> scenes", but ones that were not being named. Was this the pleasure principle holding forth supreme? Was this the motoric discharge of accumulated stimuli? Bion (1957, p. 267; 1967a, p. 45) had already alluded to Freud's (1924a) "Neurosis and psychosis" paper, in which the neurotic was capable of suppressing aspects of the id in the service of the reality principle, whereas the psychotic's ego withdrew from reality in the service of the id. Elaborating upon what he termed "ideo-motor activities", Bion now regarded the patient's need to mutilate the analyst's interpretations as more than a withdrawal from reality, but a result of an internally-mediated attack on his own mind. Since the patient was far too disturbed to have any sanguine understanding of his own internal situation, he could only evacuate it into the analyst (i.e., the fear that he had lost his sight and could only project "filthy things" into the analyst, which he in turn, by means of reversal, would be forced to evacuate from his person).

However, amid these fragmented and confusing bits of "ideo-motor activity", there was also a potentially redemptive side, namely the neurotic islands that existed inside the psychotic. Segal (1956) had pointed out that even highly disturbed schizophrenics can occasionally attain the cusp of the depressive position—and here Bion (1957) adduced the patient's ideograph of "dark sun glasses" he had seen his analyst wear some months back. Bion in effect marvelled at the "*tour de force*" of the use of pictorial illustrations to communicate a rich and otherwise indecipherable message—primitive modes of thought, characterised as agglomeration of bizarre objects instead of verbal thought:

> Now the surprising, and even disconcerting, improvement of which I spoke touches this point of skilful agglomeration (which is successful in conveying meaning). For I have found not only that patients resorted more and more to ordinary verbal thought, thus showing an increased capacity for it and increased consideration for the analyst as an ordinary human being, but also that they seemed to become more and more skilful at this type of agglomerated rather than articulated speech. The extraordinary thing is the *tour de force* by which primitive modes of thought are used by the patient for the statement of themes of great complexity. (Bion, 1957, p. 274)

Bion also remained sanguine about how the analyst's understanding could simultaneously be appreciated and yet remain the object of envious attacks. Yes, it was true that at times he felt like a "thing" with this patient, as if he was not a real person at all. Yet it was also true that the patient could trickle into, however momentary, the depressive position, when there was a momentary brush with reality, which was otherwise an elusive goal and a hardship for the psychotic patients.

In other papers from this period, Bion (1958, 1959) continued his supplemental, revisionist view of Freud's work. In "On arrogance", he delineated another aspect of the Oedipus complex by extrapolating from his experience with psychotic patients. Bion (1958, p. 145; 1967a, p. 88) wrote:

> If we now turn to consider what there is in reality that makes it so hateful to the patient that he must destroy the ego which brings him into contact with it, it would be natural to suppose that it is the sexually oriented Oedipus situation, and indeed I have found much to substantiate this view.

Yet in this instance, Bion went in a different direction, marginalising the sexually oriented Oedipus situation as an explanation in favour of another factor, namely Oedipus' urge to know the truth, to want to face reality no matter what the cost. In another case study (concerning a male patient sounding quite similar to the patient already described in the "Differentiation" paper), the moment of truth came when the patient, who had spoken in an unintelligible but highly fragmented way, had made it appear that it would be impossible to establish any viable or potent form of analytic relationship. Together patient and analyst formed what Bion termed a "frustrated couple". Then, in a moment of lucidity:

> ... the patient said he wondered that I could stand it. This gave me a clue: at least I now knew that there was something I was able to stand which he apparently could not. He realized already that he felt he was being obstructed in his aim to establish a creative contact with me, and that this obstructive force was sometimes in him, sometimes in me, and sometimes occupied an unknown location. Furthermore, the obstruction was effected by some means other than mutilation or verbal communications. The patient had already made it clear that the obstructing forces or object was out of his control. (Bion, 1958, p. 146; 1967a, p. 90)

In Bion's distillation of Freud's notion of the reality principle and Klein's epistemophilic instinct, he now understood that it was one of the analyst's functions to pursue the truth, as it was all too frequently the case that the patient evinced difficulties in his capacity to tolerate aspects of his psychic reality, which in turn led to its projective evacuation. For his part, the analyst had to evince a capacity for containing (and this seems to be the first instance of Bion's use of this important term) the discarded, split-off aspects of the various patients who consulted with him, all while retaining a balanced outlook (Bion, 1958, p. 145; 1967a, pp. 88–89). Bion further expanded upon these ideas by looking at the inverse relationship between curiosity and arrogance. In an ideal sense, the analyst who can bear their curiosity also bears the responsibility for shouldering whatever painful and uncomfortable psychic truths emerge from the patient. Inversely, the "arrogant" analyst becomes intemperate and insists on privileging a verbal form of communication as a way of making the patient's problems explicit. This narrow-mindedness can sometimes fail to take into account that the analyst's words can be experienced as primitively attacking by the patient. It is a form of stupidity insofar as it represents the analyst's failure to learn from experience—or to listen to how his understanding is being heard by the patient.

Aftermath

After Klein's death in 1960, Bion then set out his distillation of what he had learned from both Klein and Freud. In laying the ground work for his epistemological project with "The theory of thinking" paper as well as his monograph, *Learning from Experience*, Bion (1962a,b,c) drew upon their work to arrive at an over-arching metatheory that might explicate how the mind operates—all the way from the most thought disturbed psychotic to the highest functioning physical scientist (Bion, 1962b). Could the practising analyst find ways of thinking of the actual theories he deployed in his everyday work? Could a system of notation be evolved so that the analyst might have some objective way of recording crucial developments in the work with his patients, but do so in such a way as to generate fresh hypotheses?

In posing such questions, Bion's trajectory was towards the unknown, towards a way to ground as firmly as possible what the analyst could know—and also communicate what he had learned to his colleagues. In taking on this massive project, Bion now also effected a disjunction from his previous work on the understanding of groups and psychosis: he wrote in a more abstract, opaque way, giving the barest clinical examples in books rather than in brief articles. The new work reflected a form of cross-modal, interdisciplinary thinking, where he borrowed ideas from other disciplines—philosophy, mathematics, and literature—and pressed them at times violently into service in fashioning a meta-theory, which in effect was a thinking man's guide to how to think about the psychoanalytic situation and its theoretical underpinnings.

In setting out a model that might be inclusive of the most enduring findings of both Freud and Klein, Bion continued to privilege Freud's (1911b) "Two principles" and Klein's (1946) "Notes on some schizoid mechanisms'. (I add here that this was the one Freud paper that Bion cited more than any other.) He abstracted from these two systems of thought in an attempt to both transform and learn from his psychoanalytic experience to that point. Right from the outset however, Bion's preference was for concepts that could be loosely defined, "unsaturated" to use his term—neither being too specific nor too general. Bion (1962c, p. vi) preferred these types of terms because they lent themselves to a "penumbra of associations". He thought for instance of the various values (or factors) that fulfilled the requirements of the mathematical function: perhaps one could set out the necessary and sufficient elements required for the thinking "function", which Bion called "α-function". Perhaps this might be one way in which the mechanisms by which "thinking" could be approached from the perspective of the analyst bearing the curiosity of wanting to know the patient's undigested emotional experience. Perhaps this approach might also fill in crucial gaps left undeveloped by both Freud and Klein.

In setting out some of his ideas regarding a theory of thinking, Bion (1962b) continued to transform the work of his analytic forbearers. For instance: while he drew upon Freud's (1911b) depiction of the pleasure and reality principles, he did so in a Kleinian fashion, positing that the infant from the outset struggled with both the demands of reality and pleasure vis-à-vis how Freud had depicted an infant dominated by primary narcissism, where autoerotic pleasure would dominate the infant's psychic experience long before the capacity to mediate the claims of reality would set in. Yet despite this bit of textual distortion, noted by perceptive observers like Guntrip

(1965), Bion, like other creative analytic theorists, had to distort his reading of Freud in order to arrive at new meaning. So implicitly building upon another one of Klein's undeveloped concepts of "epistemophilia", Bion fashioned a model of the infant that effectively birthed him into a situation where he existed as a series of "thoughts without a thinker". In other words, given the numerous instinctual demands placed upon his immature psyche, he was born in profound need of an object-relationship that could minister to those needs in a thoughtful, containing, and comforting fashion. Thus, in positing maternal "α-function", the infant's ideo-motor activities were both received, processed by means of maternal reverie, and potentially returned back to the infant in the form of contained and metabolised understanding.

In setting out this relational matrix of how mother ministered to her infant, Bion also accepted, while he simultaneously altered, some of Klein's key concepts. While accepting the central mechanism of projective identification, one that he had previously (Bion, 1955, 1959) expanded by emphasising its communicative aspect, Bion now delineated how normal development might occur within the matrix of the infant's relationship with its mother, something that complemented Klein's predominant emphasis on the infant's phantasmic relationship to the maternal body. Bion simultaneously transformed Klein's work by now providing additional conceptual ballast to her emphasis on the infant's pathological development in his relationship to a factor she held as a "constant" in her system. The mother was now regarded as an end in and of herself, someone whose emotional processing capacities had to be factored into the matrix of the infant's psychic development. In Freud's terms, the reality principle now operated at the intersection between a subjectively attuned mother to a subjectively receptive infant. It also included Kleinian formulations as well. For instance, while still holding to Klein's findings that an infant with an aggressively envious predisposition could toxify mother's best attempts at ministering to him, Bion now added looking at how a variable infant could be received by a variable mother, thus producing different admixtures of emotional matching and mis-matching to produce different varieties of interactional outcome (Britton, 2007). So Klein's pathological view of the infant could now be complemented by a different model in which the infant's nascent "α-function" could be developed in relationship to a containing maternal "α-function" that he assimilated through a felicitous "learning from experience" ("pre-conception", "realisation", and "conception").

At the end of his reworking of the findings of both Freud and Klein, Bion (1963) enshrined his distillation of their enduring findings in the Grid. In this rather complex conceptual matrix, Bion attempted to categorise what kind of thought was emitted by the patient—and the use to which he put it. Of the various concepts elucidated by Freud in the "Two principles", Bion chose "notation" and "attention" (which became the vertical columns 3 and 4 of the Grid). Notation often merely related to the analyst's reminding the patient of something he believes might have happened on a previous occasion; while attention served as the analyst's way of highlighting a particular phenomenon in the presence of his patient (Bion, 1963, pp. 18–19, 33). Lastly, Bion elaborated upon Freud's dream theory when he complemented the view that dreams were in the service of the pleasure principle by saying that they also operated under the aegis of the reality principle (Brown, 2012, p. 1196).

Clinical vignette

In ending this brief contribution, it seems fitting to provide some illustration of Bion's theoretical and clinical distillation of Klein and Freud's ideas. To the question of how one presents clinical Bion, I answer it here by talking in approximations insofar as Bion left relatively few examples of how he worked clinically. But in connection with a recent clinical seminar at which I was asked by *Societat Espanola de Psicoanalisi* in Barcelona to present a Bionian-inspired illustration, I did so in three parts:

Part I: I started by giving very sparse details about the patient.

Part II After this brief introduction, I presented a recent session, asking the group of seminar participants, which consisted of candidates, graduates, as well as senior training analysts, to provide immediate associations to the back and forth exchanges between myself and the patient.

Part III After this discussion, I presented the same session material, only this time sharing with the group what a "Grid" analysis of the interactions yielded in terms of incremental understanding.

Part I: F, the patient is in his mid-fifties, divorced with two young adult sons; he was in a dilapidated, near psychotic state, depressed and barely functional when he started analysis twelve years ago. While he has progressed more in his external career, he has extreme difficulties managing an intimate relationship with a live-in girlfriend of several years. I see him four days a week.

Part II: The discussion focused on realising what Bion (1967a) has termed a "lateral communication", where any group of clinicians listening to material effects a transformation of that material by the specific ways in which they listen to, then finally interpret the significance of what they have heard. We clarified the nature of the group"s understanding of the material by way of their "lateral communication".

I present here the beginning of a session in question:

> F arrived a couple of minutes late, appearing a bit dishevelled in his rumpled clothes; he laid down on the couch and started talking in a disconnected tone with frequent pauses, anywhere from thirty seconds to a minute: "It's interesting ah, . . . what pops into my head . . . but I can't get back to it . . . very appropriate . . ."

The analyst thinks to himself: this fragmented way of talking is somewhat elliptical and refers to conversations F frequently says he has with me when he is on his way to his session; but then once he physically is in the room with me, these conversations seem to evaporate as he cannot either remember or bring himself to tell me more fully what he had just thought.

> *F continues*: After yesterday's session, my agent R called me again, but I didn't take the call. I needed time to prepare to talk to her about not getting this next book project . . . I finally called her back; and she told me that I actually got the job, I got the book project. (F proceeds in a grim, non-expressive tone). That was good news and all this after I had "written" the conversation on a piece of paper that I thought I was going to have with R.

F was certain he would not get the job; so he had written his thoughts on how to console his agent R about this latest failure.

> *F*: Well, it is out of the way. I wonder if R thinks this is a good book project for me to take on. She told me to take real time and relax; and I did tell her I was happy. But I also thought about

what would have happened had I not received it. After all the contacts I have called upon to vouch for me . . .

As I listen to myself, I think that my conversation is insane. I *got* the book project; it is a major coup. I could be having a great day. Yet I thought about telling my girlfriend and all she would have said was: did you get paid well enough?

Analyst: I said that it seemed easier to organise his experience around others, whereas he becomes disorganised when talking just about himself. Rejection is a relied upon meaning that organises his sense of misery.

F: I am not surprised that it has turned out this way. I think of all the times I have imagined how much I think you loath me, like when I thought you saw me smoking in your courtyard; or when we run into each other at the coffee house next door. Once again, I had no information but automatically assumed that I would not get what I wanted and I would not receive the job offer.

A: Misery is your constant companion—when you are not self-loathing, you have me in the position of loathing you. Seeking comfort in misery has been a great emotional constant of your life; it makes sense of your world; others like myself will shun contact with you, yet you fear remaining in analysis until one of us dies.

Part II. In terms of the seminar's reactions to this material, participants found the patient self-loathing and depressively self-devaluing. He appeared to be quietly and stubbornly adhered to intruding his self-contempt into the analyst—(e.g., isn't it enough that the analyst has to suffer sharing a common office space with him; it must be unbearable to feel polluted by F's presence just outside the office)? F appears to organise the analytic couple to be contemptuous of him. There was also some comment on how near-delusional and insistent R was on his profound misperceptions, as if there was no other way to take his behaviour into account. Others commented on the intense difficulty F had with direct emotional contact. He at least twice in this session appeared withdrawn, poring over how to minimise catastrophic anxieties in unrealised encounters with others that he has secretly anointed (e.g., his analyst whom he fears he has offended; or the much idealised agent who has consistently looked out after his best business interests). One other participant also was of the view that the interpretations appeared at a level a bit removed from a more disorganised emotional experience.

Part III: I then shared the results of a "grid" analysis with the group. What I found most instructive was how using this table of categories in effect made it possible to appreciate more specifically the level at which the patient was communicating. Since most case reporting involves presenters giving a bountiful amount of contextual material ("I said", "he said"), the use of the grid asks that a discrete, non-contextual analysis be made of the type of thinking reflected in the way the patient talks. Coming back to the beginning of the session, I realised that I had overly compensated for R by elevating his speaking in fragments rather than listening more intently to a patient in chaotic distress. Putting it quite simply, I had been speaking over the patient's head. I talked in complete sentences while I did not sufficiently realise that the patient was stammering and barely managing to get out mere fragments, which in effect were mutilated bits of speech. All in all, the group's "lateral communication" (defined as when an audience of analytic listeners transform the clinical meaning of the clinical material they are presently listening to) amplified the grid analysis, so that subsequent session had more elements of genuine contact and less those of one person talking past another.

Concluding statement

I have illustrated Bion's creative reading of Freud's "Two principles" paper in the context of his evolving a bi-personal psychoanalytic model of treatment. Bion more fully realised the Kleinian implicit assumptions present in such notions as projective identification and countertransference as an instrument of research, innovations that led to a greater realisation of a two-person than the more restricted one-person model. I lastly provided a case illustration of a Bionian-inspired method of understanding analytic session material.

Editors' introduction to Chapter Two

We are very fortunate to have David Bell's contribution to this book. As a leading figure in the London Kleinian group, he brings to his paper a valuable perspective. In his second paragraph, Bell tells us of the importance that he accords to the "Two principles" paper,

> It would be hard indeed to think of a single paper written by Freud that does not to some extent depend upon the kinds of distinctions brought in this paper, and for many it is central.

This comment sets the tone for the remainder of this chapter in which Bell considers Freud's paper from multiple points of view. He also sees the death instinct, which Freud (1920g) proposed in *Beyond the Pleasure Principle*, as broadening our view of the pleasure principle by introducing a "darker colour" to it through pleasurable acts of destructiveness.

Bell also expands on some basic Freudian concepts that are essential elements in "Two principles". He views the tendency to equate the pleasure principle with primary process and with the repressed unconscious as overly simplistic and reviews some of Freud's later writings that cast doubt on such analytic assumptions. Likewise, he also considers Freud's idea that the reality principle replaces the pleasure principle: Bell argues against this "static" view and opts instead to see these two in collaboration, as in works of art. In this connection, he quotes Freud's (1932) own words that demonstrate the evolution in his (Freud's) ideas from the earlier "Two principles",

> We cannot do justice to the characteristics of the mind by means of linear contours . . . but we need rather the areas of colour shading off into one another that are to be found in modern pictures.

Thus, we see Bell as successfully tracing important concepts promulgated in "Two principles" and the evolution of these foundational ideas in Freud's later work.

He also expands on Freud's distinguishing between the polarities of fantasy and reality thinking, which Bell sees as too reductionist. Referring to Bion's notions of the psychotic and non-psychotic parts of the personality, Bell asserts that neither of these in their pure form would help the adaptation to reality. Instead, he convincingly argues that just as the psychotic and non-psychotic areas of the mind interrelate, so fantasy and reality thinking mutually enrich each other. Indeed *psychic reality* depends upon constant input from external reality, which is then embellished and altered by unconscious phantasy to create the inner world that is manifest in dreams, daydreams, and children's play. Bell comments that

> The pull towards wish fulfilling fantasy is of course never overcome, it remains a continuing register of our psychic lives, with qualities that are very far from being only problematic for phantasies give our lives resonance and meaning.

Bell also casts a wide net when he discusses the apparent paradox of how thinking itself, the highest achievement of human development, is rooted in primitive bodily experience. He notes that the *capacity for judgment*, which Freud considered a central aspect of the reality principle, is based upon taking in something orally, "chewing" on it and "digesting" it or, in other cases, rejecting the idea, "spitting" it out. Taken from this perspective, Bell states that the pleasure principle is based in the primitive acts of either taking in or spitting out while the reality principle is seen as taking in and swallowing something that is good for us, though we may find it offensive in the short run.

Bell continues his discussion of "Two principles" by examining its further reaches through its relationship to the death instinct, the depressive position, art, literature, and its later echoes in Klein's notion of the *epistemophilic instinct* that Bion impressively extends. In all, Bell's paper is a good read and an intellectually stimulating contribution.

2

The world as it is *vs.* the world as I would like it to be: contemporary reflections on Freud's "Formulations on the two principles of mental functioning"

David Bell

Introduction

Freud's writing has a curious doubling back quality as he returns repeatedly to themes that had occupied him at the beginning.[1] "Formulations of the two principles of mental functioning (hereinafter referred to as FTPMF) has exactly this quality and it is perhaps this feature that lends it a somewhat puzzling nature, for it seems at one and the same time to be saying something that is both new and old.

The editors inform us that this work amounts to a kind of stocktaking, namely that Freud is bringing findings from an earlier period into line with his current thinking and also laying the basis for the major theoretical works to come. Yet in a certain sense this is too static a view, for the paper is not best thought of as *one* of the building blocks of Freud's developing theory, it addresses concerns that are foundational to the whole psychoanalytic project. It would be hard indeed to think of a single paper written by Freud that does not to some extent depend upon the kinds of distinctions brought in this paper, and for many it is central. "On narcissism" (Freud, 1914c) shows how we only *seem* to abandon the illusions that serve to maintain our infantile narcissism, while secretly maintaining them (in our attitudes to leaders, to our children, and so on), the *Future of an Illusion* (Freud, 1927c) provides an apt illustration of the ways in which we keep alive a satisfying falsehood to protect ourselves from the harsh realities of life. And, of course, an important dimension of psychopathology lies in our capacity to sustain illusions and self-deceptions that defend us from realities we cannot tolerate, while the psychoanalytic method affords us the opportunity to witness these illusions at the moments of their construction, as living phenomena in the consulting room. Once Freud had formulated the death drive (Freud, 1920g), the models of psychic activity that serve the pleasure principle take on a darker colour, as pleasure in destruction of the self and others becomes a focus of attention.

I will start with an exploration of some themes of FTPMF as they are refracted through Freud's developing theory and will then move on to bring them into relation with the work of Klein and Bion. Finally, I will bring some broader reflections as regards the relevance of this perspective on mental life to the understanding of some sociocultural phenomena characteristic of our current historical conjuncture.

This approach assumes a view of psychoanalysis that needs to be made explicit here. Psychoanalysis, as a body of knowledge of mind and human culture, Janus-faced, looks at one and the same time inwards towards the working of the mind and outwards towards culture in general. Although there are certain key works that have as their explicit reference human culture (such as *Totem and Taboo* (1912–1913), *The Future of an Illusion* (1927c), *Civilization and its Discontents* (1930a) it would, I believe, be a serious error to look upon these works as representing Freud's main contribution to knowledge of this kind, for the conviction as to the cultural relevance of Freud's work runs through his whole oeuvre, something that FTPMF makes particularly clear.

Some initial reflections on the paper

Freud's paper, then, brings together a number of foundational distinctions upon which much of psychoanalysis rests: the dynamic (repressed) unconscious *vs.* consciousness, primary process *vs.* secondary process, and pleasure (or pleasure/unpleasure principle) *vs.*

"reality principle". To put it briefly and somewhat tersely, Freud described a system of thinking that is largely unconscious, which functions in a different way (the primary process) and is governed by a principle whose aim is to provide pleasure or to reduce unpleasure (Freud oscillates as to whether the organism aims towards pleasure or a reduction in unpleasure. I will comment further upon this below). The paradigm situation is of the early organism maintained in kind of pure pleasure state where all basic needs are either actually (that is materially) satisfied or, alternatively, are satisfied though hallucination. This latter, that is satisfaction through hallucination, provides the genetic precursor for a "mode of thought"[2] that continues throughout life and which for Freud constitutes a fault line in the mental apparatus—for we are all fated to misunderstand or misrepresent the world in a manner that corresponds not to reality but to our wishes. Shakespeare provides us with the following fine illustration:

> *Prince Henry*: I never thought to hear you speak again
>
> *King Henry IV*: Thy wish was father, Harry, to that thought.
> (Shakespeare, 1600, Henry IV Pt 2 Act 4 Sc V)

Note here the precision of the King's response. He shows Harry not only that he has a hidden wish, that is to murder his father and seize the crown (and of course Shakespeare speaks through King Henry and the Prince for all fathers and sons) but, further, that he misrepresents reality in such a way as to make it accord with his wishes.

In the scene prior to this Prince Henry has removed the crown from the king's pillow (and in some performances even tries it on) and so, if we can be allowed this licence, we might imagine him as here indulging a daydream, one of our most transparent locations for witnessing the activities of the pleasure principle.

If Henry daydreams of being king, in the daydream he *is* king, he rules, and experiences the satisfaction appropriate to his station. This is a fully conscious event to a very significant degree dominated by the pleasure principle. However, to the extent to which he recognises even while daydreaming that this is not reality, he remains in touch with reality. But even so, when fully immersed in his daydream there will be moments in which he lives it as true. What is unconscious then is not the content of the daydream but the wishes that it both represents and conceals. In his daydream Prince Henry may imagine his father as having died a natural and noble death, happily passing on the crown to his beloved son—what remains unconscious is the death wish towards the father and the wish to triumph over him.

However, a daydream, although significantly determined by the pleasure principle, and thus characterised by its tendency to equate thought reality with external reality, at least to some extent retains a real narrative quality with logical connections, and so must be distinct from the activities of that we think of as unconscious.

This discussion reveals a difficulty: we must resist the tendency towards a tidy categorisation of psychic processes and qualities, one provided by the equation unconscious = pleasure principle = primary process, for things turn out to be more complicated as this discussion of daydreams reveals.

We tend, perhaps, to think of the division *Ucs./Cs.* in over-categorical terms, something that, elsewhere, Freud warns us against. In *The Ego and the Id* (Freud, 1923b), having brought to our attention that what is *Ucs.* does not equate with what is repressed he writes:

> we must admit that the characteristic of being unconscious begins to lose significance for us. It becomes a quality which can have many meanings, a quality which we are unable to make, as we should have hoped to do, the basis of far-reaching and inevitable conclusions. (p. 17)

Although Freud talks of *substituting* the reality principle, this should not be taken too literally or it would suggests a rather static stage-like theory. In fact, Freud writes:

> With the introduction of the reality principle one species of thought-activity was split off; it was kept free from reality-testing and remained subordinated to the pleasure principle alone. This activity is phantasying, which begins already in children's play, and later, continued as day-dreaming, abandons dependence on real objects. (Freud, 1911b, p. 221)

This alternative reality, as Freud says, although leading a kind of independent "split off" existence, is highly consequential for the way we live our lives. In this domain thought reality is equated with external reality, wishes with their fulfilment.

This *psychical* reality dominates over material reality in the neuroses and thus to a varying extent in all of us. Freud described these phantasies as having strong ties to the sexual instincts and thus subject to repression, becoming manifest in daydreams and children's play. This introduces a further problematic that it is as well to foreground now. For do we not usually take it that the kind of phantasy activity in daydream, in dream, and in unconscious phantasy are quite distinct from each other? I think Freud, and here I follow Laplanche and Pontalis (1973),[3] is as much pained to emphasise the links between these aspects of our psychology as he is to differentiate them from each other. The boundaries between different aspects of the mind should not be regarded as discrete and fixed, he offers us a better representation:

> We cannot do justice to the characteristics of the mind by means of linear contours, such as occur in a drawing or in a primitive painting, but we need rather the areas of colour shading off into one another that are to be found in modern pictures. After we have made our separations, we must allow what we have separated to merge again. (Freud, 1933a, p. 105)

This has a bearing on an important tension as regards the way we use the word fantasy[4]—on the one hand to refer to mental activities that bear a stamp of lightness, whimsy, perhaps most characteristic of wishes and daydreams, and on the other hand to refer to something more profound, namely phantasy as the deep content of our psychic lives. When we use the term in the former way it tends to depreciate the importance of psychic reality:

> Again, the word 'phantasy' has often been used to mark a contrast to 'reality', the latter word being taken as identical with 'external' or 'material' or 'objective' facts. But when external reality is thus called 'objective' reality, this makes an implicit assumption which denies to psychical reality its own objectivity as a mental fact. Some analysts tend to contrast 'phantasy' with 'reality' in such a way as to undervalue the dynamic importance of phantasy. (Isaacs, 1948a, p. 80)

An example of a dream representing simple wish fulfilment is offered by Freud in his account of the famous dream of his daughter: having been denied food during the day she was heard saying in her sleep "Anna Freud, stwawbewwies, wild stwawbewwies, omblet, pudden!". The dream here provides, in the most direct manner, the hallucinatory fulfilment of a wish and the prototype of a mode of mental functioning. The pull towards wish fulfilling fantasy is, of course, never overcome; it remains a continuing register of our psychic lives, with qualities that are very far from being only problematic, for phantasies give our lives resonance and meaning. Further, it is through the medium of phantasy that defensive structures take root in our minds and we all have our peculiar and individual areas of difficulty from which we escape by use of the corresponding default fantasy.

Ms H was a woman in her forties who was displaced by a younger brother when she was three years old and, as we came to understand, this event had permanently coloured her way of thinking about herself and the world. She was always late for her sessions and yet it was clear that she never intended to be late, it was just that somehow she always felt she could deal with one last thing before she left home to come to her session. For instance she could make a call that "only needed a few minutes" or deal with some other matter that was, she thought quite straightforward. However, these last minute tasks always took more time than anticipated and so, as a result, she was again late. One day, when we were discussing this she suddenly recalled being at an airport and seeing a young couple with their (only) child. They bought one of those small presentation boxes of very expensive chocolates in which there were only four chocolates. She said "So it was one chocolate for each of the parents and two for the child". She then lapsed into a thoughtful silence that ended with her saying "If they have another child, then it will be only one chocolate each".

We were then able to understand how she had continued throughout her life to think of herself as having once occupied a very special privileged position, where she could, so to speak, have twice as much as ordinary people (represented by the parents who, in contrast to the child, only have one chocolate each). The arrival of her brother toppled her from this special position and she fell into the world of the ordinary reality (represented by one chocolate each), which, however, she had never really been able to accept—following Freud we might say "one species of thought-activity was split off; it was kept free from reality-testing and remained subordinated to the pleasure principle alone". In that world she could do her e-mails or phone calls or whatever, *and* be on time for her session. That is, she was still trying (and failing) to maintain a position in which she had twice as much reality.

These kinds of difficulties we understand as narcissistic, in that they attempt to restore a picture of ourselves and our lives that harks back to a much earlier time. To some extent we all do a kind of "double bookkeeping",[5] that is for particular events we inscribe one version of it in the ledger of reality and the other in a more secret place. It is in this latter location that a success in life is registered as proof of more omnipotent claims on the world. Among those in high office there will always be some for whom the inscription in the ledger of omnipotence carries particularly heavy weight and, as a result, it is they most at risk when they step down from their position. For this readjustment as to their place in the world can bring crashing in upon them an awareness of the illusoriness of the omnipotent world they have occupied, and the result can be serious breakdown.

A further difficulty in our reading of Freud arises from the natural tendency to counterpose phantasy to reality—phantasy here becomes a kind of mistake. This view of the mind goes back, at least, to the *Project* (Freud, 1895a) where Freud described one set of neurones the "nuclear neurones" as registering needs and giving them representation, and a different set of neurones "the pallium neurones" as giving representation to the object wished for. From this structural arrangement arises one of the major faults in the psychic system: if the flow of energy is excessive, then what arises is "not simply a memory image of the wished for object but an image invested with the strength of perception" (Wollheim, 1971). That is, the an idea of reality is mistaken for reality, a wished for object mistakenly thought of as an object actually present: that is, hallucination. Phantasy here then is clearly a species of error. Wollheim writes:

> . . . for it seems to have been Freud's view that the perils to which the mind is exposed by this highly precarious biologically necessary, way in which thought comes into being can never be totally got rid of, that is thinking will always retain its provocative character. (p. 57)

But, and this is my point, would it be at all desirable for thinking to completely lack this provocative character. If a lover waiting in anticipation for the appearance of his love, finds his mind filled with anticipatory thoughts about her, it would be entirely natural for this thinking to have a provocative character, that is, at some level he would have the feelings appropriate to her actual presence; but we would not regard this as an error, indeed if thinking lacked this provocative character it would not really be thinking as we ordinary understand it.

Further, thinking in terms of this kind of polarity between phantasy and reality might tempt one to think that in some sense the acme of maturity would be to live a life dominated by the reality principle, positing some state in which "error" can be transcended. But, a moments reflection demonstrates that such a life is neither possible nor desirable—there can be no phantasy free state. After all, it is the penetration of phantasy into our real perceptions of the world that gives those perceptions resonance and meaning; a life severed from this connection would be deprived of all the qualities we naturally think of as being central to what it is to be human. Such a creature would be more like Mr Spock from *Star Trek*[6], someone we might imagine as being ruled exclusively by the reality principle: but we soon recognise his way of thinking as being logical but not human. One is reminded here of Bion's description the psychotic part of the personality as denuded, left with only logical thinking to deal with what once were emotional problems (Bion, 1965).

In order to further problematise this binary opposition of phantasy and reality let us consider an imaginary scientist at work. If we consider an astronomer looking through his telescope, we may imagine that his wonder and curiosity, as he gazes at the heavenly bodies, might hark back to his earliest experiences, that his work might be supported by his ancient strivings to understand the wonders of his mother body. Here the investigation of the world is supported by phantasy, an understanding of the function of phantasy that is core to the Kleinian development.

However, although this opposition of phantasy/reality or phantasy/error has its problems, it is a problematic that cannot be dispensed with, it retains some necessary force. For there are, of course, many kinds of error that *can* be best grasped as instances of misperceiving reality through the lens of phantasy. The philosopher Sebastian Gardner has suggested to me that the relevant distinction here might be thought of as that between background phantasies *vs*. phantasies that obtrude into consciousness, and that do so in ways that disturb cognition. In the case of our astronomer, were the phantasies to obtrude, he might get so excited that he ceases to be able to observe properly, may imagine he has seen things he could not possibly have seen, or alternatively he may become, like Klein's patient Dick (Klein, 1930), so inhibited that he ceases to be able to do his work at all. For Segal this latter case would be an instance of a symbolic equation replacing symbolism proper (Segal, 1957), in Bion's terms a failure of alpha function (Bion, 1962c).

Freud's paper "Negation" (1925h) casts a new light on the central issues addressed in FTPMF. For here he shows one of the highest human capacities, that is judgement, take its origin in primitive bodily activity. Accepting something as true has a genetic link to swallowing, rejecting something as false to spitting out or evacuating from other bodily orifices. Wollheim puts this clearly:

> Before this (judgement) can happen, a thought is first assimilated to a physical thing that at one moment can be in and the other moment be out of the body; a piece of food or faeces . . . . Thinking is then a physical activity which can bring a thing into or expel it from the body: for example swallowing, vomiting, retaining, defaeceating. Bringing this thing in is the origin of assent; expelling the thing from the body is the origin of denial . . . a child curious about his mother's body, assimilates its curiosity to this physical exploration. (Wollheim, 1984, p. 144)

These are not just bodily metaphors for cognitive acts, for the ego itself is modelled on the body, the ego's activities are lived as bodily activities, "the ego is first and foremost a bodily ego" (Freud, 1923b, p. 26). Further, we never outgrow this deep connection between cognitive functions and their original bodily inscription, they retains their influence.[7] The archaic bodily theory of the mind will for evermore stain and illuminate the minds image of itself.[8]

Thus, under the aegis of the pleasure principle we swallow what we like and spit out or defaecate what we do not like, whereas under the influence of the reality principle we "swallow" something because it is true even though we do not like, and then have to tolerate, its presence inside us.

The death drive

Perhaps at this juncture it might be helpful to think of FTPMF as describing both a general principle and a content. The general principle here would be the tendency of the mind to misrepresent reality, that is to misrepresent as being the case that which it wishes to be the case. The content refers to the kinds of wishes that are gratified in this manner (such as infantile sexual wishes). The introduction of the concept of the death drive in 1919 introduces not just a new kind of content but a new kind of pleasure that is quite distinct, in the kind of things that it is. It is *not* a principle of mental functioning as such but a new drive of the psyche. In his initial introduction of the death drive Freud describes a kind of passive lure into a peaceful world of nothingness that he links to Nirvana.[9] Later (see *Civilisation and its Discontents* (Freud, 1930a) and "An outline of psycho-analysis" (Freud, 1940a[1938])) the drive becomes understood in an entirely different manner: that is, as violent form of mental activity aimed at destroying the self and the object, a principle "[whose] final aim is to undo connections and so destroy things" (Freud, 1940a[1938], p. 147).

There is thus a sense that what is beyond the pleasure principle is not beyond it, in that it is not to do with pleasure, but *is* beyond it in the sense that it is not to do with any particular pleasure.[10,11] It is not the pleasure derived from the satisfaction of any particular desire, but a pleasure that derives from the *negation of all desire*. Thinking places a demand upon the mind for work whereas the pleasure aimed at through this Nirvana-like principle is a pleasure that arises from the absence of work, mindlessness. It is an anti-thought principle and it is this aspect that has been most developed in the work of Bion as I will describe shortly.

Phantasy reality and the depressive position

Melanie Klein's work takes us into a completely different conceptual register as regards our understanding of the pleasure principle, one that although not departing from drive theory understands those drives as materialised in internal object relations. O'Shaughnessy captures well Klein's development of the paper under discussion here. She writes:

> In "Formulations on the Two Principles of Mental Functioning" Freud described the aim of the pleasure principle as the avoidance and discharge of unpleasurable tensions and stimuli (Freud, S.E. 12). In "Notes on Some Schizoid Mechanisms" (1946) Melanie Klein described something similar to the pleasure

principle from a different perspective—an early mechanism of defence which she named projective identification. In her view the young infant defends his ego from intolerable anxiety by splitting off and projecting unwanted impulses, feelings, etc., into his object. This is an object relations perspective on the discharge of unpleasurable tensions and stimuli. (O'Shaughnessy, 1981 [reprinted in 2014, p. 56])

The stress here, it would seem, is thus more on ridding the mind of unpleasant realities as opposed to the construction of alternative pleasure giving realities.[12] But it may not be so easy to distinguish in life between these two kinds of activity. When young Prince Harry believes his father to be dead, this can be understood both as his ridding his mind of an unpleasant reality (the continued existence of his father as an obstruction to his occupation of the throne), and as an escape into a pleasurable reality (himself as king and father safely out of the way). I suspect in life these two processes are inseparably bound up with each other. Thus if we return to O'Shaughnessy's description of Klein we could perhaps add that the avoidance of unpleasure is associated with the creation of a world of pleasure.[13]

K is a nine-year-old girl returning to her first session after a summer break. As I go to meet her in the waiting room she does not rush past me as she normally does. Instead I find her sitting calmly, legs crossed, reading a newspaper. I stand there not quite knowing what to do and clear my throat, somewhat pathetically, to attract her attention. She peers over the paper and says "I will be with you in a minute".

My young patient has managed the break, or maybe the return from the break, through creating an alternative reality, one that avoids the disturbing awareness that she has been waiting for her analyst. She has rid her mind of this unpleasant state she becoming identified with a calm superior analyst occupied with his own concerns, locating in her analyst a more difficult part of herself.

On my appearance she enacts this psychic rearrangement, and does so with remarkable success, that is the inner situation, has been actualised (Sandler, 1976b) in her meeting with her analyst, so that he ends up *really* feeling small and pathetic.[14]

In the paranoid–schizoid position the relation to the world is more dominated by wish than by considerations of reality. However, the establishment of a more securely internalised relation to a good objects, brings confidence and the capacity to tolerate frustration thus lessening the need for splitting and projection as a way of managing mental distress. And so the mind is able to secure a firmer relation to reality, internal and external, these being distinguished from each other and so allowed their own separate existence. The world of the depressive position is thus much less dominated by wishful phantasy.

Freud suggests that in the earliest phases of life the mind is dominated by the pleasure principle although he concedes that such a situation must be to some extent a fiction, but one that can be sustained if one includes the mother in this system. An alternative view, and one that I find more persuasive, is that even from the beginnings of life there is already present some primitive and rather fragile capacity for recognising what is real in the world, which exists in some kind of dynamic relation with the world of pleasure principle. Klein developed Freud's suggestion of an epistemophilic drive, namely a drive to know about the self and the world that cannot be reduced to other drives (such as the sexual drive), although may have close relations to them. The establishment of the depressive position brings a more secure foundation to the drive for knowledge derived from the capacity to bear frustration (the frustration brought by not-knowing), essential to the process of finding out about the world and oneself. In the paranoid–schizoid position the activity of knowing is associated with sadism bringing a deep terror that knowledge can destroy the object, and so a tendency to a paranoid dread of being known (equated with being taken over); the new confidence of the depressive position establishes a world where knowing can be linked to more reparative aspects and so less fear for the fate of the object that is known.

Bion: the English return to Freud

Bion, in the course of his work, revisits again and again a relatively small number of Freud's works, but in so doing gives them explosive new significance. These works included *The Interpretation of Dreams* (1900a), the papers on "Neurosis and psychosis" (Freud, 1924a,b), and the paper under discussion here. Bion's use of the term "thinking" is very close to, though not identical with, Freud's "judging" and his model of the development of thought, as with Freud, places great stress on our capacity to manage the frustration arising from the non-appearance of the desired object.

> The choice that matters to the psychoanalysts is one that lies *between procedures designed to evade frustration and those designed to modify it. That is the critical decision.* (Bion, 1962c, p. 28 italics in original)

Ideas of Freud's that seem abstract and theoretical acquire, in Bion's development of them, *clinical reference*. Where Freud describes a mental apparatus that seeks to rid itself of an accumulation of stimulus, Bion sees these processes as clinical events. He asks, for example, whether a patient's smile is a communication of affection or might be better understood as a use of the muscles of articulation in order to rid the mind of unpleasant sensation.

Returning now to the central statement of FTPMFI:

> It was only the non-occurrence of the expected satisfaction, the disappointment experienced, that led to the abandonment of this attempt at satisfaction by means of hallucination. Instead of it, the psychical apparatus had to decide to form a conception of the real circumstances in the external world and to endeavour to make a real alteration in them. A new principle of mental functioning was thus introduced; what was presented in the mind was no longer what was agreeable but what was real, even if it happened to be disagreeable. This setting-up of the *reality principle* proved to be a momentous step. (Freud, 1911b, p. 219, italics in original)

"The non-occurrence of the expected satisfaction", is somewhat problematic for if it is taken to refer to an external situation (the non-appearance of the desired object), then, as Bion has pointed out, this would run into the problem of equating an external fact (the absence of the desired object) with an internal or "endopsychic" situation. Although the object may not be present and thus real satisfaction may not have occurred, in order for this to be a truly psychological situation there is a further condition that must be fulfilled, that is there must be *awareness* of this situation. In other words, the actual absence of the object is a necessary but not sufficient condition for the mental development that Freud describes.[15] Similarly considerations apply to the experience of loss and separation that is consequential for psychological development.

Freud's "objects shall have been lost which once brought real satisfaction" (Freud, 1925h) becomes Bion's,

> the "no-breast" becomes a thought. Where the capacity for this transformation is lacking, that is when the awareness of the absent object cannot become a thought about an object, its fate is to become the presence of a malign object; here the "no breast" becomes a bad object. (Bion, 1962a, p. 306)[16]

Thinking then, in Bion's sense is an expression of the epistemophilic drive of Freud and Klein; it brings thoughts together, links them with emotion so giving them significance.

Returning now to "Negation", Freud (1925h) provides a description of two radically distinct modes of dealing with unwelcome thoughts. In the first type, negation is a way of "taking cognisance of what is repressed". He gives the example of the patient who says "You ask who this person in the dream can be. It is *not* my mother." In other words the patient has had the thought "it *is* my mother" but the continuance of repression is denoted by the addition of the negation sign to the thought. Such a process one might regard as a kind of half-way house to thought and judgment. On the other hand there is something *qualitatively quite different*, which Freud terms "the negativism which is displayed by some psychotics", which he links to "the instinct of destruction". What is being described here is *not* a passive loss of a capacity, but its active destruction—one is reminded of Freud's drawing on Goethe's *Faust* to grasp the psychotic violence of the Schreber's destruction of his world:

> Woe! Woe!
> Though hast it destroyed
> The beautiful world
> With powerful fist!
> In ruin 'tis hurled,
> By the blow of a demigod shattered
>
> (Freud, 1910k, p. 70)

Bion (1962c) described a Mephistophelian principle, "–K", that has similar properties. It opposes thought, separates thought from feeling, strips ideas of significance, and attacks all meaning. Negation under the aegis of this principle is *not* a first step toward judgment but an attack on the function that makes any judgments possible.

A question naturally arises as to whether hatred of thought is a kind of irreducible datum or is a manifestation of a deeper process. It seems to me that at a very fundamental level the ego has a hatred of anything that presents itself to it as an obstruction.[17] Reality, including the reality of other minds, imposes exactly this kind of obstruction. But again this only becomes a truly psychological problem when there is *awareness* of these features of the world. From this perspective thinking, at some level, therefore always presents itself to the mind as an obstruction both because it is thought (and not action) and because such thinking brings to the mind the awareness of the features of reality just described. It is for this reason that such thought is hated. In a sense it is a case of shooting the messenger (awareness of reality) because the message (the limitations and obstructions imposed by the world) cannot be borne.[18]

Mr G a successful businessman declared early on in his analysis that: "The thing that I want that I cannot have does not exist."

As I got to know Mr G I realised that this compacted statement had a number of articulations in his mental life. If an object appeared that he desired but could not control or possess then it immediately ceased to exist as an object in his world, it was ejected from awareness. On other occasions the object continued to exist but what was annihilated was his need for it and sometimes with it his need for anything at all.

In other words Mr G dealt with the awareness of the non-identity between what he wished for and what was available by destroying his own awareness of this situation and so the momentous step described by Freud could not be taken. Such a step would bring to the mind the awareness of need unsatisfied with all the attendant frustrations, something that for various reasons could not be borne.

There is in some cases a peculiar kind of ultimate pleasure associated with this destruction of the capacity to think, felt as a hated burden—it is perhaps one of deadliest of pleasures. I can well remember, as a psychiatrist on the ward, witnessing the envy of the borderline patient for the schizophrenic, the latter was regarded as finally free of the hated burden of thought.

This whole process is opposed by the drive towards knowledge and integration. There is a special kind of pleasure associated with coming to know, and in this dimension truth is to the mind what food is to the body; Bion suggested that a lack of capacity for truthfulness leads to a kind of mental rickets.

Life, death, and imagination

The difficulties as regards the use of the concept of phantasy discussed above (that is when we counterpose it to reality), trench upon considerations of literature and imagination. Our recognition that it is to literature that we turn in order to have access to deep realities of our lives, has to be protected from opposing it to "reality". The artist's capacity for imagination, and our capacity to enter into an invented world, are highly developed aspects of our psychic functioning, one of our most deeply valued forms of inner enrichment and one of our main points of contact with psychic reality.

Yet there is also a kind of literary activity that, though appearing similar, functions in a completely different way.[19] Far from enriching life it serves to anaesthetise, providing release from pain and thus from thought. Its results are deadly—one might think of various forms of "pulp fiction" and some soap operas. The *inner* register of this activity is a kind of daydreaming that has a malignant quality and perhaps one of the greatest works of literature exploring its consequences is Flaubert's *Madame Bovary* (1857). Emma Bovary turns away from her boring life with a country doctor into the imaginary world she creates with her lover, replacing the disappointments of reality with an alternative world, with catastrophic results. Ignes Sodré has explored this aspect of Flaubert's work in some depth in her very aptly titled paper "Death by daydreaming" (Sodré, 1998).[20] Arthur Miller's *Death of a Salesman* (1967) does similar work for a contemporary audience. Willy Loman's addiction to an entirely fictional view of himself as the all-American successful salesman can only result in his ruin and eventual suicide; but Arthur Miller uses his character to show us how the dominant ideology draws individuals into this imaginary world, requires them to live in it, and so the play expresses at one and the same time an individual and deep cultural pathology.

Perhaps one can posit that where imagination is coupled to the life drive it brings exploration, curiosity, and knowledge; it is growth promoting and brings pleasures of a deep nature. On the other hand, imagination when linked to the death drive brings an "as if" world that merely repeats the same contents in thinly disguised forms, offers simple pleasure. It prevents growth and has an addictive inner momentum. However, one needs to bear in mind that these are not static categories but mobile dimensions. What starts off as a lifesaving defence (the retreat into a pleasurable world to avoid unbearable pain) can transform into an excited addictive part of character, now serving far more perverse aims.

Enactment and its relation to the pleasure principle

Freud's discovery of the centrality of the transference revealed the way in which the analysis although manifestly serving one aim (the development of understanding, the overcoming of symptoms) more secretly sought to fulfil another, namely to provide the vehicle for the fantasied gratification of infantile wishes. But, as in the whole history of psychoanalysis, what starts out as an apparent obstacle to treatment moves to the centre of our understanding of the nature of psychic change. For analysis provides a context for these wishes to come to life, while at the same time creating the possibility for them to be recognised, tolerated, and understood—a unique form of understanding. Insight of this type involves the acceptance of the existence of unrealisable wishes and the recognition of our tendency to misrepresent the world as if it were fulfilling them. The capacity of the analytic setting to provide such insight depends upon allowing these wishes and illusory gratifications to have their proper place, yet not to dominate to the extent that any thinking is impossible. In other words, it is, to borrow Freud's term, a quantitative consideration.

We have now become much more aware of the subtle ways in which emotions, anxieties, defences, and object relations are brought to life as "total situations" (Klein, 1952b; Joseph, 1985) lived out between analyst and analysand—different parts of the narrative being distributed between them. For example, a sadomasochistic scenario may be enacted where the analyst becomes somewhat cold and strict, the patient submissive. I have already had cause to acknowledge Sandler's (1976b) very helpful term "actualisation" to describe these situations and suggested (Sandler, 1976a). He has suggested that there is some basic force within us all that seeks to create a complete symmetry between inner and outer, that is, an "identity of perception" (this term is used by Freud in *The Interpretation of Dreams* (1900a)).

So, the enactments within the transference have a double valency. From one perspective, they provide the possibility for the development of thought, from the other they aim in exactly the opposite direction; where through transference enactment, outside is made similar to inside to the degree that they can no longer be properly differentiated then this foundational distinction, essential for thought, is lost.

It is not difficult to think of the kind of beliefs that suggest simple wish is gratified—one might think of the patient believing themselves to be a special patient, to be particular interesting, etc. However, there is also a different kind of gratification:

Mr A, from very early on in his analysis, claimed that his analyst did not like him. He seemed at times to work very hard, usually unsuccessfully, to achieve this result, and would even claim, on little evidence, that his contention was now proven. When on occasion a note of irritation might enter the analysts voice—this was quickly noticed with some satisfaction and any other aspects of the situation that might suggest other possibilities, were wiped out, thus confirming an inner picture of the analytic situation that the patient believes in, and often thinks the analyst shares but will not acknowledge.

One might think that the evident pleasure was derived from masochistic submission and there may have been an element of this. But over and above the pleasure derived from the gratification of this kind of wish there is, I am suggesting, another kind of pleasure, which functions at a more "meta" level. That is, the pleasure derived from the achievement, through enactment and distortion of perception, of the illusion of "identity of perception", something that seems to have its own peculiar satisfactions—a pleasant state of absence of conflict, opposed to thought. Although at some level, this urge to create symmetry between internal and external[21] may be just a simple fact of mental life, a kind of default system, it can I believe be brought into service of the most deadly aims. If thinking places a demand upon the mind for work, the pleasure aimed at through this nirvana like principle is a pleasure that arises from the absence of work.

> ... the effort to reduce, to keep constant or to remove internal tension due to stimuli ... is one of our strongest reasons for believing in the existence of the death instinct. (Freud, 1920g, pp. 55–56)

The fact that the individual has to act upon the world to create the necessary actualisation is testament to both the presence of sanity and its unbearability. Where such contact is very limited this "identity of perception" can be achieved in the original manner, without effecting any real change in the world: that is, by hallucination.

It needs to be noted that actual identity of perception can *never* be achieved, it is always an illusion and the degree of distortion that is necessary to maintain the illusion is a measure of the patient's contact with reality.

Some broader cultural implications

In the introduction I gave emphasis to the cultural significance of psychoanalysis, and here in this closing section I return to this theme for it would be hard indeed to think of anything in psychoanalysis that has more significance for human culture in general than the recognition of the fragility of the distinction between "the world as it is" and "the world as I would like it to be". The promise of fulfilment of infantile wishes permeates the discourse of everyday life both overtly (in advertising, political sloganeering, celebrity culture) and also in ways that are more subtle—perhaps nowhere moreso than in our relation to money, whose power derives in no small measure from its peculiar location within our psychic economy.

Freud thought that money could not bring happiness:

> Happiness is the deferred fulfilment of a prehistoric wish. That is why wealth brings so little happiness: money is not an infantile wish. (Freud, Jan 16th, 1898, letter to Fliess)

However, one could perhaps add that money represents itself as if it could remove all obstructions to the realisation of those wishes. Freud like Marx recognised that money, like the commodity form itself, has a fetish like quality.[22] We cease to see money for what it is, that is for the social relations that it embodies, and imagine that it is the object itself has magical powers.

Throughout history humanity has created cultural objects whose function is to appear to gratify our desires in a simple way and the extent to which they do so is the extent to which they obstruct our capacity for thought. For Freud the paradigmatic example was religion, a system of beliefs that serves to protect us from the painful burden brought by our recognition of mortality, limitation on our powers, ageing, and human vulnerability in general.

However, a kind of religious sentiment inevitably attaches itself to the ideology that comes to dominate an age which then functions like a mass religion seducing the populace into submission. We are all subject to pressures arising from a conjunction of internal needs and external interests, which draw us into the childish belief that those in power know what they are doing, are looking after our interests: that is, to treat them as parental figures. What is most impressive is the resilience of this belief in the face of the evidence, and perhaps nowhere is this clearer than in the management of the economy discussed as if it represented brute (mathematical) facts of nature rather than socio-political processes. Economic crises are presented not as revealing the fault lines of our manner of socio-economic organisation, but as unpredictable chance happenings that can be well managed by the actors who are most closely implicated as the causal agents of the catastrophe. But crisis, that is a periodicity of crisis and recovery, and further crisis, has been characteristic of capitalism since the beginning.

Viewing the crisis *historically*, gives emphasis to structures that endure in time: that is, the systemic fault lines along which fractures will take place. But when a crisis occurs there is a natural tendency, and this is massively bolstered by the needs of the dominant ideology, to view it *as of the moment*, horizontally. So the crisis, instead of revealing what is immanent/systemic within the structure, is seen as a deviation, some bizarre accident that needs another explanation.

In a parallel manner, a psychoanalyst views a breakdown as revealing what is immanent in an individual's character structure, the fault lines that are long established. But individuals and their families, like societies, have a deep vested interests in viewing the breakdown as the eruption of something new, not the revelation of what was always there. A patient entering analysis in a crises very soon loses the wish to understand the crises and seeks the restoration of the status quo ante—he loses the ability to see that the crisis is in fact the continuation of the so-called normal and that solving the crises cannot remove the systemic problems that continue to manifest themselves.

There are certain aspects of the current crisis arising from the financialisation of the economy that make it peculiarly prey to these primitive processes. Financial products because of their non-material nature readily appear in our world as "fantastic objects"; financial dealers gripped by these objects are driven into a mania they cannot resist and as this mania gathered momentum, some almost seemed to believe that money could be made out of nothing.[23]

However, there also needs to be a word of caution here, as this understanding might seem to unwittingly imply that the market freed from these fantasised projections would then reveal itself to be rational (a wish fulfilling representation of reality)—whereas what the crises make manifest are the contradictions at the centre of our mode of socioeconomic life, and do so with a peculiar and unwelcome nakedness.

In *Group Psychology* (Freud, 1921c) showed how much of the typical phenomenology of groups can be brought under the heading of regression. That is, in groups we seem to be particularly prone to lose the capacity for that momentous step described in FTPMF and fall back into more infantile modes of functioning. Groups are thus capable of actions that, if they had been carried out by an individual, would have landed him in a psychiatric hospital. This is most clearly evident in war where under the influence of leaders and group pressure, individuals who on Monday were friends and allies, on Tuesday see their erstwhile neighbours as the embodiment of evil and set about annihilating each other. What we witness here is a kind of terrible longing to be rid of the capacity for thinking so that action can proceed unobstructed. In "Freudian theory and the pattern of fascist propaganda" (Adorno, 1951)—perhaps one of the greatest interweavings of Marxist critical theory and psychoanalysis—Adorno points out that the fascist and his followers do not really believe in their heart of hearts that the Jew is evil. He goes on to say:

> It is probably the suspicion of this fictitiousness of their own group psychology that makes fascist crowds so merciless and unapproachable. If they would stop to reason for a second, the whole performance would fall to pieces and they would be left in panic.

Thought is the enemy of this system and so must be resisted at all costs. Here one can see the dual action of the need to avoid the unpleasure that thought would bring, combined with the pleasurable exaltation that results from release from reason, bringing a world free from doubt and guilt, thus leaving the way open to pure pleasure in destruction.

Segal (personal communication) used Bion's model of group functioning to make an important contribution to understanding the degradation of politics in our contemporary world. She pointed out that differentiation between the "work group" and the "basic assumption group" (the basic assumption group for our current purpose can be thought of as the wish-fulfilling group) does not hold in the case of politics, at least in politics as it is now lived. In a sense there is no work group, as the work of the politician is to create and foster basic assumption mentality: that is, to attract support, not through argument, but through the promotion of regression, "Follow me, I will transform the economy, make everyone safe, increase freedom and create law and order" and coming not far behind, "get rid of those parasites (that is immigrants) from abroad and shirkers at home, who leach on the civilised values of England's honest decent working people."

Here, promotion of regressive projective systems becomes the key to political success. This ideology with all its absurd propagandistic proclamations has its attractions—particularly for those who are the most insecure, who feel their place in the world is under threat, are burdened with a sense of their own superfluousness,[24] actual or threatened. This intolerable situation is dealt with in the way with which we have become disturbingly familiar: the hated uncertainty/sense of superfluousness is projected into others—it is not *us* who have no place, who are superfluous, it is *them* (immigrants, social security scroungers, etc.). This does bring some relief. But because the "belonging" it provides is based not on understanding but on projection, because the community created is not a real community but a pseudo-community, founded not on real shared ties, but only on negation—we are alike because we are *not* them—this whole situation is precarious. The sane awareness of the self-deception and lies that are at the foundation of these delusions is never completely eradicated, and so the drive for projection is ever more desperate.

A philosophical note

Freud's paper is embedded within a philosophical *Weltnashauung* founded on the centrality of the distinction between the "world as we would like it to be" and "the world as it is". This broadly realist ontology has, however, come under some attack from a "postmodernist" epistemology that celebrates the relativisation of all truth. This current has been widely influential especially within the humanities and some have thought it a natural philosophical "home" for psychoanalysis; bringing psychoanalysis within the postmodern is regarded as liberating it from what is characterised (or, more properly, caricatured) as a naïve scientism that makes omnipotent claims for objectivity and truth.

Postmodernism, as an epistemology, is not a child of modernism, which broke with old forms that constrained knowledge to discover deeper and often more disturbing truths, but instead stands in opposition to all claims of knowledge/truth/reality. The tragic vision of man battling against the world and himself, is transformed into a celebration of fluidity, plurality, change. As Eagleton (1996) and Harvey (1990) have pointed out, the world that is depicted is profoundly schizoid (by which they mean fragmented, alienated). But this form of existence does not bring the emptiness and despair that one might imagine is its counterpart, but instead becomes the basis of celebration. Harvey puts it this way:

> Its total acceptance of ephemerality, fragmentation discontinuity . . . .. It does not try to transcend it . . . or even define it . . . postmodernism swims, wallows in the fragmentary currents of change, as if that is all there is. (Harvey, 1990, p. 14)

Identity as an enduring characteristic ceases to exist as identities and beliefs can be *chosen* to suit ones needs. Tragic man weighed down with sedimented layers of his own personal and cultural history is at a stroke transformed into light-hearted postmodernist man watching on with a knowing and ironic smile. The painful apprehension of complexity becomes "the world can be what I want it to be", all struggle disposed of at one blow. Some psychoanalysts have collapsed the idea of truth into "what works" (see, for example, Renik, 1998). Here what was knowledge has become something one can choose to have or not have, not unlike an object on a supermarket shelf—and so this form of extreme relativisation reveals itself as the penetration of the commodity form into epistemology.

There are many other problems of this position that I have discussed elsewhere (Bell, 2009) but crucial in terms of our discussion of FTPMF is that where there is no truth, there is no place mark for lies or self-deception.[25] Where all is surface, the crucial distinctions, illusion-truth, appearance, and reality, dissolve as does all that depends on these crucial differentiations. And so, as I see it, a major foundation of psychoanalysis falls away.

Concluding comment

"Formulations on the two principles of mental functioning" covers in the space of a few pages, a territory that has remained foundational, not only to psychoanalysis, but also to a form of thinking in which psychoanalysis will continue to find a natural home. I am referring to those modes of engagement with the world in which concepts such as illusion/deception *vs.* truth, surface *vs.* depth will continue to have a place. For the distinctions that Freud draws remain essential in order for us to be able to engage critically with ourselves and the world. They commit us to an endless struggle to achieve a firmer relation to ourselves and the world, while recognising the nature and intransigence of the forces we are up against, the limitations under which we struggle—a truly tragic position. There is, however, no alternative for the struggle for truthfulness and the struggle for our human survival are inseparable and in this spirit I will end with a quotation from Hannah Arendt, who well understood the critical nature of this position.

> Could the activity of thinking as such, the habit of examining whatever happens. . . . could this activity be among the conditions that make men abstain from evil-doing or even actually "condition" themselves against it? (Arendt, 1978, p. 5)

Notes

1. For example in *Beyond the Pleasure Principle* (Freud, 1920g) Freud returns to issues that were the focus of his attention in "A project for a scientific psychology" (1895a) and *The Interpretation of Dreams* (1900a); right at the end of his life in "The splitting of the ego in the process of defence" (Freud,

1940e[1938]), he addresses, in a different register, the implication of the process of vertical splitting that had been central to *The Studies of Hysteria* (1895d) (he writes: "I find myself for a moment in the interesting position of not knowing whether what I have to say should be regarded as something long familiar and obvious or as something entirely new and puzzling . . .").

    2.   I have put "mode of thought" in quotation marks as one could argue that this is a system of "unthinking", serving to undo the capacity for thought.

    3.   It would seem that the Freudian problematic of phantasy, far from justifying a distinction in kind between unconscious and conscious phantasies, is more concerned with bringing forward the analogies between them, the transitions that they share and the transitions that take place between one and the other. (Laplanche and Pontalis, 1973, p. 317)

    4.   This is of course the reason for the convention of using the term "phantasy" to describe unconscious psychic processes, to distinguish it from the more common use of the term "fantasy".

    5.   The term "double bookkeeping" comes from classical German psychiatry where it referred to certain psychotic people who kept "one book" in reality and another more private one in their delusions.

    6.   In fact, Spock was half-human and half-Vulcan and thus to some extent never quite free of the potential intrusion of emotions although he seemed to have had the capacity to somehow make a choice in favour of pure logic.

    7.   We retain this knowledge in colloquialisms and slang—for example, someone may express disagreement by saying "I will not swallow that"; an individual may tell someone who they experience as forcing an unwelcome view upon them "don't try to fill me with your shit" or "keep your shit to yourself".

    8.   The term "the mind's image of itself" I owe to Richard Wollheim who used this as the title for his Ernest Jones Lecture, subsequently published (Wollheim, 1969).

    9.   Freud's use of this term (which he borrowed from Barbara Low) is not correct as Nirvana more refers to an emptying of the mind in order to access deeper layers of psychological experience.

    10.   I have discussed the death drive at more length elsewhere, see Bell, 2015.

    11.   Laplanche deals with this difficulty as regards the nature of the pleasure associated with the death drive by distinguishing between the sexual life instincts and the sexual death instincts (see Laplanche, 1976).

    12.   It is not clear in Freud whether the experience of pleasure and the ridding the mind of unpleasure/pain are regarded as separable.

    13.   If, following Bion's suggestion, we imagine a small child in pain and distress, being provided with love, care, and the breast, and then at that moment defecating—we might imagine him as being unable to distinguish between the pleasures of being fed and provided for and the pleasure derived from the feeling of having evacuated an object (faeces) imagined as being the source of his difficulty.

14. As Elizabeth Spillius (1988, p. 83) has pointed out, projective identification remains a phantasy and the effect upon an external object is a matter quite distinct and so cannot, I believe, enter into the definition of this process. The effect upon an external object is better understood, and here I follow Feldman's (1994) building on the work of Sandler (1976), as the actualisation of the phantasy, something conceptually quite distinct.

15. This is in reality only a re-framing and clarification of Freud's original formulation. (For further discussion of Bion on this topic see Bell, 2011.)

16. It is reasonably assumed that the idea of absence is too sophisticated for the infantile mind that conceives not of absences but malign presences. In Mozambique the popular word for breakfast is the Portuguese *Matabicho*, a compound word made up from *matar* (to kill) and *bicho* a disgusting animal. Thus breakfast is the object that kills the bad object (the *bicho*) that is the source of inner persecution. That is, the colloquial language retains in poetic form the archaic experience.

17. This has I think some relation to Freud's (1915c) description of "the narcissistic ego's primordial repudiation of the external world" (p. 138).

18. Although it is not my focus here it needs to be emphasised that the capacity for thought also brings deep feelings of integration and pleasure.

19. Hanna Segal was an enthusiastic reader of science fiction and suggested that good science fiction explored the question "what if?": that is, what would life be like if such and such was the case (e.g., if people could read others' minds). Here imagination expresses curiosity/exploration, which is in contrast to that kind of writing that seeks to replace one reality with another without exploration—not "what if?" but "as if".

20. Dennis Potter, particularly in his masterpiece *Pennies From Heaven* (1978) has brilliantly explored this territory.

21. The satisfaction derived from an opinion being right seems to take precedence over the desirability of the content of the opinion.

22. I am using the term fetish in its quite ordinary sense—that is an object endowed with magical and spiritual powers. Freud natural understanding of our peculiar relation to money is grounded in the theory of infantile development. For Marx this understanding derived derives from his more general recognition of commodities as social object. The monetary value of a commodity appear to the workman as if something that arises directly from the object (a magical quality), whereas in reality it expresses the social relations between the different producers. Marx called this "commodity fetishism" (see Marx, 1976).

23. David Tuckett has carried out an extensive study of the phantasy structures that dominate the functioning of those whose task is to administrate finance capital (see, for example, Tuckett, 2011).

24. For Hannah Arendt, the category of superflousness was a critical component of the elements of totalitarianism.

25. As Bion has pointed out, because truth is something that we apprehend alongside others, it cannot be possessed whereas the lie, because it is self-constructed, can be possessed, which accounts in part for our preference for lies.

Editors' introduction to Chapter Three

Dr Busch's paper examines how Freud's structural theory and its further development by ego psychologists expanded on the "Two principles" paper in important ways. He begins this chapter by clarifying what he believes is the unfounded equation of primary process thinking with the unconscious and, analogously, secondary process thinking with consciousness. Similarly, Busch writes, after the introduction of the structural model Freud no longer considered consciousness associated with the ego just as the repressed and the unconscious had formerly been connected. Thus, by the 1930s, Freud had all but abandoned these assertions; noting, in the *New Introductory Lectures* (1933a), that parts of the ego and superego could be unconscious. These later theoretical developments added another dimension to what Busch calls the *frustration hypothesis* in the "Two principles" paper to account for the origin of reality testing and the ego. He refers to the work of Hartman following Freud's later thinking who offered a view of the ego (in its role of relating to reality) as having its own line of development and Busch claims that, "Over time Hartmann's developmental view of the ego (and reality testing) proved more accurate than this early frustration hypothesis". Additionally, Busch importantly reminds us that Freud ultimately came to understand that parts of the ego and superego were unconscious, thereby further dispensing with his earlier equation of the ego with consciousness. This advance in his thinking allowed Freud to describe the role of the *unconscious ego* in defences.

Regarding the psychoanalytic theory of thinking promoted in the "Two principles" paper, Busch carefully discusses how Freud's early *frustration hypothesis* as the origin of thinking and reality testing (because hallucinatory wish fulfilment failed to provide *real* satisfaction) was significantly elaborated in the work of Hartmann and Rapaport. For Hartmann, the ego had its origins in an undifferentiated state in earliest infancy and later had its own line of development that was relatively independent of other factors. Busch concludes that, "what Hartmann developed was an alternative to Freud's *frustration hypothesis* in the development of reality testing, and later the ego, that dominated his views in 'Two principles' ". Busch widens his exploration of this topic by linking the ego psychologist's views with some contemporary Bionian perspectives that outline an object relational component to what is traditionally regarded the "ego". For example, Bion's concept of alpha function (Brown, 2009) seems to be an unconscious ego mechanism involved in the unconscious creation of meaning, while some of Ferro's ideas about the development of an "apparatus for thinking" also expand our understanding of the nature of thinking (Ferro, 2006).

3

Second thoughts on Freud's "Two principles"

Fred Busch

In this bold, audacious article, Freud, in a very few pages, presents his first attempt at a purely psychoanalytic understanding of how humans come to face reality and the development of two types of thinking.[1] As noted by Strachey (1958), the main theme is the "distinction between the regulating principles (the pleasure principle and the reality principle) which respectively dominate the primary and secondary mental processes" (p. 216). In this chapter I will focus on the distinction between primary and secondary process thinking and the view, still held by many, that unconscious thinking is equated with primary process thinking and that conscious thinking is the same as secondary process thinking. I will elaborate on Jones' (1957) summation of Freud's thinking at the time, and what happened after.

> When Freud wrote his important metapsychological essays in the spring of 1915 he felt he had completed his life work, and that any further contributions he might make would be of a subordinate and merely complementary order. His followers would doubtless have taken a similar view at that time. Had his work come to an end then we should have possessed a well-rounded account of psychoanalysis in what might be called its classical

form, and it would not have been easy to predict its future development at the hands of his successors. There was not the slightest reason to expect that in another few years Freud would have produced some revolutionary conceptions, which necessarily had the effect of extensively remodelling both the theory and the practice of psycho-analysis. (1957, p. 256)

In short, Freud's determined search for the truth led him to realise there were some difficulties with his first model of thinking, which led to a series of corrections. It is noteworthy that by the time Freud (1923b) wrote *The Ego and the Id*, the concepts of primary and secondary processes all but disappeared. By 1933 Freud finally came to the conclusion that the system *Ucs.* became more and more "to denote a *mental province rather than a quality of what is mental*" (1933a, p. 71, my italics). In short, the primary process could no longer be equated with the system *Ucs*. By the end of his writings, Freud felt the distinction between primary and secondary process, and their relationship to the unconscious and consciousness, was no longer useful. I will briefly review how Freud came to this conclusion, and his revised view of how thinking develops and its consequences for a model of the mind and psychoanalytic technique.

Corrections

The distinction between primary and secondary processes became less clear as early as Freud's (1915e) paper on "The unconscious". In a diversion from his main thesis Freud points out that, "*A very great part of this preconscious originates in the unconscious . . .*" (p. 191, my italics). In an elaboration, he noted the thoughts he referred to had all the earmarks of having been formed *unconsciously*, "but *were highly organized, free from self-contradiction, have made use of every acquisition of the system* Cs., *and would hardly be distinguished in our judgment from the formations of that system*" (p. 190, my italics). So now Freud presents us with a thought formed in the unconscious, but had all the qualities of secondary process thinking. However, this observation was put aside for the moment.

Freud (1923b) returns to this in another form in *The Ego and the Id*. After noting the various components of the ego, which he first associates with consciousness, Freud comes to the issue of unconscious resistances, which became one of the most important factors in his move to the structural model. This became a crucial part, also, of Freud's recognition of the difficulty in keeping the connection between the primary process and the *repressed unconscious*.

> Since, however, there can be no question that this resistance emanates from his ego and belongs to it, we find ourselves in an unforeseen position. We have come upon something in the ego itself, which is also unconscious, which behaves just like the repressed—that is, which produces powerful effects without it being conscious . . . .. (1923b, p. 17)

By 1933 Freud makes the break final when he states,

> It is a fact that ego and conscious, repressed and unconscious, do not coincide. We feel a need to make a fundamental revision of our attitude to the problem of conscious-unconscious. (1933a, p. 70)[2]

This fundamental revision was the structural model, where "portions of the ego and superego (were now viewed as) being unconscious without possessing the same primitive and irrational characteristics" (p. 75, parenthesis added).

Finally, I would like to briefly touch on Freud's view of where the *energy* came from in his models of thinking. Throughout almost all his writing, Freud was consistent in his view that the energy for development of secondary process thinking and then the ego was *borrowed*—first from the primary process and then from the id. This borrowing came about because of the demands of the external world. However, in his final work, Freud (1940a[1938]) states, "Originally, of course, everything was id; the ego was developed out of the id by the continual influence of the external world" (p. 43). However, shortly before this Freud had a different idea. In a footnote to "Analysis terminable and interminable" (Freud, 1937c) notes:

> When we think of "archaic heritage" we are generally only thinking of the id and we *apparently* assume that no ego is present at the beginning of life. But we must not overlook the fact that the ego and id are originally one, and it does not imply a mystical over-valuation of heredity if we think it credible that even before the ego exists, *its subsequent lines of development, tendencies, and reactions are already determined*. (p. 240, my italics)

This idea, elaborated in the work of Hartmann (1939, 1964) and many others, was to become a source of great controversy over the next decades, along with strong negative reactions that seem more than reactions to a scientific disagreement.[3]

The ego: elaborations and misunderstandings

Freud (1933a) was prescient in his *New Introductory Lectures* when he stated,

> I must, however, let you know of my suspicion that this account of mine of ego-psychology will affect you differently from the introduction into the psychical underworld, which preceded it ... I now believe that it is somehow a question of the nature of the material itself and of our being unaccustomed to dealing with it. In any case, I shall not be surprised if you show yourselves even more reserved and cautious in your judgment than hitherto. (p. 58)

In line with this it is fascinating that the major clinical reason for the switch to the structural model (i.e., unconscious ego resistances) has remained a source of controversy (Busch, 1995, 1999, 2013a). As early as 1934 Sterba pointed out, "It is my impression that this newest addition to our science [the defense ego] has not been sufficiently recognized and that it has not yet penetrated the thinking and the therapeutic technique of most analysts (p. 117f). It is a point emphasized some years later by Gray (1982) and others.

However, it was the work of Hartmann,[4] and his attempt to expand Freud's 1937 view of an inherited development of the ego, which was the source of the greatest controversy. Starting in 1939, Hartmann presented the view that the ego was more than just a developmental by-product of the clash between the reality and the instinctual drives, and that it had an *independent origin*. He does not rule out the role of the instinctual drives and the demands of reality, but also sees it as based on a set of factors that cannot be identified with either one of them. In a later article he sums up his position by saying, "not all factors of mental development present at birth can be considered part of the id" (Hartmann, 1950, pp. 119–120), and that later development is, in part, dependent on *maturation*. In short, Hartmann portrayed a view of the ego as beginning in an *undifferentiated phase*, where the ego proceeded to develop, *in part*, according to its own line of development. In short, what Hartmann developed was an alternative to Freud's *frustration hypothesis* in the development of reality testing, and later the ego, that dominated his views in "Two principles". As stated by Freud (1911b),

> It was only the non-occurrence of the expected satisfaction, the disappointment experienced, that led to the abandonment of this attempt at satisfaction by means of hallucination. Instead of it, the psychical apparatus had to decide to form a conception of the real circumstances in the external world and to endeavour to make a real alteration in them. (p. 219)

Over time Hartmann's developmental view of the ego (and reality testing) proved more accurate than this early frustration hypothesis. For example, authors like Peterfreund (1978) and Pine (1981) pointed to evidence of a beginning ego almost from birth, thus raising questions about an *undifferentiated phase*. Peterfreund writes,

> Everything now known about infancy—from behavioral and biological studies—argues against any conception of an undifferentiated phase in which the infant supposedly cannot distinguish inner and outer stimuli or distinguish between himself and inanimate objects, and against any idea that in the human infant the function of and the equipment for self-preservation are atrophied. (Peterfreund, 1978, p. 433)

Sander (1977) made this observation:

> Current research in early infancy is beginning to provide provocative evidence that human existence normally begins in the context of a highly organized relational system from the outset. This relational system interfaces two live, actively self-regulating, highly complex, living (and adapting) components—the infant and the caregiver, each already running, so to speak. (p. 15)

Sander's observation, which points to an early ego in the first days of life, has been repeated by many researchers (e.g., Stern, 1991; Tronick, 2002).

Studies and psychoanalytic reflection have shown the validity of many ego functions that have an *independent, but not an autonomous,* line of development. That is, there are certain universal timetables for the development of certain ego functions, but these are always subject to influences from such factors as the strength of the instincts, parental capacities for containment, and traumatic developmental interferences, just to name a few. Piaget's (1926; Piaget & Inhelder, 1959[5] studies on the development of thinking, and Pinker's (1994) work on the development of grammatical structures are just two of the notable examples of a universal developmental time-table of ego functions.

Green (2000a), one of many critics of Hartmann, believes it is not "possible to defend the idea of an ego that would be, in the beginning, in a position to have its own existence aside from the id" (p. 111). He cites the limitations of the ego (e.g., the strength of the unconscious and the compliant aspects of the ego) as based on "the scars of his ancient relationship to the id or its derivatives" (p. 111). In support of Green, even casual observation causes one to see that the earliest life of the infant, when alert, is driven by instinct. However, the data suggest there is an additional way of thinking about this issue. I would suggest that very rudimentary ego functions are in existence from the beginning of life, it just takes a much longer time for ego functions to develop, and the infant is dependent on the external world to serve as an auxiliary ego until more mature ego functions emerge according to their developmental timetable. [6] It is well documented that the child's capacity for self-regulation takes place very gradually, and is dependent on external forces far longer than other species. Seeing the ego's susceptibility to influence from the id at an early age says little about how the ego emerges.[7]

Musings on Bion's model of the mind and ego psychology

Brown (2009) pointed to Bion's reliance on Freud's "Two principles" as the basis for much of his theoretical contributions on the development of different levels of thought processes. Thus, Brown's article on Bion's *ego psychology* is interesting to follow in the light of Freud's jettisoning many of the ideas in that article as noted above.

Brown sees Bion's major contribution to the infant's early relationships as "the infant, in collaboration with its mother, comes to know reality, gives emotional meaning to its experiences, and learns from those experiences" (p. 30). While the mother's influence on the infant's experience of the world and the mutual regulation of the parent–child couple was something Freud, as well as Hartmann and his colleagues were well aware of,[8] but what Brown captures in Bion's writings *is the specific affective colouring the mother gives to experience*, which was implied but not so well represented in Hartmann's more scientific way of writing.

> And again what we find here is the closest interaction with *object relations*: while the development of object relations is codependent by ego development, *object relations are also one of the many factors that determine the development of the ego*. (Hartmann, 1950, p. 105, my italics)

However, in the early 1950s Escalona (1953) had already noted the way different types of mothers interacted with different types of infants, and its effect on temperament. Drawing from her psychoanalytic experience and work at Menninger, Escalona noted how similarities in maternal approaches could have profoundly different effects as a function of infant characteristics. Escalona saw how some infants may be overly sensitive and overactive, or under-sensitive and under-reactive, and how a more active or passive mother has an important effect on different temperaments. Over the years, of course, the effect of interpersonal relations on infant development became a staple of psychoanalytic research. Yet there was much resistance to the significance of this data in the international psychoanalytic community, and there was an inability to integrate these findings into ways of thinking about the analytic situation and technique the way Bion did.

Having trained with analysts who came from the Anna Freud Centre[9], I was most familiar with the detailed elaboration of the ego in Anna Freud's (1963) lines of development, and in the child and adult profile that came from the Hampstead Clinic (A. Freud et al., 1965; Nagera, 1963). Brown highlights Bion's addition of a previously unspecified function, an alpha function, as a "superordinate ego function responsible for ascribing emotional meaning to experience" (2009, p. 30). In adding this function, *Bion captured elements of what I would call, an ego function that is more experience-near, and clinically useful for the practising clinician*. In one sense Bion's views exemplified the essence of what we are trying to help our patients accomplish:

that is, to help change the more primitive states that cannot be digested (beta elements) into thoughts and feelings that can be observed and played with[10]. Integrating Bion with my own way of thinking, I suggest we are constantly gauging where a patient is in relationship to his transformative *alpha function*, to know best how to intervene, if at all. Further, I think Ferro (2005a), mentioned by Brown, did have a unique Bionian conception of working with the ego when he stated, "there is not *an unconscious to be revealed*, but a capacity for thinking to be developed, and that the development of the capacity for thinking allows closer and closer contact with the previous non-negotiable areas" (p. 102). Here, in his own terms, Ferro may be suggesting working through resistances[11] to the emergence of non-negotiable unconscious content before interpreting it. That is, freeing the patient to think about what was unthinkable before being confronted with it. However, in general, it is difficult to see how Bion could account for unconscious defences in his allegiance to Freud's pre-structural model.

Bion's main focus seems to be on what Freud called the descriptive unconscious: that is, the more primitive feelings and urges that have not been transformed. As described by Bion, the patient "has feelings, but cannot learn from them; sensations, some of which are extremely faint, but cannot learn from them either . . . Sense-impressions can be seen to have some meaning but the patient feels incapable of knowing what the meaning is" (1962c, p. 18).

It is clear that many analysts see the most crucial and complicated part of analysis, using Bionian terms, is in transforming *beta elements*[12] and the beta screen into alpha elements and the *contact barrier*. While these are not the terms Bion would use, as he saw what was repressed as already thought alpha elements, I would suggest that the beta elements seem to be the equivalent of what is descriptively unconscious. While alpha functioning is associated with a *contact barrier*,[13] the beta screen is composed of beta elements. "Clinically this screen of beta elements presents itself to casual observation as indistinguishable from a confused state and in particular from any one of that class of confused states which resemble dreams" (1962c, p. 22). As Bion points out, what makes these beta screens so difficult to understand is that the patient's confusion has an unconscious purpose, which is to have some effect upon the analyst, and that his *use of words is much closer to action*, and most frequently arouses countertransference feelings. The difficulty for the analyst, as I would understand it, is that these initial countertransference feelings in the analyst are closer to beta elements, and thus difficult to sort out (i.e., apply alpha functioning). In my own understanding the analyst, via reflection (Bion's dreaming), eventually becomes aware of these disturbing feelings (has a sense- impression) that allows for the work of alpha functioning to sort out his feelings, and see what Bion called "the *consistency* in the characteristic of beta-elements" (1962c, p. 24, my italics).

Approaching this topic from the standpoint of the ego,[14] I (Busch, 2009, 2013a) have focused on the term "language action".

> What this label attempts to capture is that the patient's thinking, at these times, is without meaningful verbal representation and closer to action. That is, where words become attempts to bore, seduce, anger, etc. It is where words become more like concrete acts. (2013a, p. 48)

I have elaborated that:

> this special language, *language action*, is the primary method the unconscious speaks to us in psychoanalytic treatment, and why this is. *Transformation of words as actions into symbolic, representational thinking is part of helping the analysand to develop a psycho-analytic mind as the capacity to play with thoughts is dependent on their being representable.* (2013a, p. 50)

In different terms I describe the clinical method of working with language action similar to Bion's:

> Language action stirs up the analyst's countertransference, eliciting a reaction like being taken aback, wanting to reach out, or turning away from the patient. Once we recognize this countertransference reaction, and reflect upon it, this action has already begun to be translated, i.e., represented within the mind of the analyst. From here the analyst can formulate the language action into words as a necessary step in helping patients find increasing degrees of freedom to think and feel. That is, we try to understand what a patient is *doing* with us in their words, tone, phrasing of sentences, and ideas expressed. (2013a, p. 52)

Finally, Bion ultimately comes closest to recognising Freud's structural model when, in describing the analyst work, he summarises:

(1) The ego is a structure that, as Freud describes it, is a specialized development from the id having the function of establishing contact between psychic and external reality. (2) Alpha-function is the name given to an abstraction used by the analyst to describe a function, of which he does not know the nature, until such time he feels in position to replace it by factors for which he feels he has obtained evidence in the course of the investigation in which he is employing alpha-function. It corresponds to that function of a number of factors, including the function of the ego that transforms sense data into alpha-elements. (1962c, pp. 25–26)

Differences in approach

As I have noted previously (Busch, 2013a), I find an increasing common ground among diverse theoretical perspectives in the way we describe the goals of analysis, and the methods of reaching these goals. However, there are differences in the specifics of how we apply these methods. For example, Ferro (2015) describes the necessity for working close to where the patient is emotionally, and not dismissing what is preconsciously available for the patient.

> The container is developed through the ability to be in unison with the patient, the ability, that is, to pursue the same emotional line: this develops the threads I mentioned above and implies the courage to share the manifest meaning of the patient's narrative as well—for as long as it is useful. (Ferro, 2015, p. 136)

In my own work I have described something similar, as have André Green, Betty Joseph, and many others (Busch, 2013b). However where Ferro (2015) and the Kleinians tend to focus on the symbolic transference meaning of most communications, I see the transference as something that is only in the patient's "neighbourhood"[15] after longer periods of working in displacement.

As you will see in the following vignette, I first try to work within those spaces where a patient has come to a certain point in their thinking (dreaming), and then how their thinking has stopped or there has been an emotional change in the analytic atmosphere. In this way, I try to demonstrate how there has been interference in the freedom to think and feel (unconscious ego defence), and *gradually* work towards what is terrifying rather than pointing out the fear immediately. At those times we become aware of countertransference reactions, and reflection and reverie becomes our guide to understanding. However, there are important differences in how we use our reflections. I tend use them to clarify how the patient is using words to *do something*, rather than interpreting them more directly as an unconscious communication.

Clinical vignette

Below I will present a brief vignette from a supervisee that highlights some basic components of defence analysis, and why I believe it is important to first work through the fears leading to a resistance. Basically any unconscious ego resistance has two parts. The first is the dangerous affect first experienced in the unconscious ego. Second is fantasy that leads to the fear. We have to help the patient recognise and appreciate the first, before dealing with the second. In Bionian terms, one could say that by working through resistances, we are trying to transform beta elements into alpha elements at two levels. First, the frightening feelings leading to the resistance, and second the primitive fantasy that is part of the frightening feelings.

From an ego psychological perspective, we attempt to show the moment when anxiety was aroused in the ego, leading to a shift in content or affect. We pay special attention to how this is represented by the analyst so that it may be *preconsciously grasped by that part of the patient's ego not immersed in the conflict of the moment*. This involves a first description of the resistance in *concrete* terms.[16] Our intent is to try and represent the disturbing affect in the ego that led to the disruption in the patient's association, which is basic to any understanding of resistances. Clinically, what one finds is that as treatment progresses the analysand will preconsciously note the disruption, and his associations will give depth to our understanding. I see this as a key to Ferro's (2005a) idea of developing "the capacity for thinking allows closer and closer contact with previous non-negotiable areas" (p. 102).

> Jeff[17] typically showed excessive concern for his wife's feelings, and rarely disagreed with her. In one session he came in reporting how he cleaned out books from his library but had not yet removed them from his home. He told his wife he was going to

his weekly golf game, and reported that she said, in what sounded like an order, "You are not going anywhere until you get rid of those books." He responded, "I'm going to play golf, and I'll take care of the books later." Immediately after telling the analyst of this uncharacteristically assertive stance, Jeff began to justify his wife's behaviour, saying, "She had every right to make that request of me and my anger was not appropriate."

We can see here how after telling the analyst of his taking an assertive stance toward his wife, Jeff has to quickly undo it. The resistance at this moment is not to the assertiveness with his wife, but in *telling the incident to the analyst*. It is immediately after this moment that "something happens" that makes him uncomfortable. It is this "something happens" moment, just before Jeff undoes the expression of assertiveness, where we see the resistance set in. This is what we are trying to help the analysand understand. What is it at this moment that leads to the undoing?

I would work with this resistance this way: "I wonder if you noticed that immediately after you told me of your new found assertiveness with your wife, something seemed to happen and you immediately started to justify your wife's behaviour. It was as if telling me about your assertiveness with her made you uncomfortable." In short, I would represent in the transference that it is the moment after Jeff told the analyst of what happened with his wife that he became uncomfortable, expressing his anger in the analytic moment with the analyst. I would not be representing anything else but the discomfort, as there is no way the analyst can know what part of this discomfort, if any, the analysand will be able to explore at this one moment. It is the discovering of the multiple reasons for the discomfort as they become preconsciously available in the analysis that is the essential component of the working through process. That is, each resistance has multiple parts and over time each one will need to be explored. In exploring the resistance in this unsaturated fashion, we allow the patient the greatest degree of freedom to point us in a direction they are most able to work with at this moment. If the patient cannot capture the resistance in his own mind at this point, there is no point in pursuing what happened at the moment.

Without labelling it as such, Brown (2009) works in a similar manner. After he compassionately helps his overwhelmed patient,

Sally, with a flat tyre by finding a number she had in her car for roadside assistance, Sally seems to have forgotten the event. He notes his working with a rigid resistance when he states, "Any suggestion, however gingerly given, that she might be keeping herself from uncomfortable feelings about relying on me was met with a blank response, as though I were speaking a foreign language" (p. 40). He goes on to suggest that for Sally it was a foreign language as she was more preoccupied with other matters. Thus, Brown sees the interpretation of the resistance as having been ill timed. In my way of thinking it may have been too *saturated*. That is, by linking Sally's avoidance of the topic with her difficulty in *relying* on him, it may have been too dangerous for her to approach this issue. Brown points to how Sally often experienced sensory overload so that her reluctance to approach what happened with her car may have been more of "too much Dr Brown" rather than relying on him.

Antipathy towards change

It remains puzzling as to why Freud's revision of his thinking after the "Two principles" was not embraced in many psychoanalytic cultures. This is especially true of the *models of thinking* developed by the ego psychologists around an ego with an *interdependent* (i.e., not autonomous) trajectory from birth, which has received support from numerous sources for the last seventy years. Even given the excesses of those who highlighted the taming of instincts, there were those who saw the importance of their transformation (e.g., Kris (1952) *regression in the service of the ego*). We seem to have thrown out the proverbial baby with the bath water. Further, a careful reading of the early ego psychologists show an appreciation and understanding of Freud, and in no way do they attempt to dismiss the significance of unconscious thinking in life and as an essential part of the curative process. Yet it is clear that, even today, ego psychology is met with disdain, and even rage. [18]

At least a part of what made ego psychology indigestible can be found in the observations recently made by a number of analysts of the difficulty we have when faced with a new idea (e.g., Bolognini, 2010). Paniagua (2001, 2008) focused on what seems like the pull of the unconscious as a single unitary explanation for our patients' behaviours. Of course, this was the single greatest discovery of Freud, and at an earlier time it seemed like attempts to broaden the psychoanalytic inquiry were seen as a threat to this basic foundational idea. However, the threat seems to go on. Greenberg (2001) succinctly captured our dilemma in dealing with new insights.

> We might hope that, as new ideas emerge, there would come a point at which their adherents could step back and undertake a cooler assessment of their scope. The new idea could then be seen as supplementing, or productively competing with, but not rendering obsolete everything that had come before. Whether by integration or through a constructive competitive dialogue, new ideas would over time be contextualized and tempered. Unfortunately, this tends not to happen in psychoanalysis. (p. 361)

Final comments

As I have noted recently (Busch, 2013b), there is a growing common ground among seemingly disparate theories on clinical technique that follows the structural model, and the ego's role as Janus-faced. This includes such things as:

- Working more closely with what is tolerable to the ego rather than what is deepest in the unconscious.
- Working through unconscious ego defences rather than overcoming them.
- The necessity for making our interpretations more concrete, and in the *here and now* as thinking in the midst of conflict is pre-operational.
- The necessity for distinguishing words as communication and words as language action.

It is my experience that these ideas are universally accepted as long as one does not label them as based on a growing understanding of the ego and its role in psychoanalytic treatment.

Notes

1. As described succinctly by Woody Allen, using the imagined existential philosopher Cloquet, who hated reality, but realised it was still the only place to get a good steak.

2. In fact, Freud's 1933 diagram of the id, ego, and superego, the ego goes even deeper into the unconscious than in his 1923 diagram (Busch, 2006).

3. The ego psychologists saw their work as the continuation of Freud's thinking in his later writings, and in many ways I agree with them. However, there was a tendency to see the goal of the ego to tame the drives rather than integrate them as seen in this quote from A. Freud (1945), who saw maturation in childhood as aiming "at perfecting [ego] functions, at rendering them more and more objective and independent of the emotions until they can become as accurate and reliable as a mechanical apparatus" (p. 144).

4. Many others were involved in the development of ego psychology. David Rapaport especially, deserves notice, although, for reasons that are not clear to me, he seems to be on the receiving end of even more criticism than Hartmann.

5. For excellent early summaries of Piaget's work and its relationship to psychoanalysis see A. Sandler (1975) and Silverman (1971).

6. Freud (1911b) already touches on this in the "Two principles" when he points out that, due to delayed development of the ego, the sexual instincts are under the domination of the pleasure principle for a longer period of time.

7. Much of the other criticism of Hartmann's work is based on misunderstanding. These criticisms rest "on reading 'adaptation' to mean 'conformity' or 'superficial adjustment', and reading 'ego psychology' to mean a 'psychology of consciousness'; also, viewing all such theorizing as sterile, abstruse formalism" (Schafer, 1995).

8. Spitz' (1945) studies on hospitalism were well known.

9. Those I trained with were from the time it was called the Hampstead Clinic.

10. Freud's (1933a) where id was ego shall be.

11. It is not so well remembered that when Freud (1914g) referred to *working through* he meant working through *resistances*.

12. According to Bion, "If alpha-function is disturbed, and therefore inoperative, the sense impressions of which the patient is aware and the emotions which he is experiencing remain unchanged. I shall call them beta-elements. In contrast with the alpha-elements the beta-elements are not felt to be phenomena, but things in themselves. The emotions likewise are objects of sense" (1962c, p. 7).

13. Bion describes the contact barrier in the following manner. "The man's alpha-function whether in sleeping or waking transforms the sense-impressions related to an emotional experience, into alpha-elements, which cohere as they proliferate to form the contact-barrier. This contact-barrier, thus continuously in process of formation, marks the point of contact and separation between conscious and unconscious elements and originates the distinction between them" (1962c, p. 17).

14. Noting the clinical experience of patients using language action, I puzzled over why this occurred and how to best analyse it. I came to the

conclusion that the reason for this "action" type of thinking has to do, in part, with the way thought processes develop. As Piaget has shown, one of the major characteristics of all intelligence is that it is a matter of action. Imaging is not the foundation for thought; action encoded in sensory-motor schema is that foundation. The main distinction between different stages of intellectual development is the degree to which actions become internalised and behaviour is based upon representations rather than a motoric underpinning. I came to the conclusion that much of what is unconscious is encoded in non-representational form.

15.   In his paper on " 'Wild' analysis", Freud (1910k) noted the centrality, among the principles of clinical technique, of the preconscious (the patient's neighbourhood). The patient must be able to make some connection between what he is aware of thinking and saying, and the analyst's intervention. No matter how brilliant the analyst's reading of the unconscious, it is not useful data until it can be connected to something the patient can be consciously aware of (Busch, 1993, 2013a)

16.   This is a patient's way of thinking in the midst of conflict (Busch, 1995, 2009, 2013a).

17.   This example comes from Busch (2013a).

18.   C. Gariepy-Boutin (2012) in a review of a recent book, quotes the author as saying "the literal destruction of psychoanalysis came at the hands of the ego psychologists" (p. 548).

Editors' introduction to Chapter Four

Dr Cassorla is one of the leading figures in Brazilian psychoanalysis and we are fortunate to have many of his papers published in English. In this contribution he examines Freud's "Two principles" paper through the lens of the analytic couple"s capacity for symbol formation and mutual dreaming. In this regard, he addresses Freud's (1911b) ideas about the nature of thinking and discusses "post-Kleinian and Bionian developments regarding some technical aspects that allow us to deal with patients who have deficiency in their thinking capacity." Freud, of course, emphasised that thinking develops through the postponement of the pressure to discharge unpleasurable experience and that, therefore, thinking is "experimental action". But what follows when this process does not develop as Freud suggested?

Cassorla turns his attention to the growth of the capacity for symbol formation, which underlies contemporary perspectives on the subject of thinking, and the consequences of difficulties in symbol formation. Drawing on Melanie Klein's early work on symbol formation and especially the contributions of Bion, Cassorla explores the unique challenges that face the analyst when treating patients whose capacity to form symbols is deficient. Naturally, such difficulties impair the ability of these individuals to communicate their emotions through ordinary means of verbal exchange. They instead rely upon evacuative forms of projective identification that have the effect of evoking powerful, but unrepresented, emotional experiences in the countertransference. It is then up to the analyst to use his thinking abilities to bring meaning to the patient's projected and unprocessed emotions. The analyst may find that his ability to think clearly is restricted in the face of the pressures such patients place upon him and that the traditional channels of listening to the analysand's verbal productions for unconscious material do not engage the patient.

Building on his earlier papers that address the need for the analyst to "dream"-process the emotions evoked in him by the patient, Cassorla describes his concepts of "dreams-for-two" and "non-dreams-for-two" as two modes of interaction. In the former, the analyst and patient are capable of unconscious exchanges that result in the creation of emotional meanings for psychic events that were unrepresented. However, in the latter case (non-dreams-for-two) there is an arrest in their capacity to generate meanings, which frequently leads to chronic enactments that grow out of some shared area of conflict between analyst and analysand that cannot be dreamed. Cassorla presents an interesting analytic vignette in which he and a patient became unconsciously involved in a chronic enactment about coming late for sessions that remained un-dreamed until the analyst examined his countertransference and reveries.

4

Dreaming the analytical session: between pleasure principle and reality principle

Roosevelt M. S. Cassorla

The analyst can feel lost and helpless when working with patients whose symbolisation capacity is deficient. The difficulty can be increased if the patient discharges raw elements into the analyst, attacking his capacity for dreaming and thinking. The analyst might be aware of what is happening but often his perception is numb. In these situations non-thought elements are not contained by the analyst who also discharges them. Occasionally he can give them back to the patient in raw state. Some impasse or interruption of the analysis might happen, sometimes traumatically. If the analyst recovers his mental functions he might later become aware of what happened.

In this chapter, based initially on Freud (1911b), I discuss post-Kleinian and Bionian developments regarding some technical aspects that allow us to deal with patients who have deficiency in their thinking capacity.

The development of the dreaming and thinking capacity

Freud (1911b) in "Two principles" states that "Neurotics turn away from reality because they find it unbearable—either the whole or parts of it" (p. 218).

In order to live in reality the psychic apparatus modifies itself. The *consciousness* seeks to know the reality beyond the pleasure and displeasure sensations. The *attention* searches the external world before it imposes itself. The results of this activity must be registered in the *memory*. The *judging capacity* verifies, in an impartial way, whether something is true or false: that is, whether something exists in external reality or it is a product of the mind.

The motor discharge, which "under the dominance of the pleasure principle, had served as a means of unburdening the mental apparatus of accretions of stimuli, . . . was now employed in the appropriate alteration of reality; it was converted in *action*" (p. 221, italics in original).

The development of the thinking capacity is described in economic terms. The discharge is restrained "by means of the process of *thinking*, which was developed from the presentation of ideas" (p. 221, italics in original). Thinking occurs when the mental apparatus tolerates an increased tension of stimulus while the process of discharge is postponed. This is considered as an experimental action that substitutes for hallucinatory realisation of desire (Freud, 1900a). Regarding the restriction of the excitement Freud (1900a) tells us "the mechanics of these processes are quite unknown" (p. 598).

On the other hand it is frequently known that the problem is less the reality than the perception one has of it. The lack of "necessary adaptation" results in a mental apparatus incapable of perceiving, representing, and dealing properly with the reality.

The study of symbolic representation and the construction of meaning (Bion, 1962b; Isaacs, 1948b; Klein, 1930, 1952a; Segal, 1957) shows us how symbols transform into a mental form that which was initially corporeal. Unconscious fantasies are forms of symbolisation of object relations that are signified in this way. Symbols make the absent reality present, representing and expressing it, initially for ourselves. Symbols attract each other, and create links among themselves by means of affects (love, hate, and knowledge), and constitute a symbolic network that is in constant modification and development. The reality (material and psychic) and its perception can be transformed into new emotional experiences, which become connected to the symbolic network of thinking when they are symbolised. When the capacity of symbolisation is adequate, we can "learn from experience" (Bion, 1962b). This way, the human being potentially can give meaning to his own life.

When the function of the mental apparatus is not adequate the reality cannot be sufficiently symbolised. The apparatus might not be able to transform the reality because it is too traumatic and therefore unthinkable. This traumatic reality may additionally traumatise the mental apparatus and make it incapable of functioning properly. Under these conditions the reality is felt as unbearable and the mental apparatus resorts to discharge. This discharge is accomplished through what Klein (1946) has described as the projective identification of excess stimulation, split off parts of the mental apparatus, including what Bion (1962a) calls *bizarre objects*. The gap between the motor discharge and the process of thinking is better understood when the functions of the "other" (initially the mother) are valorised in order to develop the thinking capacity. This intersubjective model is introduced by Freud (1911b) when he states that the child "learns to employ these manifestations of discharge intentionally as methods of expressing its feelings" (p. 220). It is known that the baby's expressive communication stimulates the object who receive the discharge and gives meaning to it.

Bion (1962a,b, 1992) links Freud's ideas about thinking in "Two principles" with his concept of *alpha-function*. This function, first performed by the mother, begins the process of symbolisation of somato-sensory elements without meaning (beta-elements). An important factor of the alpha-function is the capacity of reverie of the mother. Alpha function initiates the process by which concrete "facts" are transformed into symbolic emotional thoughts. These are manifested as affective pictograms (Barros, 2000): that is, images which are connected with each other through affects. They constitute a contact barrier that simultaneously separates the unconscious and the conscious as well as permitting communication between them. This way, conscious perceptions are symbolised and repressed while repressed aspects may later be re-admitted to consciousness when the defence of repression is lifted. Therefore, attributing meaning the alpha function works to make contact with reality. The alpha-elements constitute the initial material of daydreams and dreams. The thinking apparatus, therefore, is a symbolisation apparatus that generates thoughts that, when they are thought, broaden the capacity for further thought.

When Freud (1911b) describes the necessary modifications in order for the mental apparatus to deal with reality, he does not refer directly to dreaming. The main function of the dream in Freud's (1900a) view is to hallucinate the fantasy of the unconscious wish. The function of the dream is to disguise the forbidden desires through figurability, condensation, displacement, and secondary revision.

Freud (1900a) advises us not to confuse unconscious dream thoughts, resulting from the symbolisation of unconscious wishful impulses, with the manifest dream. The latter communicates to the dreamer (and to the analyst) the unconscious dream thoughts that have been disguised in order to escape notice by the censor, which would block the dream thought from consciousness. The dream is connected with verbal symbols and in this way the dreamer transforms imagetic symbols, initially unconscious, into conscious verbal thinking. This transformation allows new conscious and unconscious connections with other experiences and thoughts, broadening the thinking capacity.

This broadening can be exemplified by the discovery of the benzene formula: the chemist Kekulé transformed his emotional experiences derived from his researches into unconscious thought. The work of dreaming transformed this unconscious thinking into an image in which some snakes bit the tail of each other, suggesting an hexagon. Only when Kekulé woke up did he associate the dreamed image with what he was seeking: that is, the benzene formula.

It is known that a nightmare can wake up the dreamer. These dreams or non-dreams are interrupted (Ogden, 2005) because the symbolising process is inadequate to contain the powerful affects; thus the sleeper is awakened. In contrast, at other times the dreamer wakes up in order to make contact with the solution of a problem realised during his unconscious dream, which has been expressed in some way by the manifest dream. The creative awakening of Kekulé is different from being awakened by a nightmare/traumatic non-dream.

The idea that the dream can be thought of as a "theatre generator of meaning" (Meltzer, 1983) refers, therefore, to the constitutional and transformational processes of the symbolic unconscious network. The generated meanings (i.e., dreamed unconsciously) also search for unconscious comprehension by the dreamer (Grotstein, 2000). When we state that the subject dreams both during the day and during the night we are referring to the unconscious dream thought, which like breathing and digestion, occurs twenty-four hours a day. The manifest dream, whether an awake or asleep dream, reveals the conflict between the truth and the mechanisms that try to hide it. During the analytical session the patient unconsciously dreams what is happening here-and-now and these thoughts are expressed through the verbalisation of conscious fantasies, feelings, and ideas that cross the patient's mind. The analyst is included as a transferential object into these dreams and the understanding of the transference/countertransference, as total situations (Joseph, 1985; Klein, 1952b) reveals the meanings of these dreams. The statement: "the analyst dreams the session" (Bion, 1992) can be broaden into "patient and analyst dream the analytical session".

The capacity to symbolise is dependent on having a mind of one's own (Caper, 1999), which is achieved through the complexities of oedipal triangulation that overlaps with the depressive position. As Klein (1952a) has stated, both the depressive position and the oedipal stage involve the child's discovery of his own separateness, including having his own unique world view apart from that of the mother. The capacity depends not only on the ability of the container (mother, analyst, etc.) to transform beta-elements into alpha elements, but also on the proper oscillation between disperse facts of the schizo–paranoid position (PS) and the organisation (including oedipal) of the depressive position (PS↔D) (Bion, 1962 a,b).

The capacity to symbolise is connected to the patient's ability to observe himself and to realise his separateness from others; including his independence of the parental couple. The patient's occasional confusion between internal and external reality is acknowledged by the patient through his self-reflection or when it is pointed out by the analyst. Here we are describing a non-psychotic or neurotic area of the personality (Bion, 1962a), in which dreaming is possible—whether sleeping or awake. The patient is able to realise that he dreamt during the night or that he had been daydreaming during the day.

In this area of the personality (non-psychotic) the patient externalises aspects of his internal world that contain representations of drives and defences. As we have seen, the analytical field is composed of dreams that are dreamt by the patient—here-and-now—and that include transferential fantasies regarding the analyst's dreams and the analyst himself. The dreams have an impact on the analyst who, through the use of his analytical capacity, re-dreams the patient's dreams, thereby broadening their meaning. At the same time, the analyst is able to take a distant view and observes what is happening between the two members of the analytical dyad. The analyst's dreams (which includes the patient's) can be transformed into interventions, which in turn broaden the patient's and the analytical dyad's dreaming capacity. As the analytical process develops itself the dreams of both members of the analytical dyad constitute a complex, dreams-for-two, in which it is not always possible to differentiate the contribution of each one. It constitutes an "analytical third" (Ogden, 1994), which is an intersubjective product of the dialetic between the individual dreams of the patient and of the analyst.

In the psychotic part of the personality the oedipal triangle has been disturbed and the patient cannot discriminate himself properly from the object. The capacity for symbolisation is impaired and a confusion between the internal and external world occurs. The analytic field is dominated by formations that can be called non-dreams (Cassorla, 2005). The non-dreams manifest themselves through discharges in acts and in the body, through compulsions, repetitive scenes and plots, fanaticism, omniscience, other delusions and transformations in hallucinosis (Bion, 1965). The non-dreams penetrate the analyst's mind who must transform them into dreams. On occasion, the analyst may be so penetrated by the patient's non-dreams that his symbolic capacity is attacked; thus giving rise to non-dreams-for-two.[1]

The non-psychotic area coexists in all human beings with the psychotic one. The latter should be expanded to include the traumatic and primordial areas that are part of the non-repressed unconscious.[2]

It is known that psychoanalysis faced serious problems when the first analysts became more involved emotionally with their patients. The analytical process became stagnant and frequently ended in repetitive dual collusions. In such situations, access to the symbolic network was impaired and the analyst's capacity to dream was also compromised. The technical recommendations of Freud (1912e, 1913c) indicated how to deal with such facts, aiming to transform discharge into thoughts.

In recent decades psychoanalysis has been searching for ways in to work with borderline, perverse, psychotic, and autistic configurations in which difficulties, blocks, and attacks that impede the adequate development of the symbolic network of thinking are found. The analyst, facing these configurations, works in hazardous conditions and is subject to having his own mental functions attacked.

Technical developments

The technical recommendations suggested by Freud also pointed to non-dream situations when he referred to *Agieren* (acting out) (Freud, 1914g) and to hypothetical constructions or reconstructions in relation to traumas which do not have the potential of being recalled (Freud, 1937d).

Significant technical advances were developed from object relations theory. The idea of projective identification as something that described a phenomenon beyond unconscious fantasy (Bion, 1959; Grinberg, 1979; Rosenfeld, 1987), that is, which evokes powerful emotions in the analyst, reinforced the importance of the use of countertransference as an instrument of the analysis (Heimann, 1950; Money-Kyrle, 1956; Racker, 1957). Even though controversies persist, countertransference is seen as an important instrument and as a common ground by which to compare contemporary psychoanalytic approaches (Gabbard, 1995). When countertransference is effectively used, it becomes a powerful resource that allows the analyst's capacity to get in touch with areas of impaired symbolisation. The emphasis on the intersubjective nature of the analytic dyad, a characteristic of contemporary psychoanalysis, has developed from these clinical ideas (Brown, 2011).

There is a tendency to broaden the concept of counter-transference with that of reverie which would now encompass (Barros & Barros, 2014; Civitarese, 2013c; Ogden, 1997) previously unappreciated aspects of the analyst's imagination, visual images, fantasies, perceptions, feelings, daydreams, and nightdreams. As it occurs with the mother of the baby, the analyst also uses his reverie capacity during the session. It is necessary that the analyst allows himself to be immersed in his thoughts and feelings until the reveries start to make some sense. The non-trained analyst tends to ignore his reveries or considers them as products of his own perturbations and thus does not bother to investigate them (Ogden, 1997).[3]

Freud (1911b) compares the life of fantasy to "natural reserves" (or reservations) in which fantasy activity is akin to natural resources/life where repression and secondary process were not present. Using Yellowstone Park as a model of "natural reserve", he states that

> With the introduction of the reality principle one species of thought-activity was split off; it was kept free from reality-testing and remained subordinated to the pleasure principle alone. This activity is *phantasying*, which begins already in children's play, and later, continued as *day-dreaming*, abandons dependence on real objects. [and furthermore that] In the same way, a nation whose wealth rests on the exploitation of the produce of its soil will yet set aside certain areas for reservation in their original state and for protection from the changes brought about by civilization. (E.g. Yellowstone Park.). (p. 222)

The reverie capacity involves an active mental state that searches for contact with this kind of "natural reserve": an area of fantasy or daydreaming. The analyst allows himself be immersed in the reveries but, at the same time he observes them and tries to comprehend them. Therefore, the primary process coexists with the secondary process, which allows the analyst to think about the content of the reverie. The boundaries between them are not rigid and both processes interpenetrate.

The state of reverie allows raw emotional experiences to be captured and transformed into unconscious waking dream thought and here we can see alpha function at work. These experiences are connected to other emotional experiences, either conscious or unconscious, which had already been signified and/or are being signified. The analyst's reverie images constitute fantasies or manifest daydreams and reveal the unconscious dream thoughts that are actively being transformed and worked on unconsciously by the analyst and by the analytical dyad (dream-for-two). Besides the figurability, the reveries are also formed through the other mechanisms of dream-work: condensation, displacement, and secondary revision. These mechanisms also rely on what happens in the analytical field, which is manifested in the transference/countertransference experiences being dreamed in the here-and-now of the session. It is likely that the secondary revisions produced during this process are more sophisticated since the patient, being awake, has access to the secondary processes. It is for this reason that the way the patient presents his ideas may seem logical and organised.

Non-dreams that manifest themselves through evacuative discharges, somatisations, transformations in hallucinosis, and voids are "imagined" by the analyst who interprets the conscious and unconscious meaning of these experiences. In primordial areas of the mind, the analyst can be solicited to use constructions (via *di levare*) (Freud, 1937d). The functions of the mental apparatus described by Freud (1911b) (consciousness, attention, memory, judgment, thought, and actions) must be altered in order to allow the reverie capacity to emerge. The analyst's attention, which is used to "periodically . . . search the external world" (Freud, 1911b, p. 220), must keep fluctuating without giving major or minor importance to what is observed (evenly hovering attention) (Freud, 1912e). Memories, desires, expectations are also actively blocked. This results in an altered state of consciousness between sleep and wakefulness. This state of mind can be achieved by following Bion's (1967b, 1992) recommendations that the analyst must work without memory, without desire, and without intention to comprehend. This process becomes circular: the reverie state is a product of these recommendations that, paradoxically, are only possible when this state is reached. The analyst knows that his capacity for reverie is lost when he realises that he is dominated by desires and memories.

The factors that favour the reverie capacity and its clinical use are not clear. I think that an important factor is the active search for atemporality. When past and present (memory and desire) are ignored everything that happens in the analytical field seems to happen at the present time, although the term "present time" is opposed to the past and future time. As these categories of past and present cease to be relevant, we are in the atemporal terrain where the conscious experience of present, past, and future no longer apply. The addendum "without intention to comprehend" will not be pertinent since this "intention" is a fact that refers to the future. I think that Bion's insistence that we follow this recommendation shows that he perceived how it would be difficult to experience the "not-knowing". Thanks to this attitude of "not-knowing" the analyst can experience another type of knowledge that manifests itself in other ways—encompassing the dream thought—behind and beyond the secondary process.[4]

Through his reverie capacity, the analyst comes into contact with the dreams and non-dreams of his patient. In areas where the dream is possible, the analyst re-dreams (consciously and unconsciously) the dreams of the patient, thereby broadening the symbolic network.

> What seems to happen is that the analyst listens to the patient and watches the image that appears in his imagination. . . . he allows the patient to evoke a dream in himself. Of course that it is his dream and thus will be formed by the vicissitudes of his own personality . . . [and] every attempt to formulate an interpretation . . . could imply the tacit preamble: "While listening to your dream I had a dream which in my emotional life would mean the following, which I impart to you in the hope that it will throw some light on the meaning that your dream has for you." (Meltzer, 1983, p. 90)

When the patient externalises, areas of impaired symbolisation, leading to the appearance of non-dreams, the analyst's alpha-function may give rise to reveries; thereby transforming the non-dream into a meaningful dream in the analyst's mind.

There are situations in which the non-dream attacks the analyst's capacity for reverie and thinking, rendering the analyst incapable of dreaming and thinking. As we have seen, the analyst can discharge his non-dreams, which may result in the development of stagnant and repetitive plots that involve both members of the dyad. These are non-dreams-for-two of which the analyst is not aware. They constitute the raw material of what I have called chronic enactments (Cassorla, 2005, 2008, 2013a,b, 2014).

As the neurotic functioning (area of dream) and the psychotic, traumatic, and primordial functioning (area of non-dream) coexist; thus, it is not always possible to know either whether the analyst is transforming raw emotional experiences into dreams or if he is broadening the symbolic network by re-dreaming dreams that had already been dreamed.

I will now present some clinical material to illustrate these ideas, keeping in mind that writing about a case makes the communication of emotional experiences difficult. Nevertheless, I hope the reader will re-dream my dreams and dream my non-dreams or, perhaps, dream some of my dreams of which I am unaware.

Clinical vignette

It is dawn. I have difficulty in getting out of bed. I suppose it is because I went to bed late last night. I have a quick breakfast and leave home in a hurry. I arrive at my office five minutes late, at 7.05 a.m. I am upset with myself because of my delay but remain calm. I know my patient, John, usually arrives between 7.08 and 7.10 a.m. But, this time, I meet John in the hall waiting for me to open my office. It is the first time John arrives earlier than me. I feel bothered.

When the session starts I remember that John missed his last session, without giving me previous notice. I wondered if he had traveled on business, a common issue in his life as a businessman.

The analyst's discomfort for arriving later than John is, for a while, a non-dream in search of meaning. I am aware that there is a relation between my delay and John's constant delays. The analyst's conscious "manifest dream" does not go beyond that. The fact that "I went to bed late last night" is real, but it is a rationalisation for the delay, a false dream (Cassorla, 2008) covering my not-knowing. The analyst must bear the uncertainty of this false dream until something takes form in his imagination. Recalling that John had missed the last session is a dream-like memory (Bion, 1970), something that came spontaneously to the analyst's mind, therefore it is not an obstructive memory. However, the subsequent memories about the patient's trips must be abandoned in order for the analyst to remain receptive to new thoughts. The analyst is aware that he knows nothing about the reasons of the patient's current absence. His memory was only associated to an hypothesis, a preconception (Bion, 1962b), which will have to be either confirmed or not. If the analyst felt completely certain that John had missed the session because of his trip, his mind would be dominated by psychotic functioning and omniscience.

John starts the session by giving details about problems in his job. I observe the same moaning tone with which I am familiar. He complains and complains as if he was a victim of the world. His complaints seem unjustified to me, but I feel that if I show him that, he is going to say that I despise his suffering and that I do not understand him. I keep on listening, downhearted, trying to keep my mind in a reverie state, "without desire, without memory".

> I find my thoughts wandering. I remember that on the previous night I was trying to write a psychoanalytical text and I felt blocked in my ideas. I went to bed frustrated. In another part of my mind an idea came up—If I were not a psychoanalyst I could tell John how unpleasant he is. Later I would realise that I was attempting to transform into a dream the impotence and anger I was going through with John, which came from the previous night as well as my present frustration with him.

The analyst knows that John's complaints are evacuative discharges of some unnamed affects and that he communicates his incapacity to dream and think through them. The analyst's reveries reveal attempts at connecting facts that are happening in the analytic field with personal experiences, like the ones from the previous night. The fact of realising his annoyance and dismay alerts the analyst to the risk of being recruited by John's non-dreams and the analyst perceives the risk of giving back the projective discharges to John.

> In a sequence, I remember arriving late to the session. I can identify and name part of my discomfort: shame. This feeling connects to another memory: the one from last night in which I wondered if I could sleep some extra minutes more because John was my first patient and was always late. Having admitted my feelings of shame removes any obstructions to the expansion of my symbolic network that permits me to realise that John's delays were convenient to me—they gave me more time to read my morning newspaper . . . I had come to count on John arriving late and so felt "permission" to do the same. I feel sad and, at the same time, satisfied for being able to make contact with painful facts about myself.

> On the other hand, I know that I have not fully dealt with the issue of neither my patient's lateness nor with my failure to bring this to his attention in the analysis. Therefore, I am obliged to ask myself whether or not I have dealt with this issue with the necessary potency.

The analyst is aware that he was involved in a collusion with John and that its origins and consequences are not clear enough. These mutual and repetitive delays correspond to what I have called chronic enactments. The patient and analyst have behaved like actors in a miming theatre in which they act, without words, the mutual latenesses. These are a type of symbolisation in actions that are in search of verbal symbolisation. It was this issue that the analyst was trying to write about the previous night when his symbolic network was blocked.

The memories of the late arrivals and my difficulty writing the previous night show how unconscious dream thoughts of the analyst are revealed to himself, and are in a search for signification and broadening of meanings. Initially the analyst was unable to realise the chronic enactment, but this idea was already part of his thinking. When this realisation comes to his mind, he feels creative and knows he will register the fact through writing after the end of the session.

Subsequently, reviewing the session, the analyst will perceive that John's moaning could be in response to the analyst's delay. If he had realised this earlier then the analytic process during this session would have taken other paths.

> Now I hear John talking about a business meeting he had in city X, from where he had just come back. I can picture the city X: images of my visit to this tourist destination when I was young. I wonder about the building where John could have been in the H square. In fact, John does not say a thing about any building or places. This scenery is a creation of my mind. John talks about a former military officer who was in the meeting and who put up obstacles to the negotiations. In my mind I "see" an officer with medals on his uniform.
>
> While John tells me about the negotiation I feel bothered. This annoyed feeling is transformed into an impression that John is hiding something from me. I think about bribery, corruption. I do not know whether it is a dream of mine or it is related to what John is telling me.

When writing about the session after the appointment, the analyst will further dream the session by adding more details of his own: images, the city X, the H square, and the officer. The analyst recalls a situation when he was a teenager in which he took his first trip with other teenagers. He was euphoric with his sense of freedom while he was in the H square. He was playing mindlessly with his wallet when a thief ran by and stole his wallet. His friends ridiculed him for being distracted, "with his mind elsewhere". This brought to mind childhood memories of being accused by adults of sleeping when he got lost in his own thoughts. The imagined H square was also a dirty place, close to a neighbourhood known for prostitution. The worst consequence of having his wallet stolen was losing his ID card.

During the process of writing about the session the analyst realised that his daydream indicated the consequences of being "with his mind elsewhere", "sleeping", also as an analyst who was late for his patient because of his sleepiness. He could lose his analytic identity for not realising "thefts" (delays and absences) that were corrupting the analytical process. The H square (where there were prostitutes as well as historical museums with masterpieces) represented not only the dirty aspects of the analytic field, but also the resources and treasures that existed, and had the potential of being rediscovered. The image of the officer reminded the analyst of deceptive and destructive situations that he had experienced during his adolescence.

> Returning to the session, John says "I dreamed of you. I came to the session and you were mad at me, because I had missed the previous session. You said: 'just wait there, I do not know when I will see you.'. It was a punishment. In the waiting room there was an athletic type of guy, a sailor, who was on holiday. He was dribbling, crazy. You put a straitjacket on him, he reacted by becoming violent and then you bound him. Afterwards, another crazy guy suggested we stole G (anti-psychotic medicine) from a cabinet. We were being careful so you could not see us. Then I woke up. The dream seemed like a loony bin, madness."

> I feel invaded by a profusion of vague ideas. Although I did not have John's associations, I began an attempt at formulating an interpretation. I say that maybe John is afraid of not counting on me. I talk about his absences and our our late starting sessions that may not contain the madness permeating our sessions. We would have to resort to straitjackets and anti-psychotics. I realise that my formulation is not one of my best and I am aware that I did not wait for his associations. But, as I speak, each word attracts another word and I feel creative. But, soon I realise the risk of talking too much that might cause an "indigestion", in other words, giving him too much to mentally process; thus I interrupt my intervention and wait.

John is thoughtful. I wonder if my complicated intervention made sense to him. Then, he recounts a "hard to tell" episode. He had not come to the previous session because while in the city X he took drugs and got involved in sexual and social situations dangerous to his own life. It is not the first time that he has engaged in such risky behaviour. Hearing about his dangerous activities makes me feel dismayed and worried.

The "hard to tell" episode is a manifestation of evacuative discharges, non-dreams, happening outside of the sessions, which keep a certain invariance in relation to what is happening in the analytical field. All the stories and scenes, dreamed and non-dreamed by the analytical dyad are expressions of madness, destruction, corruption, dirt, imprudence, sedation, involving relations of John with himself, with other people, and with his analyst.

After John told the "hard to tell" episode, it became clearer to the analyst why John arrived punctually to his session. He needed my help to dream the horrific non-dream related to the dangers he lived in and outside of his mind. John intuited that this non-dream was another version of his internal deadly sabotage and corrupted relationships. The analyst also made contact with his own personal experiences that were similar to those of John.

In other words, it is as if John (like all patients) said to the analyst: "I will make you participate in my dreams and non-dreams again, in another way—please, see if you are able to signify them or give them new meanings". And, in case the analyst is unable to do so, then the mind of the patient will continue to repeatedly try until he hopes the analyst "gets it": again and again . . .

After this session, the following hours and the analysis continue without any more delays either from the patient or from the analyst.[5]

Dreaming the analytical session

The use of the reverie capacity by the analyst allows him to "dream the session" (Bion, 1992). In this model the psychoanalyst focuses on the analytical field, taking into account the functions described by Freud (1911b), but in an altered form. In this way, he is better able to make contact with both his conscious waking dream thought and his unconscious dreams that are occurring in the here-and-now of the session. While the analyst may use his conscious thinking to detect hidden unconscious meaning embedded in the patient's associations, Bion encourages the analyst to adopt a state of mind that is receptive to his reveries/waking dreams in order to intuitively "become" his patient's experience through a process of at-one-ment with the analysand's deep unrepresented feelings (Bion, 1970).

Throughout his work Bion uses other models to explicate his technical suggestions. They are related to the analyst's capacity to contain and bear the frustration of the patient's attacks and to keep himself alive as well as to think clearly. Bion (1970) proposes that the analyst develop his negative capability, an expression of which was found in a letter of Keats: "when man is capable of being in uncertainties, mysteries, doubts, without any irritable reaching after fact and reason". Bearing the capacity of not-knowing is also reinforced by the idea of Maurice Blanchot, which he took from André Green: "La réponse est le malheur de la question".

Bion (1970) also uses the term *intuition* as an instrument capable of capturing emotional phenomena. It must prevail over the observation of the sensory organs. In other places, Bion (1967b) reminds us of the letter from Freud to Andreas Salome in which he suggests that the analyst should artificially blind himself in order to see the light better.

Derived from the theory of thinking, Bion proposes that the analyst bear the chaos until the selected fact arises. This fact will make the chaos meaningful. The chaos is related to the facts of the paranoid–schizoid position (PS) and the organisation to the facts of the depressive position (D). The analyst must allow himself to oscillate between these two positions—he must bear the chaos and, at the same time, he must not attach himself rigidly to D (a premature sense of order). The capacity to tolerate fluctuations (Ps↔D) between states of relative fragmentation (Ps) and integration (D) depends upon the strength of one's analytical capacity (and also his capacity of thinking). Bion recommends patience during the PS phase in order to allow the unconscious work of dreaming to take place. As a result of the analyst's ability to tolerate states of PS, a sense of security arises as the chaos slowly organises itself (Ps↔D). This sense of security offers only a brief respite until it is undone in order to allow for new experiences to emerge. Bion proposes that the analyst have faith in the capacity of his unconscious to dream and attribute meaning to non-dreams.

Meltzer (2005) proposes another similar model:

> The state of observation is essentially a resting state. It is also a state of heightened vigilance. I compare it with waiting in the dark for the deer, grazing at night, seen by their flashing white tails. This nocturnal vigilance is on the alert for movement of the quarry, part object minimal movements which with patience can be seen to form a pattern of incipient meaning "cast before". This catching of the incipient meaning cast before is a function of receptive imagination—open to the possible, unconcerned with probability. Being rich with suspense, it is necessarily fatiguing, and fraught with anxiety. It is a trial of strength—and faith—that gives substance to terms such as resistance or retreat. However, it is a poetry generator.

And later on:

> How does he ("the analyst") know what he ("the patient") is talking about? He doesn't—he is "counter-dreaming"; he has, in fact, abandoned "thinking" (science) for intuition (art, poetry): the verbal tradition of Homer. (p. 181)

When the mind of the analyst is in a numbed state, hit by the non-dreams of the patient, he does not know that he is facing unknown or meaningless facts. Facing any evidence of not-knowing, this state of mind will be substituted by omniscience and omnipotence. The analyst's need to take control manifests itself as an excessive concern with technical procedures instead of approaching the session "without memory, without desire" and thus he will be saturated by memories, desires, theories, and supposed knowledge. In this frame of mind, the analyst is convinced that he "knows" what is happening with his patient from the past facts and/or desires, theories, and future expectations (of the analyst). Interpretations based on facts from the past, and expectations of what should happen in the future, are comments closer to suggestion than to genuine psychoanalysis. Rational or theoretical interpretations serve to label the patient and interfere with his development. I think that the analyst should be alert to exaggerated feelings of pride and unrealistic phantasies about the potency of his analytical capacity when the analytical process seems to be going very well. On the other hand, the analyst must take care not to exaggerate his capacity for patience or his containing capacity when he supposes he is dealing well with frustration and violence. This exaggerated sense of power and knowledge tends to conceal arrogance and stupidity (Cassorla, 2013c). Constant admiration and/or chronic irritation toward the patient are indicative of similar difficulties in the analyst. The analyst must struggle against a certain laziness regarding writing about clinical material of the sessions even if he does not know the reasons for this reticence. These sorts of situations suggests the need for a "second glance" (Baranger et al., 1983) at what is occurring in the session that is enhanced by paying attention to Faimberg's (1996) suggestion that the analysts "listening to [his] listening". Nocturnal countertransferential dreams and intuition of diurnal dreams can provide the analyst with other hints.[6]

I think that the analyst works simultaneously in all mental areas. Interpretations in the symbolic area indicate a present analyst that, at the same time, helps to symbolise and to create mental structures. His work, therefore, also benefits the psychotic and traumatic areas of the mind. Moreover, when the analyst works in an area of the mind where the capacity to symbolise is impaired, he is also stimulating the symbolic network that exists in a non-psychotic area of the mind. For instance, traumas could be *re-dreamed and remembered* (those traumas that had been symbolised but repressed), *dreamed and re-constructed* (those that had been transformed into psychotic non-dreams), and *dreamed and constructed* (that part of the primordial mind that can never be remembered). These processes might all occur simultaneously.

This perspective helps us to move away from moralistic view about what is "right or wrong" in the analytic work. The moralistic superego should be quieted by the validation of the analyst's work (Cassorla, 2012): that is, observe how this work creates, develops, blocks, or reverses the dreaming capacity and the symbolic network of thinking.

The analytic work, particularly with more challenging patients, stimulates self-knowledge in the analyst as he inevitably makes contact with his own traumatised areas. An analytic process promotes development in both members of the dyad. Although we expect the patient to undergo personal development more than the analyst, if the analyst does not develop personally then this is an indication that obliges us to consider that something has gone wrong.

Shakespeare (1611) wisely wrote that "We are such stuff as dreams are made of." But dreams themselves, as I have attempted to describe here, are complex phenomena comprised of the capacity of negotiation between the pleasure principle and the reality principle, between the conscious and the unconscious, between fantasy and reality, between symbolisation and non-symbolisation, between PS↔D, between dream and non-dream, between Eros and Thanatos, etc., all processes that are revealed in the analytic field. This capacity for negotiation, when introjected by the patient, will give sense to his life. As is usually the case, these ideas were already present, explicity or implicitly in Freud's work, in search of new dreamers to broaden them.

Notes

1. There is a spectrum of possibilities within the non-dream category (Cassorla, 2013a,b): registers without meaning and representations with different degrees of fragility resulting in discharges, symbolic equations (Segal, 1957), symbols that have lost their expressive function (Barros & Barros, 2011), symbols that manifest as actions, and "psychic gestures". This term was created by Sapisochin and refers to a kind of theatrical performance externalised in the analytical field, similar to enactments, and best thought of as "mental acts". These reveal a traumatic transformation of non-dreams into dreams (Cassorla, 2005, 2008, 2014) and demonstrate the always present co-existence of dream and non-dream areas.

2. Non-dream areas of non-repressed unconscious (Freud, 1923b) have been studied by contemporary authors, such as Barros & Barros (2011), Botella & Botella (2013), Ferro (2009b), Green (1990, 2002), Levine (2013), Levy (2012), Marucco (2007), Reed (2013), Scarfone (2013), etc.

3. Bion (1962c) writes: "When the mother loves the infant what does she do it with? Leaving aside the physical channels of communication my impression is that her love is expressed by reverie." And, further on, ". . . reverie is that state of mind which is open to the reception of any "objects" from the loved object and is therefore capable of reception of the infant's projective identifications whether they are felt by the infant to be good or bad. In short, reverie is a factor of mother's alpha function" (p. 36).

4. . . . the submergence of memory, desire, and understanding appears not only to run flat contrary to accepted procedure but also to be close to what occurs spontaneously in the severely regressed patient . . . There are real dangers associated with the appearance; this is why the procedure here adumbrated is advocated only for the psycho-analyst whose own analysis has been carried at least far enough for the recognition of paranoid–schizoid and depressive positions. (Bion, 1970, p. 47)

5. In the clinical material when the analyst arrives to the session later than John the dual collusion (chronic enactment) is undone. As I have described elsewhere, a chronic enactment may be brought to the analyst's awareness through an acute enactment that alerts him to the frozen state that he and the patient have been caught in.

6. Bion only briefly mentioned the analyst's countertransference dreams, but a more detailed study of this phenomenon can be found in Brown (2007).

Editors' introduction to Chapter Five

Giuseppe Civitarese is a major figure in current Italian psychoanalytic thinking and has contributed significantly to our understanding of field theory as well as, especially in his most recent writings, the study of aesthetics from an analytic perspective. Civitarese's creative discussion of Freud's "Two principles" paper begins with a quote from the end of that essay that suggests (to Civitarese) that Freud "invites a re-reading of the text, but this time with the end already in mind." Civitarese thus takes up Freud's challenge quite literally and states that "I shall proceed in my re-reading of ("Formulations on the two principles . . .") as in a film structured in a sequence of flashbacks . . . and begin from the end." His methodology in this examination of Freud's paper is to begin at the *margins* that frame the paper and to focus on those elements in the body of "Two prinicples" that may appear less relevant yet nevertheless play an important role.

For example, Civitarese references a dream about the death of a father mentioned only briefly in "Two principles", but he detects an important *intertextuality* (related to another text by Freud) to another, well known, dream discussed in the *Interpretation of Dreams* also dealing with paternal death. Both dreams in the two texts, deal with the death of a father and hidden patricidal wishes and whether the terrible reality of such wishes can be tolerated with open eyes. Civitarese's analysis concludes that the briefer dream in "Two principles" may be framed intertextually by the dream in *Interpretation of Dreams* and thus "Freud tells us that if we truly want to be realists we must open our eyes also with respect to the most inadmissible desires inspired by the pleasure principle." It is in this manner that the intertextual link broadens Freud's discussion of the reality principle and its dynamic relationship to the pleasure principle.

Civitarese also sees in the "Two principles" paper a strong influence on the work of Bion many years later, as other authors in this volume have observed. Civitarese observes that early on in "Two principles" Freud appeared more interested in considering the nature of the psychic functions that underlay the reality principle than the mental contents with which this principle deals. Furthermore, he notes that "In the end, both Freud and Bion delineate the life of man as a progressive acquisition of functions." Civitarese goes on to discuss the transition from the world of hallucination and its inevitable frustrations to the necessity for greater contact with reality in the light of both Freud's and Bion's perspectives. Civitarese deepens this discussion by comparing Freud's and Bion's views about the nature of dreaming and also makes an important connection between the various processes involved in reality testing with Bion's notion of the grid.

Perhaps the best way to end this introduction is to quote Civitarese's humbling comment about "how the beginning of the reality principle consists simply in mourning our pretensions to knowledge", a thought worthy of the reader's meditation.

5

Where does the reality principle begin? The work of margins in Freud's "Formulations on the two principles of mental functioning"

Giuseppe Civitarese

The paratext

The text of "Formulations" (hereinafter known as FTPMF) has a circular structure. At the end of the brief essay—in the very last line—requesting a good-natured disposition and an affectionate sympathy in the reader, Freud suggests that he or she pay attention to the performative aspect of the text, the plane in which enunciation and action coincide:

> The deficiencies of this short paper, which is preparatory rather than expository, will perhaps be excused only in small part if I plead that they are unavoidable. In these few remarks on the psychical consequences of adaptation to the reality principle I have been obliged to adumbrate views which I should have preferred for the present to withhold and whose justification will certainly require no small effort. But I hope *it will not escape the notice of the benevolent* reader how [*wo*, i.e., "where"] in *these pages too the dominance of the reality principle is beginning*. (1911b, p. 226, my italics)

This is a striking sentence. It gives us the feeling that something might have escaped us, and that what we have just passed through may have been written in code. So we are tempted to go through it again from the beginning. Freud's conclusion invites a re-reading of the text, but this time with the end already in mind. The game set up by this rhetorical gesture seems precisely intended to illustrate the psychoanalytic concept of "posteriority" (*Nachträglichkeit*).

And that is what I am going to do. I shall play the same game in order to try and understand Freud's precise and obscure assertion. To underline how anything may acquire a new meaning in the light of what comes after, I shall proceed in my re-reading of FTPMF as in a film structured in a sequence of flashbacks. I shall begin from the end.

In fact, we see that if it is read attentively, Freud's statement that I quoted in italics unfolds in two principal motions. On the one hand it draws attention to a certain point (the "where") to which Freud evidently attributes particular importance, while on the other hand he craves the reader's indulgence. He links the two things in this way: it will only be the "benevolent" reader who discovers the "where", and conversely, having discovered it, he will have to be "benevolent" (*wohlwollend*) towards the author. The end of the sentence reverberates back on the beginning. So the thing that should not escape us is precisely something that will require our benevolence. But why should the ideal reader invoked by Freud be benevolent? *Who* should be benevolent? *What* would he have preferred to keep silent? And why? What "psychical consequences" is he alluding to? For whom? FTPMF is certainly a text that seems to hold secrets and arouses the reader's curiosity.

So I shall adopt a second methodological principle to try and give an answer to these questions and to others that arise from them (the "what" of the "where", and the "why" of the benevolence). By going through the text backwards, taking up the exhortation to be more perceptive, and starting with what can appear to be "secondary"—for example, the sentence that closes the text—I shall above all highlight some of those textual elements that by definition stand *around* the text, and that, with respect to it, perform only the auxiliary role of influencing its reception. Doing this means receiving not only the explicit message contained in the close of the paper, but also the implicit one.

Therefore the title that I have given my re-reading of FTPMF is to be taken literally. I shall concern myself with Freud's paper from the *margins*, from that which acts as a frame for the text. In the *paratext* (Genette, 1982, 1987) and, as we shall see, in his final observation, Freud scatters various clues. And, as in the detective stories of Conan Doyle that he loved reading (Vitale, 2005)—and after all, the psychoanalytic paradigm, at least in classical psychoanalysis, *is* evidential (Ginzburg, 1979)—these often hide in insignificant details, so to speak in the margins of the text, in its paratextual components.

We consider as margins, paratext, or *parergon* (Derrida, 1978), all the elements that make up a supplement to the *ergon* or main text: blurb, preface, notes, epigraph, etc. But the letters from Freud's private correspondence—with Jung and Ferenczi—in which he speaks about FTPMF also rightfully come into this category, as well as the comments and critical notes edited by commentators: above all, once they have become canonical. More precisely these two series of productions are examples, respectively, of *epitext*[1] and *editorial paratext*.[2]

What I propose here, however, is to add to Genette's classification some elements of what we could define as the "internal" *parergon* or paratext. I mean that which appears to be less relevant *in* the main text, but which nevertheless plays an important role there: a dream, for example, however paradoxical that may seem. A dream is indeed always "only a dream" (as Freud notes in the paper "On Dreams", 1901a; p. 680). But also, of course, the concluding sentence. It does not refer to the theoretical questions addressed in the text, but is purely interlocutory. Moreover, the last two lines have the structure of a revolving door. Placed at the threshold of the text, they usher the reader out and immediately make him plunge back in again. In their liminal position, in the metaleptic nature of the appeal that the intradiegetic author, "stepping out of" the text, directs to the reader, and in the performative role it plays, we could say that while being part of the main text, the final lines play a paratextual role.

The epilogue

So I would like to accept Freud's invitation regarding the use of the text, and both propose a decoding of it and also suggest how, in my opinion, the process of understanding is acted out, even and *especially* in analysis. It is a process that addresses itself always to the past (the future too exists only as a memory of what was anticipated in the past). The analyst is an Orpheus who in every interpretation tries to resuscitate the meaning from the world of shades. Yet every time, in the very moment when it is offered—like Eurydice, the beloved who in the myth gives meaning to the life of the divine singer—it shines for a moment and then dissolves again.

But in the end what is Freud referring to?

After years of structuralism and deconstruction we may have become more worldly-wise about the way texts work, but this does not make it any easier for us to intuit what he is pointing out. It is not at all clear where, in the here-and-now of the reading, Freud begins to abandon the pleasure principle for the dominance of the reality principle. Freud writes that, against his will, he feels constrained to enunciate things about which he would stay silent if he could. But what things? I do not believe there can be a single answer to this. Like any textual mechanism that never stops intriguing, FTPMF too is reluctant to show its hand.

However, we glimpse one card almost straightaway. As we have seen, the close of FTPMF closes nothing at all: instead it re-launches the endless game of interpretation; or rather, urges us to begin reading again from the beginning, and so on ad infinitum. A reading that is therefore inevitably a *new* reading every time, and one that uncovers tracks in the text that went unnoticed before, while seeing others in a different light. In this incessant retracing of his or her steps, the reader realises that, in the ever-moving shadow of "posteriority", interpretation never reaches a definitive point. Not only this, but it will become clearer to him step by step that he is also "rewriting" the text each time, and letting himself be read (Ogden, 2012), and therefore also written, by it.

But if this is how things are, then we have already found an initial answer to the question posed in the title of my commentary: Freud continually had to go further in renouncing the positivist dream (aroused in him by his own "pleasure principle") of decoding the truth of the unconscious. In FTPMF Freud has come to a fully matured awareness that truth may be circular, rhetorical, a matter of perspective and affect, inasmuch as it is conditioned by the *manner* and the context in which one attains it—a manner and context shared with society and hence not arbitrary. Moreover, 1918 is also the year in which Freud published his book about the Wolf Man (1918b), the text in which he takes up the final challenge of the trauma theory of the aetiology of neuroses. The challenge that will close with the *non liquet* of the notes on *Nachträglichkeit* added a few years later; another splendid example of how, in an explosive overthrowing of perspective, the paratext assumes almost greater weight than the text.

The dream

Once we have identified this first re-*flection* of the text on itself, we make it easier for ourselves to bring some others to light and thereby confirm their intrinsic coherence. Two components with the function of *parergon* take on great prominence because of where they are placed: the dream about the death of the father (1911b, pp. 225–226) and note 4 on p. 219. (I further divide the text into sub-units in order to make clearer the metonymic game of retrospective significance through which each element acts first of all on the one that immediately precedes it. For example—from this point of view—the benevolence requested from the reader in the final sentence relates above all to the meaning of the dream.)

As we read this dream we cannot fail to apply an internal intertextuality (Genette, 1982; Kristeva, 1980) to Freud's work. I am referring to two of the most extraordinary dreams in *The Interpretation of Dreams* (1900a). Although the situations of the two protagonists are different—in one case the father dies, in the other the son—they address the same oedipal theme of relations between father and son. The first is Freud's famous dream on the day after his father's funeral, when he goes to a railway station and reads the notice, "You are requested to close the eyes" (Freud, 1900a, p. 317).

The second is the other way round. The son is dead, and the father who is holding a vigil for him in the next room does not realise that a candle has set alight the cloth draping the coffin. The father dreams that his son calls out, "Father, don't you see I'm burning?" (p. 509). Leaving aside the different existential situation of the characters in the dream, *the plea for pity that the son makes to the father is just the same*.

However, the dream found in FTPMF tells us, with an obvious and inevitable *après coup*[3] effect in relation to the two dreams I have just mentioned, that the father has not yet responded to the plea, he *has not* closed the eyes (he has not even closed *an* eye) and he has not ended the anguish of his son because inside him the son *is not* really dead. Instead, like a *revenant*, the father repeatedly comes back to pester him ("his father was alive once more and . . . talking to him in his usual way" (Freud, 1911b, p. 225, italics in original)). The dreamer *knows* that his father is dead and feels very sad about it. However, the father—he tells us—*does not know* that he is dead. It is as if something were stopping him. But we would think that the dreamer is himself by no means convinced that his father is really dead. If we consider that the son is the author who has put the father "who does not know" into the dream-theatre, we can in fact attribute to the event the same structure of a dream within a dream: that is, a dream in which two different levels of awareness are present. In the end, the hallucinosis of the dream reveals something that is true, even if denied by the senses, both—if we accept this similarity—in waking and in the dream that acts as a frame.

Freud interprets the dream as having been provoked by the dreamer's repressed desire for his father to die. The phrase, "his father had really died, only without knowing it" is ambiguous. To make it comprehensible, he completes it by adding the unconscious death wish directed by the dreamer towards his father. But—I repeat—the reader could also understand this to mean that the son too did not know that his father was dead, in the sense that he actually was not dead *in his internal world*. Otherwise his father's ghost would not have continued to torment him. Moreover, we could also apply this to Freud himself as composer of the text, and hypothesise that unconsciously he did not know what he was talking about. What prompts us to form this hypothesis is, among other things, the fact that at the beginning of this paragraph Freud notes the "great self-discipline" that the investigator must have in order to recognise the influence of unconscious factors upon him.

So we have identified a second point at which the reality principle imposes its dominance. Freud tells us that if we truly want to be realists we must open our eyes also with respect to the most inadmissible desires inspired by the pleasure principle. As he writes elsewhere, the child desires to possess the mother entirely for himself and for this reason would like to kill the father. In other words, we think we have certain feelings and thoughts, but we deceive ourselves. We feign a reality for ourselves that is certainly not the one of common sense, and we do this not only when we represent the world to ourselves, but also with regard to our most intimate passions.

The note

It becomes clear immediately after this that Freud is subverting the naïve realism with which we look not only at the world and at internal life, but also at the truths of science. Another significant insertion in the margin of the text—we were saying—is note 4 on p. 219 (the fourth note of Freud's own, though because of editorial insertions, it is the eighth of the text. Hereafter I shall refer to it simply as note 4). The note is justly famous. In it Freud shows himself to be aware of the limits of the psychoanalytic model he has constructed, but nevertheless justifies it. The key word in the note is "fiction". Here too— and now for the third time—the dominance of the reality principle imposes itself in the moment when Freud is compelled to acknowledge that everything he has described and theorised is no more than a scientific myth after all.

As readers we detect all the bitterness and frustration that he must have felt before reaching this conclusion. Yet, here too, he wraps them in an exquisitely personal rhetoric and makes the best of a bad job. In essence, from the systematic acknowledgement of the ego's limitedness, Freud derives an empowering of the ego, similar to that which Kant derives from the feeling of the sublime inspired by the contemplation of nature's infinity.[4] In this way weakness is overturned and becomes strength. In the modern era this is the position of Freud's contemporary Nietzsche. The transvaluation of all traditional values by the Overman does not by any means generate "a weakened subject (not in the sense of the exemption from metaphysical attributes), but one strengthened in the plurality of mortal souls and in the multiplicity of interpretative perspectives that establish a richer objectivity than that which can be ascertained by mere description" (Vozza, 2014, p. 10).

In any case, the fiction that the note addresses is that of an isolated psychic system that is "able to satisfy even its nutritional requirements autistically" as if in "a bird's egg with its food supply enclosed in its shell" (Freud, 1911b, p. 220). And yet Freudian psychoanalysis rests to a large extent on this fiction, the fiction of the "isolated psychic system". On the one hand Freud describes the development of an animal-infant and not a man-infant (i.e., affected *from the very outset* by the symbolic in language), and on the other hand confers upon him the status of an already established subjectivity, however immature: that is, he sees him as an isolated entity. The mother is assimilated as a presence that permits the child to live in this world without suffering too many of its assaults. She acts on behalf of the child to keep at a distance those external stimuli that would cause him an increase in unpleasure.

Note 4 is the return of what Freudian theory represses. The metaphor of the bird in the egg is the quintessential illustration of Freud's conception of man as an isolated subject endowed with consciousness, a solipsistic entity: and, besides, it matches the psychological and philosophical dogma of his time. Although it is obviously a dogma to which psychoanalysis will itself contribute substantially to dissolving, there is in Freud no notion that from the outset the essence of being human consists in being transposed into the other.[5]

The fact is that there is a difference between animals, which are not "world-forming" and are "poor in world" (Heidegger, 1927), and men. For the latter to become human, maternal warmth and nourishment are not enough: they need someone to help them construct an unconscious, understood as the acquisition through language of the capacity to give existential meaning to experience. [6]

I repeat that Freudian psychoanalysis is largely based on the fiction of the "isolated psychic system". However, in the note Freud anticipates the idea expressed by Winnicott in a now famous formulation, that there is no such thing as a baby if viewed in isolation from the mother. The infant's apparently closed system is in reality constituted by the infant *plus* whoever is providing the care that is necessary for its survival. In fact, the subject is already a group. It is through having the mother's mind available—and not only when prompted by frustration—that the infant is not abandoned to its own solipsistic world of hallucinatory images.

Therefore, we cannot fail to read the note also as a memory of the future, in that it anticipates and summarises—"remembers"—how psychoanalytic theory will evolve divergently from the classical model after the middle of the twentieth century specifically in order to remedy the effects of the fiction adopted by Freud. The limits that

Freud honestly acknowledges, and that he places under the aegis of recognition of the reality principle while trying to pass beyond them, will be crossed by Bion; for example, with his concept of the protomental system.

We understand why Sandler (2005) asserts that overall this brief text may be the one that most inspired the psychoanalysis of Bion. We have seen how strongly Freud relativises the certainties of his time and how he lets us glimpse the seeds of a passage to a conception of intersubjectivity. So Freud, outlining a whole series of binary oppositions in this brief paper, lays down the premises by which they could begin to be transcended, something that Bion will bring to completion, starting with the overcoming of that very fiction that Freud speaks about in the note and that informs not only Bion's theory (Civitarese, 2008), but perhaps to an even greater degree some of his later developments such as the psychology of the ego.

Indeed, there are some other themes in FTPMF that can easily be recognised as leading to Bionian theory.

For example, Bion takes up from FTPMF the idea of having to concentrate on psychic functions more than on their contents. We may note the recurrence in FTPMF of the term *function* as early as the fifth line, in relation to Janet, or the term *process(es)*.

We may also note the striking equivalence between the text and the way in which the Bionian design of the grid presents an analogous teleological development of the functions of the psyche on the philo- and ontogenetic planes simultaneously, from primitive emotions to concepts, and from concepts to moral action (Bion, 1977, 1997; Civitarese, 2013a,b,c). In the end, both Freud and Bion delineate the life of man as a progressive acquisition of functions.

Then there is the significant passage in which Freud diminishes the opposition between the pleasure principle and the reality principle, writing that the latter only replaces the former so as to preserve it better. It is as if he were saying that every form of pleasure can only be a negative pleasure. We renounce something with a view to future compensation. The satisfaction of the pleasure stems from an initial moment of negation.

In the following lines Freud reduces the distance between neurosis and psychosis, making them a matter of quantity, of how large a part of reality the subject is able to tolerate, and immediately afterwards mentions the distinction between the neurotic and "mankind in general".

Lastly he presents the unconscious psychic processes as the most ancient, and above all, as closely bound to the pleasure principle. It would only be the disillusionment suffered by the hallucinatory satisfaction of desire that makes the recognition of external reality gradually emerge: "the psychical apparatus *had to decide* to form a conception of the real circumstances in the external world and to *endeavour* to make a real alteration in them" (Freud 1911b, p. 219, my italics). It can clearly be seen how on the theoretical plane it may not be the introjection of the maternal alpha function that puts the baby more fully in contact with reality, but rather a kind of "painful decision" by the baby himself, to accept his own deep "situation of frustration" (p. 222).

Sleep brings us back every night to this primitive condition in which we know nothing of external reality, "because a prerequisite of sleep is a deliberate rejection of reality (the wish to sleep)" (p. 219, n3). The dream is introduced as a residue of the hallucinatory route to the satisfaction of desire. Dream thinking would be at the service of the latent thoughts that express prohibited desires. Dreaming, for Freud, is equivalent to suspending the reality principle. He does not by any means believe, as Bion does (1992) that dream thoughts are a rough draft of thought, that the dream designs maps for exploring the world and is not confined solely to the state of sleep. He gives no sign of dream's creative value, nor of the idea that it may be dreaming of the mother that initially acts as a complement to the condition of being "all (and only) conscious" (Bion, 1967a) of the baby at birth (Civitarese, 2011). For Freud, reality knocks on the door because dreaming never works, because it fails as an investigation of reality and not, conversely, because it succeeds in giving a "poetic" or integrated meaning to experience. Nor is the dream seen as an activity of digesting the real that also takes place in the waking state. For Freud, primary and secondary process are not a continuum, but separated by a clear caesura.

And yet, here too, if on the one hand Freud reaffirms the dichotomy of *C./Ucs.* and primary/secondary process, is he not at the same time eroding from within any metaphysical view of truth, and letting perception subtly and dangerously incline to the side of the hallucinatory? Do not dreaming, "imagining", and "pretending" end up almost superimposed on to each other? Is he not also clearly asserting that it would be a mistake to identify the dream solely with latent dream thoughts?

In a narrative crescendo worthy of Rossini, by which—I repeat—FTPMF anticipates the structure of the grid, we are present at the linear itinerary of the infant who from being immersed as he is in this hallucinatory world, step by step develops effective sensory channels, a consciousness, a memory, and finally attention; an activity that instead of passively receiving sensory impressions, goes to meet them. All that is true. But there is more. When the psyche passes from the pleasure principle to the reality principle, writes Freud, a small part of it remains attached to the pleasure principle: the activity of fantasy, which is immediately located in children's play and in *dreaming with open eyes*. Here the ego's drives are pulled away from the sexual ones, which remain much longer under the dominance of the pleasure principle. The neuroses find easy terrain in "the delay in educating the sexual instincts" (1911b, p. 223).[7] However, as soon as the two currents have diverged, in some ways they re-converge because the ego takes account of reality in order to preserve better the achievement of pleasure. And here too a caesura begins to be broken little by little.[8] The reality principle is only the servant of the pleasure principle. The hallucinatory in dream begins to infiltrate perception.

For example, if religions are able to bring about the complete renunciation of pleasure it is always with a view to a greater pleasure (in the afterlife), even if illusory.

Even the pleasure offered by the sciences is a small matter, an intellectual pleasure with a view to a practical reward. Therefore, both religion and science are animated by dream, by a subterranean fantasy life, by the pleasure principle.

But the point at which we can best pick up anticipations of the current vision of dreaming as an activity that characterises waking life as well, and of the crisis in the opposition between primary and secondary processes, is in the Freudian theory of aesthetic experience.

In this text of Freud's, art is the *via regia* for reconciling the two principles. The artist, presented initially as in some way maladapted, is an artist because he does not renounce pleasure but addresses himself to reality "by making use of special gifts to mould his phantasies into truths of a new kind, which are valued by men as precious reflections of reality" (p. 224).

Then Freud adds an essential detail, which is that the artist "can only achieve this because other men feel the same dissatisfaction as he does with the renunciation demanded by reality" (p. 224).

So we see that in this text Freud on the one hand reaffirms a series of caesuras, but on the other does what he can to destabilise them.

In confessing in note 4 that he sees his theoretical construction as a model or framework for reaching the thing that in itself, however, remains unattainable, Freud admits that scientific truth is also a myth. Here his personal life coincides with his scientific vicissitudes. Indeed, *how* could Freud have wanted to "kill" his father if not by annexing a continent new to science and hitherto unexplored? It is as if—we may speculate—Freud were telling us with the dream of FTPMF that his desire was to overcome the father and acquire a fame that he would demonstrate by means of an incontrovertible discovery. This discovery, the dominance of the reality principle imposes on him the need to recognise that *there had been no such discovery*: a "rhetorical" or "consensual" truth is only a pale reflection of it. In fact, Freud was thinking of himself as a "true" scientist, not as the founder of a discipline that could only exist in a space half way between art and science—a *Zwitterart*, as Schiller said of himself and of the poet (Reitani, 2003, p. 124). This game does not merely happen in the background of FTPMF but, well hidden, is the principal game being played in the text.

So far we have seen how Freud's most intimate personal experiences are tightly interwoven in the text with his theoretical activity. The same thing occurs also in the final element of paratext that we shall take into consideration, the editorial introduction.

The introduction

Finally we come to the first crucial paratext in FTPMF, the preface by Cesare Musatti that acts as an introduction to the Italian edition of Freud's *Works*. It is of no importance that the preface was not written by Freud. Our reading could not now overlook it. It would be absurd to think we could gain access to the truth of a text in its original purity. We are not given a text without a context that determines its reception in some way. As has been said, just like the other paratextual elements inserted by the author, the introduction is an editorial *parergon* that acts as a frame and so engages in dialogue with the main text, contributing to the outlining of its meaning.

The most noteworthy element in the introduction refers to Jung's role in the conception of FTPMF (see also Blum (2004)). Introducing the figure of a parricidal Jung in Freud's eyes, the introduction merely anticipates what we encounter in the text's opening remarks, in the lines where Freud overtakes, and so "kills" his father Janet, writing that the latter could not explain the reason for the lessening of reality function in neurotics.

But while the reference in the text to Janet is obvious, that to Jung is hidden, and in order to shed light on it we first need the introduction and then a reference to the Freud–Jung correspondence. In the letter of 19 June 1910 Freud praises a work by Jung (*Symbols of Transformation*) that will later flow into *Transformations and Symbols of the Libido*. Then he adds that he is taking up some of Jung's ideas for a paper, destined for the *Jahrbuch*, which will be called "The two principles of psychic action and education".

This letter clearly shows that the two are now at loggerheads. Freud writes (Freud & Jung, 1974, pp. 330–332):

> Dear friend, I am really sorry to hear of all your overwork and irritation and thank you very much for your friendly explanations. You mustn't suppose that I ever "lose patience" with you; I don't believe these words can apply to our relationship in any way. In all the difficulties that confront us in our work we must stand firmly together, and now and then you must listen to me, your older friend, even when you are disinclined to.

It is the tongue-lashing that a father would give a son who has disappointed him. Once we have read the rest of the letter our last doubts will vanish:

> You know how jealous they all are—here and elsewhere—over your privileged position with me . . . and I think I am justified in feeling that what people say against you as a result is being said against me.

Then Freud blames Adler, whom he describes "hypersensitive and deeply embittered" because he consistently rejects his theories. He comments that "a secession were going to be attempted in Vienna" and mentions "a step that implied calling the authority of the chairman into question", but he managed to avoid this. By and large "The goings-on in Zürich" seem to him "stupid" and the situation there "untenable". He wonders that Jung has not been able to develop sufficient authority. In the rest of the letter, if we read between the lines, we will be hit by expressions such as "internal division", "Swiss blockheads", and finally by the rhetorical but subtly provocative question directly addressed to his interlocutor "Could you have given the impression that you were indifferent to them ['. . . to *me*'?!] as individuals?"

Apparently at this point Freud intends a change of tone, adding that he would rather speak about pleasant things. Except that he continues unperturbed in a combative vein, albeit latent, when he refers to his "plagiarism" (but by whom, we may ask, and from whom?) and to some pages of FTPMF still in progress. After praising Jung for the text, now lost in its original form, which came from the conference held at Herisau and was then included in *Symbols of Transformation*, he goes on:

> Don't be surprised if you recognize certain of your own statements in a paper of mine that I am hoping to revise in the first weeks of the holidays, and don't accuse me of plagiarism, though there may be some temptation to. The title will be: The Two Principles of Mental Action and Education. It is intended for the *Jahrbuch*. I conceived and wrote it two days before the arrival of your "Symbolism"; it is of course a formulation of ideas that were long present in my mind.

As they say, *in cauda venenum*: who is plagiarising whom? And that is not all, because Freud takes up with a phrase that is impossible not to understand even in a shrewd way: "I identified your vulture only today", a sentence that can be translated as "Only now I realise that you are a vulture". Freud then again sets himself in open opposition: "I am not inclined to let you have Count Zinzendorf for the *Jahrbuch*. Don't take it amiss", and lastly complains about health problems, "a recurrence of the intestinal trouble . . . plain colitis", etc. But we can only understand the nature of these complaints by reading the list of no more than thirteen objections to Jung's text (another example of paratext!) with which Freud accompanies his missive. At the end of the letter he looks diplomatically ahead and tells Jung that he is aware that his criticisms will certainly not be received willingly, but that overall, in the end, he very much liked the work.

Jung's reply was not long in coming. A week later, 26 June, he replied to Freud in a conciliatory tone. Indeed, the *incipit* of the letter is significant in that respect: "Today being a Sunday I am using it to go over your critique in peace" (p. 361). The polemical tone is evident in Jung's discourse. It is as if he were saying, "Since it is Sunday, I am not responding in kind." But that little word, "peace", appears to have been placed there precisely to hint at the cold war that now seems to be under way, and that is reignited a few lines later when Jung firmly defends his position on sexuality, even though it had been attacked by Freud.

In the light of my observations so far, FTPMF appears as the "dream" with which Freud tries to give meaning to the strong emotions (the "psychic consequences") stirred up by Jung's rebellion. In his filicidal impulse, unconsciously denied, Freud finds yet another, stronger impulse for his parricidal drive, or rather cannot stop himself siding with Jung, except that now the father to be killed is . . . himself! Why do I say this? Essentially because the key to the three examined dreams—which, I repeat, I propose to consider similarly as paratextual elements—lies in the invocation to mercy that is always addressed by a son to the father *and never vice versa*!

In the dream about his father's death, Freud asks him to leave him in peace. The same thing happens in the other dream, not his, about the son who is burning. There too it is the son who asks the father to ease his torment. It is like this again in the dream of FTPMF and in the letter where Jung asks him to make peace. If in this incident with Jung, Freud finds himself objectively taking the other side (it is the father, Laius, who wants to kill the son who has been revealed as a danger to him by the prophecy), here he is burning above all with the suffering of Oedipus. Perhaps this was more difficult for him to admit to himself than the impulse to kill his son (while accusing him of the reciprocal), as if unconsciously it was impossible for him not to identify—against himself—with the rebellious son. If my interpretation is plausible, the accusation against Jung is in reality a self-accusation.

The work of the margins

Do we now have to conclude that, paradoxically, it is in the introduction, in the editorial paratext (the text's unconscious?) that we find the "where [*wo*]"—the thing that Freud would gladly have withheld, and on account of which he asks the reader to be benevolent towards him? As in *The Purloined Letter* of Poe, the meaning sought with such doggedness was always in plain sight.

The aspect of FTPMF that I have called performative, and to which Freud ambiguously calls our attention at the end of the text is of broad scope. It plays on a series of particular planes that intersect with each other. Not only the theoretical recognition of the fictional status of reality; nor only the admission by Freud that his too is nothing but a scientific fiction, not the real thing; nor yet the interpretation aimed at Jung of his desire to do away with him, nor the awareness of his own filicidal desire toward Jung: but perhaps, close to the core of the dream, the reappearance of the desire in Freud himself, this time unconsciously identified with Jung, to kill *his* father. Also in play here is the possibility that one achieves with greater or lesser success the "complete psychical detachment from [one's] parents" (1911b, p. 219, n. 4) that signals the end of the pleasure principle. Even though, when we think of the *incipit*, with its "elimination" of Janet and its invocations of the father in the two dreams and—in the letter to Jung—of the reader-as-judge-father, there can be no doubt about which passion prevails, what is still more important is the general principle: that one must accept we are no longer making use of a separating logic, of an absolute principle of non-contradiction.

The text's various planes follow one another in a centripetal direction, from the theoretical level to the most personal and vice versa, as if saying that, whichever way you look at reality, it is never how it appears, not even when viewed in the pure, disinterested manner of scientific research. FTPMF seems to reaffirm that at the bottom of any epistemophilic passion there is always a private nucleus of neurosis. With this text Freud is trying to treat himself. We also see, in the light of this, how effectively the oneiric participates in the construction of rational argument, and how the beginning of the reality principle consists simply in mourning our pretensions to knowledge. The dominion of the reality principle demands that we see everything in our inner or outer lives as fiction. But is this not the work of the margins? Is not the frame the component of a picture that takes on the job of marking out a space for fiction? Does not any frame warn us never to give in to the images' status as real? And is not the dream the threshold where one passes every time from internal to external and vice versa, but without our ever being able to do without either of the two termini lest we lose that which represents the quintessence of humanity? In FTPMF every time a paratextual element emphasises or nuances something that has just been asserted, it reframes it, adjusts it. The reader is confronted on each occasion with a catastrophic change of perspective on various levels. What remains in essence is this very vertigo, which Nietzsche calls the world become infinite again.

We have seen at work repeatedly in the margins how they act to join together the internal and external. This is "how" the reality principle begins, or rather where the fiction principle begins. FTPMF's discovery is that we are characterised more by the fiction principle than by the reality principle. The reality principle is merely a name we give to the occasional convergences that allow us to have a minimal common view of things.

In fact, to become human it is necessary to achieve the fiction which, in allowing us to tolerate the "no" of the object's absence, simultaneously permits us the illusion that we attain it through its name. For this reason we can say that the only reality that concerns us—given that, strictly speaking, animals do not perceive objects but are merely immersed in a dynamic flow of automatic stimulus–responses—can only be a fictitious reality. The dominion of the reality principle lies in recognising that the quality that makes us human lies in an essential principle of fiction and that every fiction has its beginning in the *no* of the name.

So where does the dominion of the reality principle begin? I would say, paradoxically, in the margins, from the start of the disappearance of the real in favour of reality. Reality is in the margins: or rather, only the frame makes a concept of reality available to us. The affirmation of the dominion of the reality principle means recognising that reality is a fiction. This is the truth imposed upon us and that we struggle so hard to accept: that reality has the qualities of a dream. Acknowledging the dominion of reality means recognising that we only possess reality by dreaming it. It means mourning our ability ever to possess the thing, the object, the truth. Dreaming is equivalent to representing, to transforming the real into a familiar and reassuring reality, to placing a desired but feared object at a safe distance that allows us the peace and quiet of thought.

Notes

1. See Genette (1987, p. 5): "The distanced elements are all those messages that, at least originally, are located outside the book, generally with the help of the media (letters, conversations) or under cover of private communications (letters, diaries, and others). This second category is what, for lack of a better word, I call *epitext* . . . peritext and epitext completely and entirely share the spatial field of the paratext. In other words, for those who are keen on formulae, *paratext = peritext + epitext*".

2. See Genette (1987, p. 16): "I give the name *publisher's peritext* to the whole zone of the peritext that is direct and principal (but not exclusive) responsibility of the publisher (or perhaps, to be more abstract but also more exact, of the *publishing house*)".

3. In this text I use the terms *après coup*, *posteriority*, and *Nachträglichkeit* as equivalent.

4. See Civitarese (2014). The passage which follows is extremely noteworthy: "The place of repression, which excluded from cathexis as productive of unpleasure some of the emerging ideas, was taken by an *impartial passing of judgement*, which had to decide whether a given idea was true or false—that is, whether it was in agreement with reality or not—the decision being determined by making a comparison with the memory-traces of reality." (Freud, 1911b, pp. 221). Here it is the moral, Kantian man who comes into view. The Freudian rhetoric sparkles as it shows the necessity for the repression of pleasure, of sexuality felt as a danger for the order of meaning. It is moreover evident that Freud is here proposing a theory of knowledge. The moral man acts correctly in reality. ("A new function was now allotted to motor discharge, which, under the dominance of the pleasure principle, had served as a means of unburdening the mental apparatus of accretions of stimuli . . . Motor discharge was now employed in the appropriate alteration of reality; it was converted into *action*". We may note here too, the coincidence with key terms from Bion's vocabulary.)

5. Cfr. Heidegger, 1983, p. 206: philosophy has propounded "the dogma that the individual human being exists for him- or herself as an individual and that it is the individual ego with its ego-sphere which is initially and primarily given to itself as what is most certain. This has merely given philosophical sanction to the view that some kind of being with one other must first be produced out of this solipsistic isolation". See also Brown (2011) who has shown in Freud's work the presence of a "proto-intersubjectivity".

6. The contemporary psychoanalysis that draws most on metapsychology has identified in the paradigm of the *Nebenmensch* one possible way to highlight the presence even in Freud of a form of proto-intersubjectivity.

7. Before subverting the laws of civilised life, a sexuality not regulated by a paternal/third function would subvert the very establishment of symbolic order, because it would tend to wipe out the space between subject and object from which all difference arises. The dominance of the reality principle begins with the introjection of the father's *no*. The father as third function prevents incest between infant and mother and allows the symbol to arise from the space thus created, but at the same time the symbol arises from the fact of keeping a link between subject and object and thence de facto transgressing the paternal interdiction. Moreover, thanks to the desire to which it always gives rise, sexuality also acts as a safeguard against the risk that this distance becomes infinite. Pleasure and unpleasure are thus both consubstantial with the capacity for symbolisation.

8. On the concept of "caesura" see Civitarese (2008).

Editors' introduction to Chapter Six

The title of Dr Ferro's paper captures the essence of his contribution: he invites us on a journey that explores the path from the roots of Freud's "Two principles" paper to its contemporary development and in particular to his personal rich contribution.

To contextualise the way in which Freud's paper influenced his theoretical and clinical posture, Ferro first starts by summarising briefly what he considers the main points of the "Two principles" paper. He then elaborates on the fundamental differences between Freud and Bion's conceptualisation of the unconscious. For Freud the unconscious is the source of drive energy that is at the source of psychic conflict. From this perspective, psychoanalysis aims at uncovering the repressed unconscious contents in order to make sense of how it affects conscious life. For Bion, the unconscious is conceptualised in a fundamentally different manner. The mind, according to Bion, is continuously occupied in the task of processing the sensory experience that stems both from within and outside of the individual. The alpha function transforms these experiences (beta elements) into alpha elements that can be used for thinking. The unconscious, conceived in this manner is continuously being created. So for Ferro, following Bion, the aim of psychoanalysis is not to unveil the unconscious but to foster the development of mental functions that will transform the sensory data into alpha elements that can be used for thinking. As Ferro states: "the waking dream function is thus a positive operation of the alpha function and leads to the capacity, during waking hours as well, to create visual images as a consequence of sensory stimulation—in some way *to dream what happens to us* (p. 132, this volume, editors' italic). This way of conceptualising the unconscious also transforms the way in which we think about dreams: as a psychic activity that serves to continuously transform sensory data into thinking and into narrations of reality. Moreover, this conceptualisation also transforms the way in which we think about sexuality: for example, not only as a drive but as a "narration" of the functioning of minds among themselves.

Ferro's reading of Freud's "Two principle" paper highlights what can be thought of as the "seeds" that became the starting point for the major tenants of Bion's theory: the alpha function and the theory of container–contained. The concept of the alpha function has its origins in Freud's notion of the recognition by the conscious mind of sensory qualities. The alpha function will then become the "great elaborator of sensoriality, and whose significant factors will be attention, notation, and memory, alongside many other that are unknown" (p. 134, this volume). The theory of container–contained has its origins in Freud's ideas about the passage from the motor discharge to action to thought processes, which open the possibility "for the mental apparatus to tolerate an increased tension of stimulus while the process of discharge was postponed" (Freud, 1911b, p. 221).

In continuity with Bion's conceptualisations of the alpha function and the theory of container–contained, Ferro introduces the notion of the bipersonal field and characters in the field. Ferro develops this in his own terms and, using strikingly evocative imagery, he proposes that if one were to describe the container in terms of a relational/field theory,

> we could envisage the container as being made up of emotional threads extending from the mind of the analyst to that of the patient and vice versa, and each time is unison between the two, another small thread is added to the container, thus expanding it continuously. As the container is strengthened and enriched by new emotional threads, this size and nature of the emotions it can contain grows. (p. 134, this volume)

With these advances in post-Bionian theory, the notion of a reality principle from Ferro's perspective is no longer a question of relinquishing the pleasure principle and using thinking as a way of affecting reality. Reality is something that "must be dreamed in order to become thinkable and digestible". For Ferro, this has important implications in the analytic work: "a very meaningful and painful mourning process must be undergone by the analyst, who must mourn the reality of the patient's communications in order to dream them and render them as representations, narrations" (p. 136, this volume).

In linking his ideas to Freud's conceptualisations of the process of living according to the reality principle, Ferro, in a creative manner, invites us to consider a perspective on the process of lying that takes it away from an exclusively negative and pathological perspective. In this introduction I will mention only a few points on this subject, the reader will find an in depth elaboration in Ferro's paper. Ferro considers that there is a process of thinking in the creation of a lie. He sees it as a sort of creation "an invention of worlds that is not dissimilar to the activity of writing. . . . The thinker of a lie must create plots, connections; he must engage in a mythopoetic activity" (p. 145, this volume). Still, following Bion, one can recognise the merit of lying in that the lie needs a thinker, that is, the lie needs to be born and maintained by a creative thinker.

Defensive activities can be thought of as lies; they provide humans with "shock absorbers" (p. 143, this volume). The truth, both internal and external is often unbearable. Internal experiences such as rage, terror, envy, homicidal feelings, etc., can be so unbearable that it can lead to the renunciation of the internal truth in favour of a truth that is more tolerable and allows thinking. For instance projecting feelings of homicidal rage on to someone, can both compromise the recognition of internal truth while still preserving the contact with it in the outside. In this manner, lying can be paradoxically considered a capacity, the capacity to preserve the pleasure principle yet at the same time preserving contact with reality.

> The capacity to lie must therefore be considered one of the markers of having reached psychic maturity . . . The ability to tolerate this defence mechanism with elegance is a sign of psychic maturity, both in the patient and in the analyst, or in the analytic field. (p. 143, this volume)

We are indebted to Dr Ferro for the different creative ideas he develops from the "Two principles" in particular a paradoxical perspective in the act of lying.

6

Freud's "Formulations on the two principles of mental functioning": its roots and development

*Antonino Ferro**

There are different ways in which to approach models of the mind—one that I would define as favouring *continuities* and the other, favouring *discontinuities*. The first tries to catch hold of their roots, the analogies among concepts developed during various periods of time; the second recognises some models that introduce new, unanticipated perspectives on a particular idea that could not have been predicted.

What is the relationship between the ego and the alpha function? This could be an interesting question for some, and for others a non-essential one.

In tackling this essay of Freud's, "Formulations on the two principles of mental functioning" (1911b), one cannot help but admire and be impressed by his genius in constructing such a clear and functional model of the mind. The route that leads from the pleasure principle to the reality principle is extraordinary and, for those who inhabit a Freudian model, an unavoidable one. I will now summarise briefly what I consider the main points of Freud's "Two principles" paper.

* Translation by Gina Atkinson, MA.

Freud leads us by the hand in considering how the patient is forced "out of real life", how there is "an alienating of him from reality" (p. 218). It is the unbearable nature of real life that isolates the neurotic from it; some fragments of reality are always denied by the neurotic.

Unconscious psychic processes are the oldest ones and are the residuals of an earlier phase of development; in that phase, the pleasure principle reigned supreme. The dream is considered a residual of this way of functioning. The psychic apparatus has had to adapt itself to new demands, to the point of latching on to the sensory qualities of the external world, and to a takeover by the pronouncement of judgmental activity (Freud, 1911b) with respect to the veracity—or lack of it—of a given representation.

Simultaneously, motoric discharge is transformed into action, and action is transformed with the postponement of discharge in thinking, "thinking", which thereby becomes what Freud calls "experimental action". Fantasising constitutes a sort of no man's land. The sexual drive is cultivated later than reality. It is fascinating, then, to consider observations about religions, which shift the pleasure principle into the future, and about education, which leans in the direction of the reality principle. The choice of neurosis derives from the particular developmental phase that the patient was undergoing at that moment. Due partly to space constraints, I have summarised Freud's clear and admirable construction in a somewhat awkward way, but all of this must be examined, in my opinion, in the light of some of the catastrophic events in the theory and technique of psychoanalysis that have occurred since the publication of the paper and that pertain to certain of its aspects.

The contrasting way of conceptualising the unconscious put forward by Bion

I would like to begin this section with a metaphor of Civitarese's (2013a) on the concept of the unconscious for Freud: he saw it as a sort of maximum-security prison, like Alcatraz, where the child's repressed desires of a sexual nature have been locked up. Every now and then, some prisoners manage to escape from this prison in disguise, and these are our dreams, slips, parapraxes, witticisms, etc.

Thus, according to Freudian theory, the unconscious is primarily made up of contents repressed during the early phases of childhood when the child must learn, according to social rules, to renounce the satisfaction of his desires of a sexual nature, which are consequently repressed and imprisoned in the unconscious. The warden of the unconscious, its censorship, functions in such a way that when we dream, the contents of the unconscious are "camouflaged, masked" by various mechanisms of the dream: displacement, condensation, and so on.

For Freud, the unconscious is a source of drive energy that is very important in an individual's life, but it is also the source of many psychic disturbances. The task of psychoanalysis, therefore, is to "unveil" the unconscious content of our mind, in order to understand how and in what ways it influences our conscious life.

In Bion, the concept of the unconscious changes completely: the unconscious continues to be formed, during the daytime and at night, through the alpha function, which continually performs the transformation of beta elements—that is, as purely sensorial elements incapable of being thought—into alpha elements, pictograms, which can then be used in dreaming. The transformation of beta elements into alpha elements brings about the construction of a sort of contact barrier made up of alpha elements themselves, which ensures that there is a separation between the conscious and the unconscious; yet also creating a permanent boundary between these two mental regions. Alpha elements formed in this way can, however, be utilised by thinking, and we find traces of them in narrative derivatives.

In other words, our minds are continually busy with this kind of digestion of the sensory based experience that strikes us both from inside and from outside. Our mental health derives precisely from the digestive capacity of our minds, and so from our capacity to create the unconscious.

With this assumption, one quickly sees that, in Bion, the aim of psychoanalysis has also changed; it is no longer the unveiling of the unconscious, but instead the development of mental functions (first of all, the alpha function) that carry out the digestion/transformation of somato-sensory data into pictograms. The pictograms that make up the unconscious can be utilised for nocturnal dreaming, but they can also be used during waking hours for the narration of our experiences and vicissitudes.

Pathology and mental discomfort, for Bion, are born of a defect in the mind's digestive capacity (that is, in the alpha function), or from an excess of beta elements, which in turn give rise to an excess of unthinkable somato-sensory experience This excessive somato-sensory experience is then projected internally that is, it brings about discomfort in the body through somatisation. Mental health, on the other hand, depends on our continuing capacity to dream what happens to us, even during the daytime. The waking dream function is thus a positive operation of the alpha function and leads to the capacity, during waking hours as well, to create visual images as a consequence of sensory stimulation—in some way to dream what happens to us.

Bion's contrasting way of conceptualising the dream

In Bion, the dream is no longer the realm of a hallucinatory realisation of desire, but in its two forms—daytime (alpha function) and night-time (the dream actually understood as an alpha super-function; see Ferro (2011) and Grotstein (2007))—the dream serves to continually transform sensory data into pictograms, into thinking, and into narrations of reality. "Pathology" as described—for example, a symptom—speaks to us of a defect of the oneiric function of the mind in transforming "that fact", "that fragmented piece of reality" into a narration that is shareable, navigable, and digestible.

Examples of this are numerous and widespread: Professor Unrat (in the novel *The Blue Angel* by Heinrich Mann (1905)) is not capable of "dreaming", of "metabolising" the limited, finite nature of life and uses massive doses of antidepressants (the dancer Rosa Fröhlich) to buffer a "fact": the aging that he could not claim as his own. The same is true for a patient named Carlotta, who lives in a circular, not yet linear time that actually prevents her from wearing a watch, both in a real sense and metaphorically. When she finally begins to dream this "fact", making it accessible, she exclaims, "Here is my new watch!" She then adds (jokingly, but not entirely so), "Santa Claus gave it to me!" Bion reminds us in his book *Attention and Interpretation* (1970) that it is the function carried out by dreams in all their forms in which we really get down to work.

A contrasting way, derived from Bion, of conceptualising sexuality

In Bion, the view of a sexuality that develops in phases is no longer operative. We come to think of sexuality not only as a drive, but as a "narration" of the functioning of minds among themselves—for example, of the way that projective identifications and reverie are linked together (Ferro, 2009a,b).

If a male patient speaks of premature ejaculation, this probably relates to an emotionally uncontainable experience and to explosive emotions that have come to be narrated in a sexual narrative genre. It is the same if a female patient speaks of vaginismus, according to this model; much thought would be directed toward a disproportionate state between insufficient containers and hyper-contained emotions, told through a sexual metaphor that could be replaced by any other narrative genre.

"O", reality, has various new destinies according to this perspective. Let me continue by summarising the vicissitudes of "O":

(a) Transformations in "O" and catastrophic change: These are the transformations that involve a sudden leap in mental growth, achieved by way of a crisis that may sometimes even include short periods of depersonalisation. Characteristic features of catastrophic change are violence and subversion of the system or of the existing structure and invariants as a process of transformation, as well as, for the analyst, awareness of the emotions arising from being unable to spare himself or his patients from the experience of catastrophic truth. Transformations in "O" contrast with other transformations in that the former are related to growth in becoming and the latter to growth in knowing about growth.

(b) Transformations of "O": I personally see these as the long journey of "O" in Column 2 of the grid (that of lies and dreams), insofar as "O" cannot normally be understood and must be "subjectivised". Alpha functions, dreams, reveries, and narrations are the main tools that transform "O", truth, into that part of truth that is bearable for our minds. As stated earlier, in Column 2 of the grid, people/histories/realities are transformed into internal objects, characters, and holograms.

(c) During this journey from "O" to dreams and narration, we as analysts undergo a mourning process leading toward reality. In other words, the psyche stems from a sacrifice of reality, when assisted by another alpha function: we need another mind to relate to—that is to say, to create a field where the characters of the narration can emerge. We need to learn how to dance across Column 2 and Row 3 of the grid—myths, dreams, and complex narrations.

I am certainly not a supporter of the "Freud already said it" line. And yet . . . and yet . . . in this brief and extremely dense paper, "Formulations on the two principles of mental functioning", seeds can be found that will be developed by others. In particular, I refer to the passage in which Freud alludes to the recognition by the conscious mind of sensory qualities, in addition to the qualities of pleasure and unpleasure. In this way, Freud's ideas about sensory qualities are pertinent to the concept of the alpha function, which will be seen as a great elaborator of sensoriality, and whose significant factors will be attention, notation, and memory, alongside many others that are unknown.

Not only this section is relevant to my comments, but also what Freud says about the passage from the motoric discharge → action → thought processes, which opens the way toward the possibility "for the mental apparatus to tolerate an increased tension of stimulus while the process of discharge was postponed" (Freud 1911b, p. 221). And here we have arrived at the little conceptual building blocks that will lead to Bion's conceptualisation of the container–contained.

The first way in which Bion described the container was from a spatial perspective. During the interplay between the child's projective identification and the mother's reverie, the notion of an internal mental space is first experienced. Finding a mental space within the mother's mind allows the child to introject the concept of an internal space. This mental space is the first epiphany of the container. The container is always solicited by the contents that need to be contained.

The second way of describing the container is in terms of a sort of relational/field theory. In analysis, we could envisage the container as being made up of emotional threads extending from the mind of the analyst to that of the patient and vice versa, and each time there is unison between the two, another small thread is added to the container, thus expanding it continuously. As the container is strengthened and enriched by new emotional threads, the size and nature of the emotions it can contain grows.

It can be seen as a kind of safety net such as those used in circuses during trapeze performances. The difference in this case is that it extends around a full 360 degrees, in every direction. This, too, is a spatial metaphor, but now I think it is better to set aside this spatial concept and turn to that of the narrative container.

If "Jack the Ripper" is alone, his presence in the city is unbearable, but if he is linked to *Django Unchained*, the connection between them lessens the "intolerability". Through narration, the more connections made between different characters within the field, the less havoc they can wreak.

Naturally, all of this pertains to mental functioning within the analytic session.

As if that intermediate area of "fantasising" were not sufficient, it will open the way to key concepts such as reverie, transitional space, and, I would dare to say, the bipersonal field, a place of all possible worlds and all possible interpretations—whether they are obstructed, navigable, mute, or expressed.

The cultivation of the drive, by contrast, is something very different from its containability, metabolisation, and transformation, as Bion reminds us in *Taming Wild Thoughts* (1963–1977). The centrality of the sexual drive has lost much ground, I think, as has the associated development in phases in regard to the development of the mind conceived as a particularly human characteristic. I am referring to that aspect of the mental that—from sensoriality through containability, the alpha function, and the nocturnal dream function—permits, in the relationship with the other, the formation of tools that make up the particularity of our minds. Even if evacuation remains a defence mechanism, in its variations in every individual mind, whether healthy or suffering, this is an unavoidable source of relationality and a necessity for alleviation.

Perhaps a few words are missing here in regard to the emotional and to the necessary presence of emotions that will become central in the concepts of the emotional pictogram, but I would like to conclude this section with a note about a short story by Chekhov entitled *The Exclamation Mark* (1886). The story tells of a clerk who for years has written or transcribed documents, always working in a scrupulous manner. One day, on a social occasion, he is accused with some arrogance of not actually having any in-depth or worthwhile knowledge or study under his belt because he is always limited to editing others' documents.

On returning home that night, he cannot sleep due to going over and over in his mind all the documents—thousands and tens of thousands—impeccably written out, and he remembers all the possible rules for the use of commas, periods, semicolons, and even question marks. But while in an agitated half-asleep state, he woke up abruptly when he finds himself thinking of exclamation points. He does not remember ever having put one in. Precisely when are they used?

He awakens his wife, who has completed all her college courses and who has proudly told him that she knows all the rules of grammar by memory. She says that the exclamation mark is used when one wants to give emphasis—to indicate an emotion, whether it is anger, joy, happiness, or any other type. It then appears clear to him how it could be used in a letter, but how can it be used in a document? He again thinks of the tens of thousands of written documents that never had a single exclamation mark, of that he is certain.

This story lends itself well, in my opinion, to an emphasis on how a routine, factual existence is possible, with everything in order, well documented and well documentable, without there ever being an emotion such as anger, joy, jealousy, or any other.

At this point, after a sleepless night, the protagonist decides to go to his department head, and in the agenda that he must write in order to see him—that is, in the book of recorded appointments—he writes his own name, Yefim Perekladin, and adds three exclamation marks after it. Chekhov concludes: "In putting down these three marks, he felt enthusiasm, indignation, joy, and a seething rage. 'Hey—look at that!' he murmured, gripping the pen tightly."

Post-Bion changes in the concept of reality itself

Indeed, reality is that thing that must be dreamed in order to become thinkable and digestible. Here a very meaningful and painful mourning process must be undergone by the analyst, who must mourn the reality of the patient's communications in order to dream them and render them as representations, narrations.

A patient invents an alternative personality for himself and presents it as real to everyone.

But what is the "fact" that he has not known how to dream or transform? It is that of being—as he himself will say after a long analysis—a small-time country lawyer, devoid of any appealing characteristics, alone and deprived of all warmth and friendliness. The lie protected him from dreaming, performing an alpha function on a story that was too painful to accept.

As I have said, the analyst is an enzyme capable of fostering the development of tools for thinking, feeling, and dreaming, which we human beings need in order to live.

An intermediate area could be opened up by this vignette: that of the lie that can be understood as an extreme, as a negation-falsification of reality, and at the other extreme, as the opening of "other" worlds in which to find refuge from anxieties that are otherwise too great to be managed.

We could also consider lies to be among those mechanisms of defence that protect us from existential truths and burning intense emotions. Here another interesting dialectic could open between the rules of reality and oneiric rules.

The lie rises to a more "elevated" degree when the liar becomes capable of constructing and sharing a non-existent world with others in reality. We can get a glimpse of this in the following clinical situations.

The liar who wanted to be loved

Marco comes to consultation at the request of his wife, who has discovered that her husband has been using an enhanced identity and some incredible inventions. Marco is said to be a member of the secret service, a paratrooper with the Special Forces, and a black-belt master of judo. Every now and then he disappears alleging he has gone on a foreign mission or claiming he is busy with top-secret activities (while in reality he holes himself up in the home of an elderly aunt to whom he is extremely attached, and where he has spent some days in the faraway small town to which she has retreated).

Marco has even "invented" a great quantity of stories of bold and daring romances he has experienced during his missions. Most recently, he has been acting as a "serial chat room visitor" on the

Internet, engaging in exchanges of secret messages with various girlfriends whom he has never met, claiming them as his contacts in his job as a secret agent.

Already at our first meeting, Marco will say he is "afraid of losing the people I love", he also says "lies are a way for me to feel appreciated". He is a country lawyer, the head of a partnership of little importance. It has come naturally to him over the years to colour this grey world with intensely bright brushstrokes, ever more audaciously. In this way, he feels himself to be more interesting in his wife's eyes, more able to evoke her feelings of admiration and appreciation for him. Had he not done this, if he had shown her only what was real—the banal face of "Demetrio Pianelli" (his expression) [1]—he would have been abandoned and betrayed.

The analyst's comment is that it seems to him that Marco is functioning as a very good lawyer for himself: he has succeeded in transforming an imprisoned man in grey, destined for obscurity and abandonment, into a sort of Superman who is capable of, among other things, keeping at bay the depression by which he sometimes feels tormented. This intervention causes Marco to open up and induces him to reveal another incredible series of lies that he has strung together, "in order not to lose" the love of people he loves and on whom he depends emotionally.

How can one forget the famous words "My name is Bond—James Bond"? A "bond" is a connection or a tie. Without connections, Marco is lost and forced to mint counterfeit coins both to implement and maintain such connections. The lie becomes something that gives him prestige and the possibility of being appreciated and loved.

Lying in order not to disappoint

Even though her parents are leading academics at a medical school and enjoy considerable professional success, Maristella has been able to be independent in her choice of profession and enrolled in a prestigious school of economics. On the threshold of her graduation, she confesses to her parents, after a suicide attempt (it was not clear how serious the attempt was) that in six years, she has taken only two exams. Her parents explode with rage and bring her back home, cutting off their support. As a result she feels forced to separate from her boyfriend, with whom she has been living but who cannot manage to meet expenses on his own.

Maristella has found a job in a small but promising advertising agency that seems to open up various possibilities for her. But failing to graduate seems impossible according to the family ethic. Therefore, at age twenty-eight, Maristella finds herself going back on her decision and promises that she will return to her studies, that she will graduate and leave her advertising job. The lie here was evidently the protective barrier that defended Maristella's autonomy in facing an avalanche of disappointment and her parents' narcissistic injury.

But this intermediate area—how could it be conceptualised? If what is described is the pathological function of a lie, in what sense does the lie render "O" tolerable on the journey to Column 2? How could a "fact" be transformed?

Let us take death, one of the most unpalatable and difficult facts to accept, digest, and metabolise in our minds. It has become the subject of many artistic works; for example, in literature, we find it as a central theme in *The Blue Angel* (Mann, 1905), *Faust* (Goethe, 1832), *The Divine Comedy* (Dante, 1321), and *Life Is a Dream* (Calderón de la Barca, 1635). That is, it has been rendered less terrifying and therefore has been made thinkable in many possible forms.

The same thing happens in sessions with whatever fact comes to be deconstructed, de-concretised, made narratable. It is the undreamt dreams that make us ill, as Ogden (2005) observed some time ago.

A lie about the "lie as such"— how could it be transformed?

Religions have been among the biggest lies—collective dreams that were invented. Lies, then, can be deconstructed, de-concretised, and narrated in a tragic dimension, from the Holy Inquisition to the Gestapo. Or a comic dimension, as in Molière's *The Hypochondriac* (1673), or still more so with Eduardo de Filippo's play such as *Filumena Marturano* (1951). More than anyone else, Pirandello made all this poetic in his play *Right You Are If You Think You Are* (1917).

Here we must stop and turn to art, literature, and film in order to see how some little lies and some big ones have been transformed. In our daily life, perhaps, after praying, "Give us this day our daily lie", we should make an attempt through art to transform it into play, narration, dream.

Reality and play

Manuela is a ten-year-old child in analysis. She is a hyper-compliant small girl in rivalry with her sister, aged twelve. The latter has recently been cured of a serious illness, at which time her parents granted her wish to have a German Shepherd puppy. Manuela's analyst is very upset at what he considers the unwise acquisition of the puppy given that his patient has a phobia of dogs. He regards it as an intrusion by the parents into the analysis with Manuela. The analyst decides to speak with the parents, reproving them for having disturbed Manuela's analysis, not having thought it over, and so on.

What Manuela's analyst is doing is abandoning a "fact" (the acquisition of the puppy) as a mere statement of fact. That is, within the therapy, the analyst adopts a state of mind that is receptive to an evolving "O", permitting a meaning to emerge "made from a concrete thing", if you will, from beta elements, K elements, and alpha elements, in narration.

In other words, and this may seem counterintuitive, the transformation in "O" paradoxically must lead through Column 2 (yes, that of lies) in order to be transformed into the subjective truth of that analysis. However, this apparent paradox is accounted for by keeping in mind that any transformation is always a *representation* of "O" and not the "thing itself", a phenomenon of which Grotstein (2009) continually reminds us.

Ultimately, according to this perspective, the puppy could be dreamed as a hooligan of whom Manuela is afraid, as something alive and new that arrives in the analysis and in the psychic lives of Manuela and her parents, who make that acquisition, from a certain point of view, as the dreamed description of the analyst's work, which has been capable of bringing something new and alive into the analysis. This look at the possible subjectivisation of "O" would have to be from the analyst's perspective, and his perspective would have to be continually trained to receive transformations in "O" and to, in turn, further these received transformations.

In the end, guiding a transformative narration involves passing through dreaming "some facts" so that they can become narremes (that is, narrative subunits; see Ferro (2005a,b)) in a completed narration. That implies having the courage to look at the dream not as a way of entering into contact with emotional and psychic truth, but as a lie capable of bending "O" to our need for meanings and narratives that organise emotions, affects, and events.

An alarming theft

After the analyst has missed a week of analysis for personal reasons, a patient dreams of having been the victim of a theft by his own son, in whom he has always had faith and from whom he would never have expected this behaviour.

If we wish to continue with this exercise, the "fact" is the cancellation of four sessions by the analyst, which when inserted in Column 2 gives rise to the dream: someone whom the patient trusts has betrayed his faith, stealing something from him. That is, the "fact" of the cancelled sessions becomes: "You, the analyst, stole something from me, and I would never have expected this—can I continue to trust you?" In other words, the dream becomes the instrument of the subjectivisation of "O", a lie that permits us to think, to feel, to make sense of things.

The lie of the pathological liar seems to construct worlds without any apparent motivation. The way in which it functions is that of negating even the Aristotelian logic by which opposing realities can be affirmed, in accord with the principle of non-contradiction. But could it also be that the pathological liar tells such gratuitous lies when he thinks he is facing a firing squad that makes it necessary for him—for reasons that only he knows—to put himself in a state of continual lying (to a primitive and sadistic superego)?

It could also be that the lying may be relatively more detailed, and that it pertains to those situations that in various people could entail attacks of jealousy, or envy, or something else, of such violence that the only salvation is to lie. That could happen in the extreme even without the other having anything to do with it, or only tangentially—let us say in the case of jealousy that could be projected, and sometimes also injected, into the other.

Those that appear to be "gratuitous lies", those without apparent motivation, could derive from a scenario constructed by the liar that is the product of his own internal scenario, which does the necessary casting and sometimes also the ongoing evacuation of that role into the other. (Unfortunately, understanding this does not mean curing it or tolerating it in whatever connection or relationship may exist; in every case, one would have to deal with a serious personality disturbance. As I said earlier, the creation of other worlds, and of those that do not provoke the feared jealousy and envy, has its own deep meaning in the management of a given psychic economy.)

What can appear perverse or sometimes ridiculous then returns to one of its human roots in the avoidance of pain and of intolerable emotions (had not the earlier Freud actually already spoken of this?). Have pity, too, for those who run into these types of personalities, in that often they come out of these encounters shattered by long-lasting contact with them. How can we not think of the unforgettable Athos and Milady in *The Three Musketeers* (Dumas, 1822)?

"A" (who is extremely jealous) tells "B" a lie because he imagines that "B", if he knew the truth, would have an intolerable, rage-filled crisis, which "A" wards off with the lie. Certainly, if this happened constantly and on a large scale, it would lead to the continual opening up of non-existent worlds and, over time, delusional ones. Often this modus operandi is a defence experienced in such a way and so successfully that it is not even perceived in its irrationality, in that it leads, at any rate, to its own disqualification (with the meaning used in soccer at the start of an offside position). How much is tolerated over time can only be revealed to us by the history, or rather, by that which will be recounted later. We think that there may be a limit to tolerable suffering.

Praise for the lie: an unpredictable paradox

The lie is a way of creating worlds that may be more easily habitable. It is common in science fiction stories, novels, and films that a spaceship coming from an uninhabitable world will try to reach Earth—or, vice versa, that spaceships from Earth, once it no longer has resources, will depart on a quest for new worlds (as in the great cartoon *WALL-E*) (Stanton, 2008). The lie is often that spaceship itself, or that new world with characteristics that make it habitable: that is, it is one of the many defences that we can mobilise in order to survive (even if not so very well, as we see in *WALL-E*: humans transferred to the spaceship are frighteningly overweight and have lost much of their autonomy and previous capacities; moreover, they are slaves to a robot that does not respect the first law of Asimov).

In fact, we have infinite examples—starting with Homer's *The Odyssey* (between 675 and 725 BC), who tells the Cyclops Polyphemus to call him "No Man" in order to save himself from the fury of the Cyclops. Polyphemus, blinded by Odysseus, asks for help from his brothers, and to their questions about who has blinded him, he answers, "No Man!"

Another famous example is Bishop Myriel in *Les Miserables* (Hugo, 1862), who saves Jean Valjean from prosecution by the authorities. Jean is by necessity a thief and steals all the bishop's possessions. The bishop then tells the gendarmes who have captured Jean that the stolen goods are nothing other than gifts that he has given to Jean.

Ultimately, Bion recognises the value of the lie both in the so-called metaphor of liars, and in his statement that the lie needs a thinker. That is—in some ways, and paradoxically so—the lie needs to be born of and maintained by a creative thought. We think of the parallel worlds that those who engage in extramarital relationships are forced to invent.

The lie, at least in some of its gradients, saves us from truths that are unbearable to think—for example, that there is nothing after this life, that we live in complete randomness, or that we no longer feel love for a person whom we have loved in the past, and toward whom we now feel only affection and so will have to leave.

The lie and the compromise open up infinite avenues of existence that are equipped with shock absorbers. All defence mechanisms, at their extremes, are nothing other than gradients of possible lies, where the truth—"O"—is not only unknowable but also often unbearable. The capacity to lie must therefore be considered one of the markers of having reached psychic maturity, and also a signal (not the only one) of terminability of the analysis.

Here we are obviously not talking about those who use the lie and lying as a lifestyle (Baranger, 1963), starting from the self, but to those who use lies in acute (and sometimes chronic) emergencies. One could add that the ability to tolerate this defence mechanism with elegance is a sign of psychic maturity, both in the patient and in the analyst, or in the analytic field (Lewkowicz & Flechner (2005)). In the end, every defence mechanism is a lie, but it is so as a reaction (a defence, precisely) to a truth that is otherwise intolerable. Sometimes the truth of an emotion is so intolerable to thinking that the latter cannot but turn to a lie in order to preserve good mental functioning.

Sara is Alberto's devoted girlfriend. She fears that a behaviour of hers could unleash jealousy that, in her judgment, would be unmanageable for Alberto. She is so afraid of his presumed and projected jealousy that she resorts to a lie in order to save herself from a feared violent impact with this tsunami-like swirl of jealousy. Thus, the lie saves her from the impact of a presumably unmanageable storm, and consequently she can tell Alberto in good faith that "I have never told you a lie to hurt you, but only because I was afraid."

In other words, the fear of overly intense emotions (which from time to time might be terror, jealousy, rage, envy, rivalry, revenge, etc.) leads to the renunciation of truth in favour of a truth that is tolerable to thinking with the use of various gradients of lying. Each of us, to a certain degree, is a liar, at least to ourselves. Thus, we can see how the lie may serve the pleasure principle by diminishing painful emotions but also functions in the service of the reality principle to allow contact with the truth.

It is not necessary to repeat that sometimes the lie can become a personality trait that causes a loss of contact with one's own emotions, thereby encouraging the construction of a compliant nature à la *Zelig* (in the film of the same name (Allen, 1983)). Or it may lead to those syndromes in which an individual becomes incapable of saying "no" for fear of unpleasant emotional reactions (or feared emotional explosions), which could bring in *the other* (even if most often this is a projection of one's own intolerance of frustrations).

Returning again to the positive side of the lie, one could add the following reflections:

- The lie is a diminished form of the evasion of rules that are felt to be too restrictive at a given moment in life—from playing hooky from school to the omission of a bad grade. As a small transgression, it can speak to us of the emergence of a need for autonomy and for a flight from symbiotic and undifferentiated elements. (On the child's first lie, which permits him to overcome the fantasy that his parents are omnipotent and capable of reading his thoughts.)

- The lie is also a "creation", an invention of worlds that is not dissimilar to the activity of writing. It is not by chance that Bion says the lie requires a thinker, while the truth does not. The thinker of a lie must create plots, connections; he must engage in a mythopoetic activity.
- We think through lies and their articulation. "O", the thing in itself, and the ultimate reality are in themselves unknowable; they require a journey along Column 2 of Bion's grid (also the column of lies and of the dream, Grotstein (2009) reminds us) in order to be thinkable.
- Bombardments of sensoriality require transformation into images (the first lie), in order to be organised in our minds as aggregates of pictograms. The sequences of the latter necessitate various forms of narration (the second lie), in order to be shared with others, according to various diverse literary genres that invariably have some side notes.

A sense of precariousness can be portrayed in pictograms by, first, the image of a tower that is shaking and whose plaster is peeling, and immediately afterward, an image of the disintegration of the same tower. This will then be narrated according to various narrative expedients that will use—as a stabilising ingredient/solvent—the narrative genre of "a childhood story", "an anecdote of everyday life", "a sexual dialect", or the story of a television show or film.

Only through these lies can we exchange some "emotional truths", where the truest exchange can take place only with the exchange of the preverbal through projective identifications (which at any rate will need lies—images—stories in order to be communicated and shared).

The time to grow

Stefano is a child who was adopted at the age of three and who, at the age of nine, is brought to consultation due to "violent and uncontainable behaviours". The parents arrive at the first consultation with perfect punctuality, well dressed, meticulously proper in their manner of speaking. Their surname does not go unobserved: they are "Mr and Mrs Canary".

They immediately speak of how Stefano has been "bullied" by bigger and more violent boys. They emphasise the lies that he tells continuously, the small thefts he is guilty of, and the excessive hunger that he has all the time. Although they make use of severe punishments, the only effective one seems to be hitting him, which they then regret.

At this point the analyst has the fantasy that, due to a quirk of fate, a little eaglet has entered the nest of Mr and Mrs Canary and is undermining the entire system. The inevitable lie arises from the fact that Stefano must act like a canary when he is in fact a young eagle. And the same thought fits with the ravenousness of a bird of prey.

Immediately afterward, a second fantasy is formed in the analyst's mind: it is as though some sheep have adopted a little one that has then revealed itself to be a puppy . . . of a wolf. There is continual lying about identities, needs, instincts, greed, theft, and hunger. Not only that, but the ways of the "eagle" are also transmitted to the parents, who—"eagle-like"—cover their child with blows. These fantasies are with the analyst as he listens in subsequent meetings.

In the very first sessions, Stefano is already talking about (incredibly) *Dances with Wolves*, sheepdogs, Dobermans, and Rottweilers. The videogames that he describes involve bloody fights in which throats are cut and enemies are murdered. Then there is an appearance by Fury, a horse from a television series. What is striking is the absence of limits, leading him to steal, to eat raw meat, and to bite other children.

After Stefano stole something small, his mother slapped him and he kicked her. Then . . ."I lost control . . . The anger, I don't know . . . I was afraid, then Dad beat me . . ."

A postscript seems necessary: the thorough and repeated reading of this article has caused me to again be in possession of my two ways of thinking and feeling (favouring *discontinuities* and favouring *continuities*). This has led me to once again conclude that the right balance lies in the continual oscillation among concepts, as occurs with the various mindsets between the autistic–contiguous, paranoid–schizoid position, and the depressive position.

Notes

1. Translator's note: Demetrio Pianelli is a character in Emilio de Marchi's 1890 novel of the same name. The novel contrasts Demetrio, an unattractive and uneducated man, with his brother Cesarino Pianelli, called "Lord Cosmetico" for his elegance and handsome appearance.

2. Translator's note: this 1979 Italian comedy was released internationally as *Hypochondriac*.

Editors' introduction to Chapter Seven

In his editorial note, Strachey's stresses that "The two principles paper" opens up a number of related topics left for investigation in the future (1911b, pp. 216–217). H. Levine suggests that one of these related topics might well be thought of as the "metapsychology of the representation of reality" (p. 152, this volume). An important part of his paper is focused on developing this concept.

Before developing this notion further, Levine helps the reader clarify, based on the work of Shur, some of the difficulties that one may encounter with the "Two principles" paper. One example of this is that Freud did not use the notion of the pleasure principle in a linear fashion. Freud also used this concept in two different and apparently contradictory ways: pleasure seeking *vs*. pain avoidance. One needs to make a distinction between,

> the trajectory of the unpleasure principle (avoidance of that which is unpleasurable) is towards withdrawal or decathexis, while that of the pleasure principle (seeking out that which is pleasurable) is towards approach and re-cathexis, although both share an ultimate goal of tension reduction within the psychic apparatus. (p. 156, this volume)

After this useful clarification, Levine's paper returns to the subject of the *metapsychology of the representation of reality*. He reminds us that Freud did not develop in depth the way in which an individual is able to acquire the reality principle. Winnicott and Bion developed this idea by taking into account the role of external objects, and a facilitating environment. Inspired by Bion's work, Levine suggests that the "Two principles" paper, is an essential background text for Bion's *Learning from Experience*. He invites us to learn about the silent dialogue between Bion and the "Two principles" paper. Starting with the notion of attention described by Freud as an "activity [that] meets the sense-impressions half way, instead of awaiting their appearance." Levine highlights how Bion pursues this notion and connects alpha function and reverie with the capacity for attention as associated to the reality principle. Linked to the notion of attention, Bion also developed further the notion of "notation", which was originally addressed by Freud. He stated that each individual develops a certain form of notation "that reflected the transformations of beta elements into alpha elements in the process of thought containment and creation and allowed for 'publication' of these transformed, now mental, contents" (p. 153, this volume). Levine illustrates well how Bion, different from Freud, was "interested in examining the vicissitudes of frustration tolerance as a central pre-condition for psychic development and the capacity for thought" instead of being interested in the regulatory principles.

In his theorising about the *metapsychology of the representation of reality* and still inspired by Bion, Levine stresses the importance of frustration tolerance in the development of thought and mind. In the process of representing reality, the role of the object is paramount. In the absence of the object, the individual not only experiences frustration, but also creates an opportunity where an internal representation of the absent object may be inscribed. It is the capacity to tolerate and withstand the frustration of a desire in the face of the absence of the object that initiates the process of thinking and therefore of representation of reality. Following this line of thought, the incapacity to tolerate frustration will lead to the destruction of the capacity to think. This ensues in an experience of hate for psychic reality that leads to projective identification, which leaves the individual more subject to frustration because, not having a representation of reality, the individual cannot act in a way that diminishes frustration. This compromises both the sense of reality and as a consequence, the capacity for psychic growth. Levine moves to elaborate on the notion of no-thing, negative hallucination. If reality is not represented in the mind, the psychic emotional space becomes infinite or incomprehensible, time is annihilated, and patients lose a coherent sense of self, reality, and/or narrative continuity.

In the last part of the paper, addressing the clinical implications of the "Two principles" paper, Levine discusses the way in which the author's theoretical elaborations can be linked to the clinical situation. The paper ends with clinical recommendations stemming from this way of conceptualising the difficulty that an individual has in bearing the pain of reality and being able to represent it. He elaborates on the importance of clarification, construction, and the creation of a myth in analytic technique. This helps strengthen the capacities for attention, notation, and frustration tolerance, which have the potential to transform the patient's functioning from avoidance of reality to tolerating and dealing with it.

7

Two principles and the possibility of emotional growth

Howard B. Levine

> "The man who is mentally healthy is able to gain strength and consolation and the material through which he can achieve mental development through his contact with reality, no matter whether that reality is painful or not."
>
> (Bion, 1992, p. 192)

In his introduction to Freud's "Formulations on the two principles of mental functioning", Strachey remarks that,

> The work gives the impression ... of a stock-taking ... as though Freud were bringing up for his own inspection, as it were, the fundamental hypotheses of an earlier period, and preparing them to serve as a basis for the major theoretical discussions which lay ahead in the immediate future—the paper on narcissism ... and the great series of metapsychological papers. (Freud, 1911b, p. 216)

The central concern of "Two principles" is a summary and review of the distinction and relationship between what Freud then saw as the two great regulating principles of the mind, the pleasure principle (sometimes called by Freud the pleasure–unpleasure principle) and the reality principle.[1] Having relied a great deal on the former in describing the formation and meaning of dreams and neurotic symptoms, Freud will increasingly turn his attention to implications of the latter in the continuing evolution of his theories.

Each of these principles was believed to be associated with a particular mode of thinking—primary process and secondary process, respectively—that was believed to be especially characteristic of a particular region of the mind—primary process: *Ucs*; secondary process: *Pcs/Cs*—and that allowed analysts to understand and explain the differences in psychic functioning that obtained in dreams *vs.* waking states, in neurotic *vs.* non-neurotic thinking, and in the unconscious *vs.* preconscious/conscious sectors of the psyche. It is important to note that psychosis was not yet clearly separated out as possessing a distinct form of psychic organisation, but was classified as a variant of neurosis (e.g., paranoid psychosis as a "neuro-psychosis of defence" (Freud, 1894a)). This development would await Freud's explorations of narcissism, the repetition compulsion, and the psychic representation of reality and reach a particularly rich crystallisation in the work of Wilfred Bion.

Translated into clinical terms, one of the central implications of the "Two principles" paper is the question of whether, or to what extent, one has the ability to tolerate frustration and take considerations of reality into account, forgoing discharge and deferring instant gratification in order to obtain a greater or more adaptive and reality syntonic pleasure at some future time. This matter of frustration tolerance and capacity to delay would prove to be of the utmost importance in the treatment of psychotic and borderline patients and in the evolving understanding of psychic development and the creation of mind.

Looked at from the perspective of subsequent theoretical advances along these and related lines in Freud's writings, Strachey notes that this work also introduces and opens up "a number of other related topics . . . the further development of which . . . is left over for later investigation" (Freud, 1911b, pp. 216–217). Most importantly, these topics include an attempt to formulate what might be termed the *metapsychology of the representation of reality* (e.g., perception, attention, notation, memory, reality testing, reality sense, etc.) or as Freud described it in the "Two principles":

... the task of investigating the development of the relation of neurotics and of mankind in general to reality, and in this way of bringing the psychological significance of the real external world into the structure of our theories. (p. 218)

The inclusion of "the psychological significance of the real external world" would have important implications for an understanding of the development of the psychic apparatus and its role and relation to adaptation and survival. The elaboration of these factors would, in turn, prove significant to Freud's (1923b) eventual proposal of his second topography (the structural theory).

Although cast in the language of tension reduction and not specifically clinical in intent, the "Two principles" paper inevitably calls attention to the interaction—and potential conflict—between impulse and adaptation, as it raises the question of frustration tolerance: whether gratification will be peremptory and immediate or considered and delayed; unthinking or mindful in regard to reality and the dictates of conscience; and the extent to which reality itself will be felt to be frustrating and restrictive or liberating and conducive to growth (Bion, 1970, p. 23).

This paper also introduces the concept of *notation*, something Freud mentions here and hardly comes back to again as such, but which will return in his subsequent theorising (e.g., Freud, 1915e) in the form of *words* (word presentations).[2] The latter are assigned a central role in containing, saturating and binding the affects and energies of the drives, and in so doing, allowing drive derivatives to become potentially available to consciousness. It is the combination of *word presentation* and *thing presentation* that implicitly underlies Freud's understanding of thought as trial action and will prove vital to his theory of representation. Notation also assumes prominence in the work of Bion (e.g., 1962c, 1970), who asserted the importance of each individual developing a specific form of notation, a "language of achievement", that reflected the transformations of beta elements into alpha elements in the process of thought containment and creation and allowed for "publication" of these transformed, now mental, contents in that language, in the service of group and object relations (what Bion called "social-ism") as opposed to "narcissism" (isolated, grandiose thinking).

From a contemporary perspective, we may also see in this paper the very preliminary groundwork being laid for a shift in orientation from a mostly *content* driven view of psychoanalysis towards a greater appreciation of process and psychic function. (This, of course, is a shift that would begin slowly and not reach its full flowering until our more recent era.) One indication of this shift may be noted in the difference of connotation contained in the titles of Freud's two works on dreams, between the foundational *Interpretation of Dreams* published in 1900–1901 (1900a) and "A metapsychological supplement to the theory of dreams", which appeared fifteen years later (1917d). "Interpretation" *vs.* "metapsychology" is the difference between decoding or discovering the hidden content or meaning of dreams *vs.* understanding the mechanism of dream work and its psychic function in the creation of mind. Of course, the latter perspective was not absent from the Dreambook—think of the very complex and sophisticated theoretical views put forward in Chapter Seven. Rather, it is a matter of emphasis, signaling what we might recognise in retrospect as already beginning a move beyond an emphasis upon the search for what is hidden but contained, towards the *interpsychic* and *intersubjective* processes aimed at strengthening, helping to develop, and even creating the psychic apparatus, especially in its functional role as psychic container.

It is the clinical implications of the "Two principles" as elaborated in the work of Bion that I wish to emphasise, noting that "Two principles" is a crucial background text for *Learning From Experience* (Bion, 1962c) and is the only paper of Freud's that Bion (1970) referred to in the bibliography of *Attention and Interpretation*. As early as August 5, 1959, Bion (1992), in his personal diary, connected alpha function and reverie with Freud's description of "a capacity for *attention* as associated with the development of the reality principle" (p. 73) and suggested that his own use of the term, attention, "may be a legitimate extension of an opening for investigation which Feud made but did not follow up" (p. 73). Thus, it may be argued that sections of *Attention and Interpretation* (Bion, 1970) were written in large part in a silent dialogue with the "Two principles" paper.

Before embarking on this exploration, however, I would like to enumerate some of the difficulties that contemporary readers may encounter in engaging with Freud's text and the concepts that it deals with. These were examined most carefully by Schur (1966) and may be useful for readers to bear in mind, as they try to engage with this and other texts in this volume.

Schur cautioned that Freud did not develop the concept of the *pleasure principle* in a consistent or linear way. Old formulations that in part had been replaced by newer ones sometimes returned in later works. Moreover, Freud often confounded two different tendencies in the concept, pleasure seeking (*pleasure principle*) and pain avoidance (*unpleasure principle*), and used both the compound term, *pleasure–unpleasure principle*, and the abbreviated term, *pleasure principle*, in different ways at different times (e.g., Freud, 1900a, 1911b, 1915e, 1920g, 1923b, 1924a,b, 1926d, 1940a[1938]).[3]

When Freud spoke about the pleasure–unpleasure principle within a metapsychological framework, he primarily resorted to economic formulations. However, within that same framework, he also used the terms, "pleasure" and "unpleasure" to indicate affects rather than regulatory principles of psychic functioning, blurring the distinction between principle and feeling, thereby causing potential confusion. These inconsistencies in Freud's writings are embedded in many of the discussions of the analysts who followed him, as they either failed to spell out precisely which version of Freud's formulations they are actually referring to or whether they are using the terms "pleasure" and "unpleasure" to refer to regulatory principles or affects (Schur, 1966, p. 126).

From a clinical perspective, Schur's (1966) study calls attention to the fact that the *unpleasure principle*, the wish to rid oneself of excitation and return to a state of quiescence,

> regulates the *necessity* to withdraw from excessive stimulation impinging upon the mental apparatus from the outside, "outside" implying both outside the organism [i.e., stimuli that originate in the external world] and outside the mental apparatus [i.e., stimuli, including the drives, that originate in the soma]. (p. 137)

Schur further noted: "Withdrawal is understood to include both the physical act of withdrawal and the withdrawal of special cathexes" (p. 137, footnote 10). Another way of stating the last point is that the unpleasure principle leads one to withdraw either from the actual situation of unpleasure, when whatever is causing that unpleasure is external to the self, or from the recognition (perception), or memory traces of that unpleasure when whatever is causing that unpleasure is external to the psyche, both types of withdrawal being in the service of reducing or eliminating accumulated tension in the psychic apparatus (Schur, 1966, p. 143).

In contrast, the *pleasure principle* regulates and determines the need to either recreate a situation of drive satisfaction, urgently and at any cost with little or no regard for the limitations of reality, or at least to recathect the memory trace of a past satisfaction of that drive (p. 141). The former often requires approach rather than avoidance of an (external) object or a memory. The goal in either case is the attempt to obtain gratification by producing a "perceptual identity" in fact or via hallucination with a previous experience of drive satisfaction. This movement implies or entails either an *actual or imagined approach response to an object in order to obtain gratification* or the recathexis of a memory of drive satisfaction, along with the attendant fantasy that the gratification has just happened or is taking place.

Thus, Schur argues that the trajectory of the unpleasure principle (avoidance of that which is unpleasurable) is towards withdrawal and decathexis, while that of the pleasure principle (seeking out that which is pleasurable) is towards approach and re-cathexis, although both share an ultimate goal of tension reduction within the psychic apparatus. Where the two come together is in Freud's assumption that the avoidance of a painful stimulus or memory, the successful approach to and interaction with a potentially gratifying object or the re-cathexis of the memory trace of a past gratification each work to reduce drive tension, albeit only temporarily in the case of the latter. Schur further cautions us to note that the aim is tension *reduction*, but not necessarily to a zero state of absolute quiescence or stasis, noting that "the term 'regulating principle' was understood by Freud, in accordance with Fechner's [usage of the] concept, to be a 'tendency' towards stability ([Freud] 1924[b] pp. 159–160), and not a mechanism which always resulted in the elimination of all tension" (p. 143).

Of further note in the "Two principles" article is that the reality principle is seen as a later acquisition, evolving from the more primal pleasure principle due to the infant's encounters with the limitations and dictates of external reality, including, of course, the actual satisfactions that are obtained. What Freud implies, but does not specifically say is that for this evolution to take place, it must do so in the context of a set of actual, external object, care-giving relationships that provide an appropriately facilitating environment. Freud never offered a more specific theory of how these developments take place. This was taken up by later analysts, such as Winnicott (1965), who emphasised dependence, "ego gratifications", and "good enough" maternal response and Bion (e.g., 1962c, 1970), who described the communicative aspect of projective identification, the role of alpha function, and the process of container–contained in affect tolerance, the development of the psyche, and the creation of "true thought" (Levine, 2010; see also Brown, 2009).

With this as background, I would now like to turn to some of the clinical implications of the "Two principles" as elaborated in the work of Bion.

The importance of frustration tolerance to the development of thought and mind is essential to Bion's theory of thinking, the basis of which was summarised by Grinberg and colleagues (1977): "all knowledge has its origins in primitive emotional experiences related to the absence of the object" (p. 99).

Absence, of course, implies the challenge of bearing and dealing with frustration and delay, both of which are inevitable parts of life's experience.

Bion's view is an elaboration of Freud's argument about the birth of thought, its role in adaptation and survival, and the development of the capacity for thinking. Freud characterised thought in the "Two principles" paper as "experimental kind of acting, accompanied by displacement of relatively small quantities of cathexis together with less expenditure (discharge) of them" (Freud, 1911b, p. 221). He hypothesised that *thinking began with and required the absence of the desired object* (the breast). Following the satiation of the first good feed, the hungry infant responds to the absence of the breast by re-cathecting a memory of that feed, thereby creating a hallucination (perceptual identity) that momentarily feels indistinguishable from the past actual experience. While this perceptual identity may temporarily satisfy the infant, the hunger pangs eventually break through causing pain, disturbance, crying, etc. If this reaction evokes the provision of the real external breast or bottle from the caretakers, then the hunger is truly sated and the infant has experienced and may learn something of the difference between a thought (memory, hallucination) and a perception (external reality), inside and outside. Successful feeding may also begin to allow for an increased ability to tolerate delay and frustration by helping to shape the concept of a hope that satisfying, responsive care-taking objects may exist, who can wish to help and will be competent to help mitigate the pain and frustration of existence. A satisfying feed also assists in the introduction of temporality by reinforcing the sequence "now!—not now—later?—OK, (ah), now."

This description serves as a model of how the psyche and the capacity for thought develop in the face of optimal frustration and adequate caretaking. Put in terms of Freud's theory of representations, the absence of the object not only produces a frustration marked by increased tension, it opens up a potential space in which an internal representation of the absent object (a contained and containable thought, in Bion's terms) can be created. This process is initially predicated upon once having had a good enough external object capable of insuring that the tension and frustration produced by the object's absence are held within reasonable limits and preventing the situation from assuming proportions that could go on to be called "traumatic". Later, this possibility, the ability to delay action if necessary, to wait and see what will develop, (i.e., Bion's (1970) "negative capability"), may be internalised and can gradually become an autonomous ego capacity. Thus, it is the capacity to tolerate and withstand the frustration and distress caused by the absence of the object in the face of the drive need (initially and often thereafter assisted by the presence of a facilitating object, who can lend the infant or patient the necessary alpha function) that initiates the process that eventuates in the capacity to think.

These processes, which are more or less implicit in Freud assume centre stage in the work of Bion (1962c, 1970), who was at least equally if not more interested in the unconscious as a function of the mind, as he was in viewing the unconscious as a repository for hidden mental contents, and so more interested in examining the vicissitudes of frustration tolerance as a central pre-condition for psychic development and the capacity for thought than he was in describing the regulatory principles themselves. Thus, Bion (1962c) writes:

> the choice that matters to the psychoanalyst is the one that lies between *procedures* designed to evade frustration and those designed to modify it. That is the critical decision. (p. 29, my italics)

In *Attention and Interpretation*, he discusses this at length, playing on the double meaning of the word, *suffer*, which means both "to experience" and "to feel pain":

> People exist who are so intolerant of pain or frustration (or in whom pain or frustration is so intolerable) that they feel the pain but will not suffer it and so cannot be said to discover it. *What* it is that they will not suffer or discover we have to conjecture from what we learn from patients who *do* allow themselves to suffer. The patient who will not suffer pain fails to "suffer" pleasure and this denies the patient the encouragement he might otherwise receive from accidental or intrinsic relief. (Bion, 1970, p. 9)

Adding Klein's description of projective identification to Freud's implicit theory of representations and his own theory of alpha function and container–contained, Bion argues that if the image of the absent, frustrating object can be maintained in the mind, it becomes a persecutory object that, punning on the presence of its absence, Bion calls a "no-thing". If frustration can be tolerated, the no-thing can become a thought. If the "no-thing" can be represented but frustration cannot be tolerated, it might form the basis for evacuation via projective identification; and if frustration intolerance is excessive and the representation of the "no-thing" cannot be formed, maintained, or is shattered, then the "no-thing" or its fragments can become "the foundation for a system of hallucinosis" (Bion, 1970, p. 17). In the latter two instances, the patient cannot create or maintain a thought, and so cannot attain the freedom and relief that Freud (1911b) describes and which Bion (1970), after Samuel Johnson, calls "the consolation which is drawn from truth" (p. 7).

What is at stake is whether or to what extent one can stand the frustration and pain that Bion believed was the unavoidable price for developing the capacity for thought and experiencing one's emotions, a price that had to be paid for being in the world, being sentient, and coming to know oneself and one's experience. This is especially problematic in the lives and treatment of psychotic patients or the psychotic portions of the mind, for whom and in which one can only:

> experience pain but not suffering. They may be suffering in the eyes of the analyst because the analyst can, and indeed must,

suffer. The patient may say he suffers but this is only because he does not know what suffering is and mistakes feeling pain for suffering it . . . Suffering pain involves respect for the fact of pain, . . . [one's] own or another's . . . Pain is sexualized; it is therefore inflicted or accepted but it is not suffered—except in the view of the analyst or other observer. (Bion, 1970, p. 19)

Bion (1970) continues:

The patient feels the pain of an absence of fulfillment of his desires. The absent fulfillment is experienced as a "no-thing". The emotion aroused by the "no-thing" is felt as indistinguishable from the "no-thing". The emotion is replaced by a "no-emotion". In practice this can mean no feeling at all, or an emotion, such as rage, . . . of which the fundamental function is denial of another emotion . . . The "place" where time was (or a feeling was, or a "no-thing" of any kind was) is then . . . annihilated. There is thus created *a domain of the non-existent.* (pp. 19–20, my italics)

In the "domain of the non-existent" thinking becomes impossible, as the capacity to think is destroyed.

The psychotic patient or the psychotic part of one's personality hates psychic reality and therefore opposes any move towards the establishment of thinking. He cannot tolerate frustration and this intolerance does not appear to get modified in the usual way so that he continues to attempt to deal with psychic tension by evacuating it, using the musculature. (Symington & Symington, 1996, p. 68)

The consequences of this hatred for mental life and emotional development are disastrous.

Frustration enforces the installation of the reality principle . . . But the psychotic with his hatred of reality evades the installation of the reality principle. His intolerance of frustration makes for intolerance of reality and contributes to his hatred of reality. This leads to projective identification as a method of evacuation. This in turn leads to dreams that are evacuations, not introjectory operations—hence "dreams" of the psychotic, which are really evacuations of such alpha as he has been unable to prevent . . .

Thus, in the psychotic we find no capacity for reverie, no alpha, or a very deficient alpha, and so none of the capacities . . . which depend on alpha, namely attention, passing of judgment, memory, and dream-pictures, or pictorial imagery that is capable of yielding associations.

But this in turn means that he destroys the capacity for thought which is essential to action in reality and which makes bearable frustration—an essential concomitant of the interval between a wish and its fulfillment. So the psychotic's attempt to evade frustration ends in producing a personality more than ever subject to frustration without the softening or moderating mechanism that would have been available through alpha and thought. In consequence he is more than ever intolerant of a frustration that is more than ever intolerable. And thus a self-perpetuating situation is created in which more and more frustration is produced by more and more effort devoted to its evasion by the destruction of the capacity for dreaming which, had he retained it might have enabled him to moderate frustration. (Bion, 1992, pp. 53–54)

That is, without frustration tolerance, there can be no sense of reality and without a sense of reality, there can be no psychic development,

because a sense of reality matters to the individual in the way that food, drink, air and excretion of waste products matter ... Failure to use the emotional experience produces a comparable disaster in the development of the personality. (Bion, 1962c, p. 42, my italics)

The process of evading and destroying a sense of reality leads to a downward spiral of mental constriction, retreat to omniscient phantasies, delusional thinking, and hatred of reality itself. But the challenge of having to face that which is potentially unpleasant and disturbing remains and is always present.

In addition,

The experience of reality can be very unpleasant because it always carries with it the recognition of one's ignorance ... So that anything that you learn immediately makes you aware of the enormous area of the unknown and the incapacity to learn it. (Bion, 2005, pp. 48–49)

Green (1998), in his paper on "primordial mind", offers a further observation about the domain of the non-existent. There, he argues that this domain is created by means of negative hallucinations aimed at representations of reality in a process he calls "effacement" (Freud's *Verwerfung*). In contrast to repression (*Verdrangung*), where the unacceptable, anxiety arousing mental content—thought, feeling, perception, or fantasy—remains intact, even as it is banished from conscious awareness at the behest of the superego, in effacement, "the processes of symbolization are impaired" (Green, 1998, p. 652) as *negative hallucination is directed against the perception of thought and representations* (p. 658), *including representations of reality* (p. 655).

In his 1924e paper on "The loss of reality in neurosis and psychosis", Freud described "representations of reality" as "ideas and judgments which have been previously derived from reality and by which reality was represented in the mind" (p. 185). In modern parlance, these representations are the grid or "Google maps" of our existence. They help us negotiate and move about the world. When they are absent, effaced by negative hallucinations in the minds of borderline and other non-neurotic patients, then psychic (emotional) space becomes infinite or incomprehensible, time is annihilated, and patients lose a coherent sense of self, reality, and/or narrative continuity. They may experience their lives as one might a book from which paragraphs and whole pages are torn away (Abensour, 2013).

To return to Green (1998) and the difference between repression and effacement:

> Repression keeps the representation as far as possible from consciousness. It [the representation] is conserved in the mind though out of reach, impossible to awaken to memory, but still there. In the case of negative hallucination, the thoughts, some capital thoughts, are lost, because they have been erased. There is no trace of their ever having existed or of their "underground" performance. (pp. 658–659)

What this means clinically and practically is that when effacement predominates *what is said by the patient or reported as felt in one moment cannot be expected to be retained and used in an emotional sense in the next*. Links between mental elements are easily lost or severed and the link between analyst and patient on which comprehensible analytic work can be constructed may be attacked. Representations of reality, especially emotional reality, cannot be maintained or securely relied upon to be present.

In states of splitting or repression, we cannot simply trust or rely upon our patients' ability to notice or recall their memories, thoughts, or feelings. Patients who are limited by these defences require our analytic help to do so. In contrast to repression, however, when effacement (negative hallucination) is active, the analyst often has little or no indication or "pointers" to symbolically indicate the outlines of what has been effaced, has gone missing, or has never been represented or formulated to begin with. What then is called for in the treatment is the *construction* by the analyst, patient, or pair of a plausible description of what the analyst believes is taking place in the mind of the patient or between the pair. This description lends further credence to Bion's (1970) assertion that the *psychoanalytic object*, which for Bion is the unique, proper subject of analysis, is not directly observable or ascertainable empirically via the data of the senses. Rather, its apprehension requires a kind of inspired intuition that can only arise in states of reverie unimpeded by memory, desire, or theoretical preconceptions.[4]

Elsewhere (Levine, 2011, 2012; Levine et al., 2013), I have attempted to begin to describe some of the technical implications of these formulations, suggesting that effacement authorises the importance of clarification, construction, and the creation of myth in analytic technique. Each of these involves on the analyst's part acts of "presentation" and "re-presentation" to, for, and with the patient, so that what has been effaced can better be attended to in order to help the patient keep facts, feeling states, and their plausible cause and effect relationships in mind. If successful, these acts may reinforce and help the patient maintain a more stable and coherent sense of self, thereby avoiding the terrors of annihilation anxiety, engulfment, and abandonment.

To these interventions, I would add the value of naming and helping the patient to create and preserve a space for free association in the analytic interchange. Unlike neurotic patients, who, with the help of the instruction to follow the basic rule, are better able to maintain a psychic space autonomously so that the repressed unconscious may be allowed to make itself known via the pressure it exerts on the patient's discourse and action, here, the goal is to help strengthen the capacities for attention, notation, and frustration tolerance through waiting, noticing, and naming feeling states.

In so doing, and if successful, one may help transform the patient's functioning from a pleasure orientation to a reality orientation, from evading frustration to experiencing, tolerating, and dealing with it, strengthening what Freud (1911b) called the "reality ego" at the expense of the "pleasure ego". But for Bion, the stakes and implications of this transformation are even greater than those emphasised by Freud. As Symington and Symington (1996) noted:

> Freud believed that the function of thought is for the reduction of tension, whereas Bion believed that it was for the *management of tension* ... The former's model posited a system whose function was the removal of pain and frustration whereas Bion posited a model where the individual was able to bear pain. Whereas Freud saw thought as a mode of achieving satisfaction for the organism, Bion saw thought in the service of truth. (pp. 7–8, my italics)

Thus,

> The difference between Freud and Bion lies in the motivation; Freud claimed that the reality principle enabled postponement of immediate gratification in order to achieve a greater measure of pleasure later on, whereas for Bion the motivation lies in the possibility of emotional growth. (p. 55)

Notes

1. He was later (Freud, 1920g) to add a third principle, the repetition compulsion, to the mix.
2. Freud first introduced the term, *word presentation*, in his writings on aphasia (1891) where he also refers to *object presentation*, a term he later (Freud, 1915e) replaced with *thing presentation*.
3. For a more thorough discussion of this point, see Schur (1996), especially Chapters Eleven to Fourteen.
4. For another language and description of this process formulated in a different theory, see Botella and Botella, 2013.

Editors' introduction to Chapter Eight

Mauger's paper highlights the socio-cultural reality at the time when Freud wrote the "Two principles" in Austria. He does this not only out of historical interest. Mauger wants to emphasise how, at that time in Austria, and elsewhere the pace of human life was increasing with rapid cultural changes and had been for several decades. Mauger's discussion begins with Freud's "Two principles" and later to *Beyond the Pleasure Principle* (Freud, 1920g). He invites the reader to consider the way in which the ideas presented in "Formulations" where later transformed and expressed differently in *Beyond the Pleasure Principle* where, in reflecting on the First World War, Freud would come to grips with the magnitude of human destructiveness. It is at this point that Freud realises what he had proposed in his previous work could no longer explain psychic functioning. Mauger explains: "He proposed to take into consideration a *beyond*, a compulsion to repeat at the heart of any drive pressure, a *beyond* without principles, or better, a new radicalism at the heart of the two principles already established: a death-compulsion" (p. 172, this volume). In this way, Freud's creative ideas were transformed as well. As a consequence, analytic listening based on the "Two principles" was also transformd; it now included a more destructive dimension of psychic functioning.

Mauger's first part of the paper focuses particularly on art; one of the four civilising attempts described by Freud to transcend the pleasure principle, the others being religion, science, and education. He highlights the crucial difference between art and the other attempts. Following Freud's idea that the artist can find his way back to reality and "mould his phantasies into truths of a new kind, which are valued by men as precious reflections of reality" (Freud, 1911b, p. 224), Mauger will develop the argument that artistic creation becomes part of the culture that both simultaneously expresses and contains a collective hostility to reality.

As a way of illustrating this argument, Mauger describes the evolution of dance that went from court dances to the Viennese waltz, which sought to maintain the illusion of harmony in the wake of political forces that led to the disintegration of the system, to Ravel's *La Valse*, which expressed the despair and destructivity of that age. Ravel's *La Valse* is a new "precious reflexion" that leaves the listener with the impression of an overwhelming intensity in the pace of life and a disintegration of the political world. Mauger's title "Time is short" attempts to capture this sense of overwhelming intensity with its urgent quality.

One of the most important contributions of Mauger's paper, is his weaving together of the core ideas of "Formulations", *Beyond the Pleasure Principle*, and *Civilization and Its Discontents* with a thought provoking reflection on the different ways in which psychoanalysis can take into consideration the concept of time. The author moves from a description of time that feels incomprehensible in spite of our attempts to control it, to the time that is the object of psychoanalysis, the reality of the unconscious, which is considered to be atemporal. He highlights the paradox implied in the time required by the analytic method in great contrast with the fast pace of political and social change in Freud's time.

By following the rule of abstinence and refusing satisfaction the analyst sets up the condition for the appearance of unbidden manifestations of another time. The analytic frame in this sense is the practical embodiment of the reality principle. His reflection on the question of time ends with a discussion of the time of "our" civilisation with its pressing qualities and its lack of consideration for the need to take time to wait for development, that is, to wait for things to come about. He claims there is a collective propensity for the "present" time, which seeks to reduce the experience of time to its simplest expression (we think about the virtual time of information technology). Following this argument, Mauger reminds us that in *Civilization and its Discontents* Freud was deeply concerned about men's need to gain control over the forces of nature. He cites Freud "Men have gained control over the forces of nature to such an extent that with their help they would have no difficulty in exterminating one another to the last man. They know this, and hence comes a large part of their current unrest, their unhappiness and their mood of anxiety" (Freud, 1930a, p.145).

Mauger finishes with a troubling question: "Might there be a connection between our difficulty elaborating any reflection on the possible disappearance of psychoanalytic practice and our collective refusal to take seriously the possible disappearance of the human species, as we spiral headlong into the accelerated whirlwind of climactic changes? Time is short . . . but we do not believe it . . . as in the time of the *Valse Folle*" (p. 180, this volume).

8

Time is short

Jacques Mauger

At the beginning of the twentieth century in Paris, the composer Maurice Ravel, in homage to Johann Strauss II, came up with the idea of writing a symphonic poem for a ballet, a sort of commemorative celebration of the Viennese waltz as practised in the nineteenth century. From its popular origins, the waltz had grown up in opposition not least to the court dances, which were very formal and danced in a line, such as the minuet at the time of Versailles. The waltz, on the other hand, would intertwine couples face to face—no trifling difference. At the end of the eighteenth century, the French Revolution had encouraged this practice, which had become widespread in the West. In Austria, the whirling form of the waltz paralleled socio-political gyrations from left to right: the decline of an aristocratic empire, the fleeting hopes of liberalism, and the rise of mass political parties. Popular music and classical music by turns took their part in this dance that sought to maintain the illusion of harmony in the tempo of the waltz. Johann Strauss junior was known as the "King of the Waltz" and Ravel wished, as early as 1906, to exalt him. Under the circumstances, the ambiguity of such an endeavour must have been one of the reasons why the project struggled to materialise.

Meanwhile, in Vienna, Freud was apparently somewhere else in his mind. Though searching, like Ravel, for a new way of listening to human reality, he made a point of denying any musical capacity of his own, perhaps unnerved by a "real" that was immaterial, yet inscribed in time. In 1910, he was preoccupied with another kind of intangible reality, in a text that would certainly perplex his colleagues: "Formulations on the two principles of mental functioning" (Freud, 1911b, p. 226). (By his own admission, this was a "short paper, which is preparatory rather than expository" (Freud, 1911b, p. 226) but he hoped that it would "not escape the notice of the benevolent reader how in these pages too the dominance of the reality principle is beginning" (p. 226). Freud's enigmatic choice of words should be noted for its apparent invitation, reminiscent of Ravel's musical vision, to conceive reality as a kind of infinite regress (*mise en abyme*).

Despite what he already knew of the political situation in Austria, of the centrifugal forces triggered by reforms bringing nothing in their wake but disintegration of the system, he took part, as did a number of his fellow citizens, in a kind of retreat from the socio-political domain, favouring instead a more psychological approach to the situation, both individual and collective. By his own admission, Freud remained "a liberal of the old school" (Freud, 1930, p. 21). He continued to hope that his modernist and rationalist vision of psychoanalysis would contribute to the *Enlightenment* of the masses. Published in 1911, "Formulations" took up this theme where he had left off in the *Interpretation of Dreams* (Freud, 1900a). In the latter half of the text, he reviews various civilising attempts to transcend the pleasure principle, starting with *religious* illusion, which he would further elaborate in 1927; then *science*, also viewed as a cultural creation that is rooted in instinctual sources and thus not exempt from the risk of illusion; and also *education* as "an incitement to the conquest of the pleasure principle" (Freud, 1900a, p. 224), a sort of reinforcement of the ego, whose libidinal source he also suspects. Freud is forced to conclude that "Actually the substitution of the reality principle for the pleasure principle implies no deposing of the pleasure principle, but only a safeguarding of it" (Freud, 1900a, p. 223). Naturally.

But then Freud comes to the question of *art*. In this realm of human endeavour, as he argues, things proceed in a quite different manner. The artist first "turns away from" restrictive reality, like the neurotic Freud mentions at the beginning of the paper. But in contrast to the ordinary neurotic, the artist "finds the way back to reality . . . by making use of special gifts to mould his phantasies into *truths* of a new kind, which are valued by men as precious reflections of reality" (Freud, 1900a, p. 224). Freud adds a crucial condition: "But he [the artist] can only achieve this because other men feel the same dissatisfaction as he does with the renunciation demanded by reality, and because that dissatisfaction, which results from the replacement of the pleasure principle by the reality principle, is itself a part of reality" (Freud, 1900a, p. 224). These sublimated *truths*[1] become part of the culture. They nevertheless express, while still containing, a collective hostility to reality, linked with the renunciation demanded by civilisation itself, no less than the duplicity of the human ego towards it.

In the meantime, Ravel was back in Paris, wounded during the First World War. Encouraged by his friend Diaghilev, the great dancer, he went back to work on his Straussian waltz project. But the first time Diaghilev heard the piece, though he recognised it as a great symphonic work, it was clearly not a ballet. This would be the end of their collaboration. The war had left its mark, shattering into pieces what the promised "apotheosis" (Orenstein, 2003, p. 32) had struggled to contain. Indeed, *La Valse* of 1919 had become, in the composer's own words, a "fantastic, fatal whirling" (Orenstein, 2003, p. 32).

Now more than ever, time was pressing. After an opening measure in which the music seems to emerge from a dense fog, before the first ghostly echoes of the three expected beats become audible, everything rushes inexorably towards disequilibrium and noise, reminiscent of a cataclysmic event. The anguished savagery of that enormous crescendo completes the deconstruction of a work that was to have been called—before the war—*Vienna*. But since then the city of Vienna itself had become for Ravel the enemy; the gentle muffled decadence of the era was suddenly giving way in his music to the discordant din of destructivity. It is not surprising that, through these "reflections of reality" (Freud, 1911b, p. 224), the score should convey so explicitly a sense of despair over lost time and the runaway destruction of the age. Even before the war, in the very same city, the composer Arnold Schoenberg and his acolytes were deconstructing tradition by featuring the "emancipation of dissonance", which would afford a new freedom to the forces in motion during the early years of that century (Rosen, 1975, p 22).

This "truth"(Freud, 1911b, p. 224) (or effective reality) created by the artist is a new kind of reality, "precious [cultural] reflections" (Freud, 1911b, p. 224) of reality for all. Ravel's *La Valse* is of this order: a *precious reflection* leaving an impression of unbridled eccentricity in the pace of life, of the disintegration of a political world—not to mention the overthrowing of the Viennese waltz and its "King". This was the *danse macabre* as "truth", or *presentation*, of the sexual death drive as "effective reality". Yet for all its faithfulness to the reality of the modern crisis of culture, it is no less a work of art—something to be sharply distinguished from reality. "To this strange coexistence, this reality within reality, this world which arises at the same time as man, at the heart of the real world . . . Freud gives the name civilization" (Imbeault, 2006, p. 103). As we saw with the reality principle, Freud understands culture as inseparable from its malaise—"both civilization and its discontents". Thus, for Freud, the artist manages to condense the compromise of the human condition itself, in the daunting face of the real. This coexistence of reality with an "effective reality", which is a psychological translation of the real world, might be described as the artist's *refusal of a refusal*: through the work of art, the pleasure ego (not only of the artist) unwittingly consents to recoup the painful reality it cannot bear, rendering in its own way what was imposed from without.

In Vienna, after the publication of the "Formulations", Freud would barely have time to write his 1913 introduction to narcissism before war broke out and Western civilisation would sink deeper than ever into murderous destructivity. For him too, the First World War would open his eyes to certain cruel realities. "It strips us of the later accretions of civilization, and lays bare the primal man in each of us" (Freud, 1915b, p. 299) he would comment in "Thoughts for the times on war and death" in 1915. Amid the deprivations entailed by the rationed lives of the Viennese, against the wretched backdrop of a decadent capital, Freud, like many of his contemporaries, experienced a sudden upsurge in speculative innovation. The following years would give rise to a creative maelstrom in which Freud himself would be virtually undone, dispossessed. The pressure of time was relentless. The twelve papers of his *Metapsychology* were drafted in such a white heat that in the end he would agree to publish only three of them and would destroy the other seven, though they were already completed.

In the immediate post-war period, Freud published *Beyond the Pleasure Principle* (Freud, 1920g). From now on, the "Formulations on the two principles . . ." of 1911 would no longer suffice to *explain* psychic functioning (the *geschehen*). He proposed to take into consideration a *beyond*, a compulsion to repeat at the heart of any drive pressure, a *beyond* without principles, or better, a new radicalism at the heart of the two principles already established: a death-compulsion—always needing to be inferred. As a result, "reality-testing" (Freud, 1911b, p. 222), that is, the test that confronted Freud-the-man with the realities of mass death, was no longer reducible to the formulations of 1911. The ego, suspected of serving several masters (as he would state in *The Ego and the Id*), was no longer deemed as reliable as previously thought, particularly with respect to its capacity to distinguish between what is represented and what is perceived. Traumatic reality demanded that account be taken both of the massiveness of what came from without and the complexity of internal cathexes.

Thus it was that the later metapsychology took form in a tumultuous period of history, as a feverish experiment in speculative thinking, a creative "sorcery" that would transform, like Ravel's *Valse*, how we listen to the world in time. Now recast in the inferential mode, psychoanalytic listening could no longer trust its connection to the reality of the primary process. Metapsychology became the condition for hearing its otherwise inaccessible movements. Neither art nor science—or perhaps a strange integration of the two—it offers a way of working *on* and *within* culture and civilisation, approaching reality without overlooking its own share of illusion.

Counter-time (*Contretemps*)

Scientific discoveries are inseparable from the culture of the age that produces them—how could this be otherwise? Psychoanalysis is no exception. Freud was a man of his time; his invention was determined by the culture of his time, which he continually called into question. How do we reappropriate his legacy, his time no longer being our own?

The reality of time interests the psychoanalyst in more than one respect. First of all, there is the time that resists us as unassimilable: the real. The representation of duration by which we measure time is not time itself. Nor can time in the strict sense be reduced to what unfolds within it. Our ordinary use of time convinces us that we can grasp its nature in phenomenological terms, in spite of news to the contrary from post-Newtonian physics. When we say, for example, that time is racing by, we are not describing time itself, but rather what we make of it as human beings, how we are stirred up when we feel that time is pressing. Even the clock provides us only a measure, a functional abstraction of time. Thus, time might be defined as that "something" that relentlessly imposes itself on us, we human beings who are always striving just as relentlessly to make "something else" out of it, according to our own timetable.

So, when we say that something is *outside of time*, what do we mean? When we say, for example, that the time of psychoanalysis is out of joint—that psychoanalysis may very well be an anachronism, out of tune with current events—what are we talking about? Are we referring to psychoanalysis as such, or is this more a question of defining the object of psychoanalysis, the reality of the unconscious, which Freud claimed to be atemporal?

Understood as a discovery, as the invention of a method for the investigation of the unconscious, psychoanalysis cannot claim to be *outside of time*. This is even more true of the individual psychoanalyst who practises the method while placing himself at a distance from the zeitgeist. The temporal distance of practice does not spare psychoanalysts from the temptation to identify themselves with their method, and then to amalgamate the method with the timelessness of its object. But the reality of the repressed unconscious cannot be said to be *outside of time* if by that we are referring to primary processes; and this is also true of the non-repressed unconscious, the reality of the repetition compulsion, since a repetition, even if it pretends to perpetuate a certain moment in time, arises by definition in a sequence: "if it is really a matter of process, a kind of *procession*, how could [this] happen without any relationship to time?" (É. Klein, 2005, p. 146).

It is another story, however, if we are referring to something that takes place outside our familiar concept and experience of time passing. Then we are talking about an *other* time which does not pass, a time that contradicts our conception of time, and our measurable experience of it.

Every analyst belongs to his time, like Freud himself. And though it did not follow automatically, Freud's method was also a product of its time in Vienna at the turn of the last century. We need to acknowledge that in any period of history, psychoanalytic practice is necessarily traversed by impersonal forces in conflict. These impose themselves from without, and press on the analytic frame, as rumours of the civilised world will do. Yet porous as psychoanalytic practice may be, it still needs, on its own terms, to hold fast the aim of discerning the organisation and nature of whatever forces are at play, however "external" they may be.

In Vienna too, at the end of the nineteenth century, time was already pressing. The industrial revolution was accelerating. Political and cultural ruptures pushed and shoved. The merry waltz in triple time no longer sufficed to sustain the harmony of an obsolete age, as it dragged reluctantly to a close. The waltz had become entirely carried away with itself.

Paradoxically, in order to probe this pressing reality of time, Freud invented a method that could only proceed on its own time. Though he refused to be swept up by the quickening pace of events, he did not disengage from the historical forces at play, whose conflictual nature he sought to understand, together with their repercussions on psychic reality, through different forms of psychic investment.

As early as 1890 he had related the course of "psychic (or soul) treatment" (Freud, 1890a, p. 283) to a state of mind that presupposes a time for waiting; an alternately trusting and anxious form of attentiveness—prefiguring the mutually supportive intertwining of the two principles of 1911. While for the first time in human history people had become fascinated with speed and acceleration, Freud suggested a methodical approach in which the tempo is slowed down, and time is spread out, as in free association—never mind the worry that psychoanalysis might seem to be a waste time.

This of course did not prevent Freud-the-man from having an ordinary conception of time as something that returns, evolves, and develops. He was personally sensitive to maturational time, to necessary time, be it cyclical or linear. He clearly knew the passing of time, its order and measurement, its acceleration; and the articulation of past, present, and future in narrative time and historical chronology.

It is against this backdrop of ordinary temporality that Freud experienced an *other* time, the immediate and unexpected irruption of a full-blown unconscious event. Thus, for both analyst and patient, there are two categories of time to contend with: the time for recounting the dream in session *vs.* the primary process time of actual dreaming; the length of the session *vs.* the atemporality of unconscious events; the development of the transference *vs.* the immediacy of the act (*agir*). On the one hand, respect for the measured time of the session, its frequency, and the continuity of the analysis; and on the other, unconscious events conceptualised as outside of time.

The analyst's and patient's measured representations of time form the precondition and framework for the psychic emergence of an *other* time, which only the psychoanalytic method renders accessible and recognisable by inference. This is an ageless infantile time, without principles, that presents itself unexpectedly, undoing the continuity of representational time.

The productive tension between these layers of analytic time find a parallel in the contrast between the rapidity of infant maturation and the slow evolution of the species. Freud postulated the existence, in the human psyche, of an indestructible archaic legacy, descended from the origins of hominisation, whereby the fate of each man is tied to the fate of humankind. This is the hypothesis of a prehistory of humanity, incarnated in the agencies of the psychic apparatus, while remaining present in the unconscious of each individual.

For Freud and Ferenczi, the emergence of the psyche and human civilisation found their true measure in the enormous span of the Earth's geological history. For them, the psychoanalytic method did well to emulate this model of slow evolution because it cautioned us against a practice overly centred on periods of crisis in our individual histories.

But now, as we face the acceleration of climate change—which reality is of specific interest to psychoanalysis? The answer remains: *psychic reality*, whether we conceptualise it as individual or collective—the "reality" that exists for us to the extent that it is revealed in the analytic session, in contrast to the reality of conscious perception. Psychoanalysis is concerned with a reality (real) that continually places the latter in doubt.

If we are referring to an actual time, a perpetual "unpast" (Scarfone, 2014), does it not follow that the actual would connote the real of time itself (Scarfone, 2014, p. 202), always there yet ungraspable? This would be the *thing* (Scarfone, 2014) at the heart of the analyst's work, a centre whose existence the analyst must forever re-postulate, since the analytic work itself involves a continual decentring. Indeed, everything accountable in terms of what we call the "real" would be subject to this complication. Freud acknowledged as much when he argued, at the end of his life, that ultimate reality "will always remain 'unknowable' " (Freud, 1940a[1938], p. 204). In this, he was reiterating the fundamental proposition of 1911: that our sense of reality is always a compromise: "Whatever the ego does in its efforts of defence . . . its success is never complete and unqualified. The outcome always lies in two contrary attitudes [leading to] psychical complications" (Freud, 1940a[1938], p. 204).

Whether it be our relationship to time, to the world, to nature, or to life, these complications were traditionally, until not so long ago, given over to the powers of God, from whom we expected protection in return. In its own way, as Freud indicated in 1911, this traditional religious culture expresses an attempt at reality testing: namely the recognition of humanity's powerlessness not only to grasp the real, but to protect itself from reality, and in counterpoint, the recognition that our sense of omnipotence needs to be relocated in a power greater than ourselves. If the time of our lives escaped our control, an eternal life beyond it was promised to us in return.

The real of nature could only be represented as hostile. It is external to the psyche, and psychoanalytic theory infers this from human anxiety, which Freud understood as our helplessness before the omnipotent forces of nature. It is from this anxiety that culture is created, in an attempt to invent a collective counterforce—religious, for example—which transcends the perceived threat of natural reality. The trauma of the real will always compel the development of culture to generate counterforces that allow us to break away from reality by giving priority back to the pleasure principle and the power of illusion.

"In time, time itself passes . . . and everything goes"[2] (Ferré, 1970)

One would think that Ferré's lyric has no bearing on us, since in our day and age we claim ownership of time. We measure it, we master it, we place it at our disposal, we profit from it like loan sharks. Yet time hurries us along. The time of "our" civilisation presses upon us. We convince ourselves all the same that even if we are short of time, this is because we want it that way: no time to wait for development, for maturation, for the time it takes for things to come about. Our ideal is waitless time, actual time, heedless of dilemma, blind to the tensions between the literal time we claim to master and the unknowable "real" of time, which is no less pressing, for it resists our best laid plans, our illusory strategies of control. If time is pressing in from all sides, we still hardly believe in a real that eludes our grasp. The whirling of the *Valse Folle* sweeps us up ever more frantically, presenting a true challenge for reality-testing as conceptualised by psychoanalysis. For psychoanalysis to be true to the times, to maintain the relevance of its ultimate responsibility to place our judgments of reality in question, should it not be constantly resituating itself within the complexity of these diverse times, which determine the need for its survival? To really do this would be quite different from the usual meaning of the expression "true to one's time"—the tendency to conformity and the carrying out of expected adjustments in our way of doing things. Nothing prevents the mounting idealisation of real time from snubbing its nose at the elusiveness of time as real.

The collective propensity to focus exclusively on present time is very characteristic of our century, seeking to reduce the experience of time to its simplest expression by adhering more and more to the virtual time of information technology. This brings about a distortion of our criteria for perceiving the reality of the world. It is in relation to this denial of the real that psychoanalysis—itself endangered if it subscribes to the strong propensity for acceleration—can reveal itself authentically as a product of its time.

A question

From this perspective, is it possible for the practising analyst to ignore the prevailing representation of temporality, as inscribed in our life and times? Can we avoid asking what kind of civilisation and culture would allow psychoanalysis to situate and justify itself? The point of asking such questions would not be to adapt to current therapeutic fashions, to risk distorting our method in an attempt to render it more productive or more palatable, but rather to recognise the hidden sources of our own resistance—like our patient's—to the demands of the psychoanalytic method itself. This would be a matter of acknowledging the conflictuality and the complexity of psychoanalytic time, including that of waiting in silent *attention*, even as the pressures of time encroach from every other angle, and events in real time come to stand for the ideal. Ultimately, we would have to face our own resistance to maintaining the conditions that allow the emergence, and the analysis, of a subject divided in time, given the challenge of an environment governed by a univocal representation of current time.

To propose the experience of a time for attention implies a willingness to engage the difficult task of refusing to satisfy not only the immediately conscious demand, but ultimately the distorting effect of the return of the repressed, namely the modalities of hallucinatory wish fulfilment. This practice of abstinence would be an extension of the real in its non-compliance to human desire. As guardian of the time-frame of the session, the analyst's implied refusal is precisely the condition for the appearance of *contretemps*, counter-time: unbidden manifestations of other times that challenge the accepted frame of reality. This practical embodiment of the reality principle lends to measured temporal reality the potential of refusing satisfaction to the hallucinatory immediacy of desire remobilised in the transference.

The analytic apparatus sets everyday life to the side: the span of both the individual session and the unfolding of the analysis entails a slowing down, which challenges the ideal of real time, since the temporal rhythm imposed by analysis is difficult to pin down. It is interesting, in this connection, to note that since the beginning of analytic practice, the length of the session has gradually decreased, going from one hour at the time of Freud to forty-five minutes nowadays—not counting the variable or short Lacanian session—while on the other hand, the average length of analytic treatment has increased steadily: analysis terminable and interminable! So the time-keeping of psychoanalysis appears to be no less under the sway of complex influences, unbeknownst to us. Indeed, we seldom raise this issue among ourselves or try to investigate the consequences of the state we are in.

The temporal framework of our sessions is thus not as well established as we would like to believe. No doubt our ambivalence about maintaining the analytic method has played a role in this. The situation also seems to have been determined by a network of forces infiltrating the discourse of each protagonist in the analytic relationship, also affecting the way they listen to each other. Yet we prefer to react rather than to reflect upon these influences from the outside—these movements in the zeitgeist.

From the Freud of "Formulations" through the post-war generation to ourselves a century later, the relation to time, the manner of interrelating past, present, and future, has changed. This is not just a question of the past no longer passing behind us, but of a future that has been fast-forwarded, folded back into the present. This would be an "actual" future, belonging to the literality of real time with no psychic dimensions, without any deferred action, afterwardness, or *après-coup*.

What then can we make of this impasse in which the future appears without distance, in which humanity, enslaved to the ideology of infinite growth, seems diminished by so much impersonality and quantification? How then to capture the living present in a time of relentless presence? How to explore the conditions for emergence, the "breach in time" (Arendt, 1954) if the regime of modernity, now become post-modern, destroys the horizon of expectation, valuing instead an immediate future and accelerated progress towards endless growth?

Freud was a man of his time not only because he was sensitive to the universal destructiveness and cruelty of the First World War, but above all for modifying his theory of intrapsychic agencies and drives as a result. Freud's understanding of the conflicting forces at play in culture and civilisation, of the work of culture, and of the ongoing struggle within civilisation, clearly expresses his preoccupation with the destiny of the human condition. It has often been remarked how, in the eyes of the post-Freudians, his cultural texts were never afforded the same clinical value as other writings, as if, in terms of relevance for psychoanalytic practice proper, they were but discretionary considerations compared to the rest of his work. This reflects the non-Freudian assumption that psychoanalysis can be practised in isolation from the realities of a world in conflict. The idea of "reality-testing" (Freud, 1911b, p. 222), put to us for the first time in his 1911 "Formulations", has evolved. It has gradually worked its way in as a necessity, at the intersection between forces at play in the cultural environment and the internal modalities of psychic investment. Without reality testing, we cannot grasp the complexity of the compromises that constitute human reality, which is always subject to the challenge of the real, yet rebellious toward it.

> Let us recall the old saying: *Si vis pacem, para bellum*. If you want peace, prepare for war. It would be in keeping with the times to modify it thus: *Si vis vitam, para mortem*. If you want to live, prepare for death. (Freud, 1915b, p. 300)

Has psychoanalysis had its day? Freud himself had no hesitation thinking, against his own wish, that its time might soon be up. We are quick to remember our survival, defying a death foretold many times since Freud. Might there be a connection between our difficulty elaborating any reflection on the possible disappearance of psychoanalytic practice and our collective refusal to take seriously the possible disappearance of the human species, as we spiral headlong into the accelerated whirlwind of climactic changes? Time is short . . . but we do not believe it . . . as in the time of the *Valse Folle*.

The deadly pulse of history

In 1931, twenty years after his "Formulations", Freud would write in the closing lines of *Civilization and its Discontents*:

> The fateful question for the human species seems to me to be whether and to what extent their cultural development will succeed in mastering the disturbance of their communal life by the human instinct of aggression and self-destruction. It may be that in this respect precisely the present time deserves a special interest. Men have gained control over the forces of nature to such an extent that with their help they would have no difficulty in exterminating one another to the last man. They know this, and hence comes a large part of their current unrest, their unhappiness and their mood of anxiety. (Freud, 1930a, p. 145)

"Control over the forces of nature" and, similarly, control over time—a time dematerialised, digitised, the time of information technology, the pretentious possession of real time. Actuality is immediate and holds up the image as proof of reality without any testing, any waiting, any beyond. Illusion has reached its culmination, without memory, interchangeable, day after day. The images shield us from paying any attention to the unconscious roots of our historical tragedies; even the most recent ones: Shoah, Hiroshima–Nagasaki . . ..

And so, in this world where time is pressuring us from all sides, while the echo of the nostalgic tick–tock of our grandfather clock still lingers, our relation to time is no longer that of the analogic clock. Our little waltz in double time—reality, pleasure; psychoanalysis terminable, psychoanalysis interminable—now takes place in digital time, in the immediacy of the electronic present. In exchange for lost time, have we found a new one: a real time, with no gap—nothing but repetition of the same?

In quite a different counterpoint, would this not suggest the paradoxical relevance of *Beyond the Pleasure Principle*, as a lucid reality-testing, without pathos, of our own becoming? (Freud, 1930a, p. 145).

Acknowledgement

The following people contributed to the translation of this paper: Sylvie de Lorimier, Charles Levin, and Caroline Williamson.

Notes

1. "Truths" does not quite render what Freud describes in the original German as "*Wirklichkeit*", translated into the French as "*réalité effective*" or "effective reality"; namely the reality of an actual event or occurrence the impression of which is suddenly made in the course of psychic functioning.

2. Léo Ferré, *Avec le temps*, Paris, 1970. The opening words of the song in the original French are: *Avec le temps, avec le temps va . . . tout s'en va*.

Editors' introduction to Chapter Nine

Some psychoanalytic thinkers such as object-relation theorists, interpersonalists, and relational psychoanalyst have questioned some of the fundamental assumptions in the "Two principles" paper. Dr Tubert-Oklander's paper focuses on these criticisms. His discussion is condensed into two questions: the first is what do we mean by "reality"? The second is who is to decide what is and what is not real?

Dr Tubert-Oklander traces the origins of these questions to the time at which Freud abandoned the seduction theory and, even though he continued to affirm that there was clinical evidence that events were also a cause for neurosis (e.g., the Wolf man), he gave priority to the concept of psychic reality. Dr Tubert-Oklander believes that ever since there has been a tendency to reject as not worthy of analytic exploration real external events. This was in fact the source of rupture between Freud and Ferenczi.

It is the impersonal quasi-physical aspect of Freud's instinctual drive theory that has become the target of much criticism by the various relational and culturalist theories, which have discarded the causal theory of drives and emphasised instead the concrete experiences of relating to other human beings and participating in social systems.

While Dr Tubert-Oklander recognises the paramount importance of personal aspects of human experience, which help us to understand an essential part of human experience, thinking, feeling, and behaviour, he also acknowledges the importance of drive theory. He states: "we still have to account for the impersonal side of our existence discovered by Freud" (p. 192, this volume). So in this manner Dr Tubert-Oklander attempts at integrating the object relational, interpersonal, and self-psychological theories with the impersonal dimension of sexual and aggressive drives described by Freud. Dr Tubert-Oklander underlines that it is a fact that both metapsychology and psychoanalytical practice have had, from the very beginning, a place for extra-psychic reality, which has to be acknowledged and taken into account by mental processes, which necessarily have to adapt to it, as Freud clearly demonstrates in his "Two principles" paper.

Dr Tubert-Oklander suggests that there is yet another impersonal current that drives humans, which emanates from the pressure of the community we belong to, which also extends in time (as in transgenerational transmission and the history of families and peoples) and space (as in the case of the impact of institutions, culture, and politics) far beyond the apparent limits of personal existence. He argues that these social processes have an inscription in the unconscious and that they need to be included in the analytic endeavour. In other words, the analyst should explore all the dimensions of reality and contrast it to wishful thinking as Freud stated in his "Two principles" paper.

Dr Tubert-Oklander believes that the term "reality", which is usually identified with our sense perception of the material world, has been taken for granted. He puts forward a definition of "real" as being,

> whatever exists independently from our will, wishes, or thought, and that resists our attempts to modify it, thus requiring work and effort in order to introduce any changes in it, and sometimes proves to be impossible to change, in spite of our efforts . . . But also other human beings, groups, institutions, and society. So are emotions. (p. 191, this volume)

So for Tubert-Oklander, social currents and their impact are mainly unconscious.

Dr Tubert-Oklander also discusses the links between what is real and the truth. He proposes different kinds of truths: semantic, syntactical, or logical; pragmatic; consensual or social; expressive and narrative. They are all characterised by their power of conviction. Dr Tubert-Oklander emphasises that the analyst is neither in a position to define what is real nor can he consider himself the bearer of the truth.

> This requires a shared inquiry, discussion, and negotiation between patient and analyst, in order to reach the partial and temporary agreements that lead to a moderate conviction about the findings of an analysis. (p. 195, this volume)

Therefore, the analytic exchange and experience creates a new form of consensual truth that is convincing for both the analyst and patient.

9

The quest for the real

Juan Tubert-Oklander

Two principles of minding[1]

In his seminal paper called "Formulations on the two principles of mental functioning", Freud (1911b) gave shape to some of the basic concepts of his theory of mind, which he had been ruminating on ever since his unpublished *Project for a Scientific Psychology* (1950a [1895]). Ernest Jones (1953, p. 349) tells us that when, on October 26, 1910, he gave a preliminary presentation of the theme before the Vienna Society, the audience found it too difficult to understand and was so unresponsive that even he felt displeased with the ideas he had presented. We can now see that the problem was that they were too abstract and condensed, so that they became practically unintelligible for a group of disciples who knew nothing about their early development in the *Project*, and could not yet grasp their relation with the equally abstract concepts he had put forward in Chapter Seven of *The Interpretation of Dreams* (1900a).

Freud began writing this essay in December and the paper was finished by the end of January 1911. Ever since its publication in the *Jahrbuch*, late that spring, this brief piece has become one of the basic texts on the fundamentals of Freudian theory. It is so clear in its formulation that it has been a keen stimulus, both for those thinkers who adhere to the basic tenets of Freudian thought and for those who criticise and revise them.

The basic concepts of the theory that he put forward are the *pleasure principle* and the *reality principle*, which are, of course, related to those of the *primary process* and the *secondary process* that had been introduced in his dream book. They are related to his theoretical strategy of comparing the organisation of the mind, "the instrument which carries out our mental functions . . . [with] a compound microscope or a photographic apparatus, or something of the kind" (1900a, p. 536). This implies viewing mind as a functional entity, a structure akin to that of the nervous system, intended to process the excitation induced by stimuli stemming from the body and the sense organs, and conduce it to its final discharge through action. Such a process must somehow be regulated, and this is where the two principles intervene.

The pleasure principle is supposed to be the primary mode of mental functioning. In such a situation, motor discharge of excess stimuli occurs without any previous deliberation and is not corrected by its consequences, fantasied mental images are not distinguished from perceptions, since the mind only represents what is pleasurable, and this precludes any learning from experience, which requires knowledge of the real.[2] The obvious insufficiency of this kind of minding sooner or later brings about the instauration of the reality principle, so that now "what was presented in the mind was no longer what was agreeable but what was real, even if it happened to be disagreeable" (1911b, p. 219).

This very simple and thought-provoking schema of the early development of mind has been taken as an essential element of a Freudian credo by some—usually referred to as "orthodox Freudians"—and firmly criticised by others—such as object-relations theorists, interpersonalists, and relational psychoanalysts—who take exception at some of its underlying assumptions. Such criticism has been basically aimed at two questions: what do we mean by "reality"?; and who is to decide what is and what is not real?[3] I shall discuss them accordingly.

Fantasy or fact?

Psychoanalysis has been, from its very beginning, a dialectic of fantasy and reality. This came about as a consequence of the radical theoretical turn taken by Freud in 1897, when he discarded his so-called "seduction theory". This was a rather unfortunate term, since it referred to an aetiological theory of neuroses that explained them as resulting from the traumatic effect of the sexual abuse of children by their parents, relatives, or carers. Hence, the use of the word "seduction" was surely a euphemism, intended to bowdlerise the subversive impact of a theory that denounced that those people who were in charge of the welfare of others could, and often did, abuse their authority and damage their charges. For, if parents and relatives could not be fully trusted, this would surely also apply to nurses, teachers, doctors, priests, policemen, and government officers, thus undermining the very basis of authority in society. No wonder that such ideas generated widespread animosity and outrage among the young doctor's colleagues!

Besides, Freud himself had quite a few doubts and misgivings about his theory. If it were true that neurotic disturbances were caused by the perverse acts of parents and other trusted adults, vis-à-vis their children, how was he to account for the presence of neurotic symptoms in his sisters and himself? The only logical explanation was that his own father had been guilty of such transgressions. In his letter of September 21, 1897 to Fliess, he voiced his surprise at finding out that "in all cases, the *father*, not excluding my own, had to be accused of being perverse" (Masson, 1985, p. 264).

This, together with the unsettling discoveries from his self-analysis and the violently hostile reactions of the medical community towards his ideas must have induced in him a distress that compounded his doubts. These were generated by the confluence of what he felt to be an essential unlikelihood of finding such a widespread prevalence of perversion in parents, particularly in fathers, inconsistencies in his patients' narratives of their childhood traumas, and the discovery of his own incestuous and parricidal wishes in his self-analysis (Jones, 1953, p. 358). All this led him to his final abandonment of his traumatic theory of neuroses.

Strangely enough, although this implied the demise of the theory from which he had hoped to attain fame and recognition, his feelings at the time were not of hopelessness or depression, but of liberation and elation. As he wrote in the same letter of September 21, 1897, "I have more the feeling of a victory than a defeat", and also,

> If I were depressed, confused, exhausted, such doubts would surely have to be interpreted as signs of weakness. Since I am in an opposite state, I must recognize them as the result of honest and vigorous intellectual work and must be proud that after going so deep I am still capable of such criticism. Can it be that this doubt merely represents an episode in the advance toward further insight? (Masson, 1985, p. 265)

This was surely a most unsettling situation for any researcher, since his whole aetiological theory had collapsed under his newfound certainty that the traumatic events he had so laboriously unearthed had not happened at all. But he emerged from this predicament through the formulation of a brilliant and audacious hypothesis: that it was not necessary for these childhood events to have happened *in reality* for them to have a traumatic effect, but that it sufficed that the subject believed in them, that is, that they existed *in fantasy*. This was the origin of the concept of *psychic reality*.

From that moment on, the dialectic between fantasy and reality, or between *psychic reality* ("internal") and *material reality* ("external") came to the fore in psychoanalytical theorising and practice. There also emerged a generalised prejudice that rejected as worthless and "non-analytic" any interpretation framed in terms of real external events, whether interpersonal or social. Indeed, the main conflicts and splits in the psychoanalytic movement have been related to the discussion of the impact of "external reality", as opposed to the exclusive emphasis on "internal" processes that defines what is usually called "orthodox psychoanalysis" (Tubert-Oklander, 2006).

It must be said, however, that Freud's stance on the matter was rather ambivalent. On the one hand, he firmly maintained that psychoanalysis dealt exclusively with psychic reality, and rejected any attempt to explain mental dynamics and psychopathology in environmental terms. This clear-cut position, which was enthusiastically shared by the initial group of analysts that followed him, was the essential disagreement that determined his rupture with Ferenczi.

But, on the other hand, he uneasily sought a material basis for early experiences in actual occurrences that could be validated by evidence, as in the case of his efforts to prove that the Wolf Man (Freud, 1918b) had *actually* witnessed parental intercourse at the age of one and a half years. This led him to publish a brief note in the *Zentralblatt für Psychoanalyse*, in early autumn of 1912, in which he wrote,

> I should be glad if those of my colleagues who are practising analysts would collect and analyse carefully any of their patients' dreams whose interpretation justifies the conclusion that the dreamers had been witnesses of sexual intercourse in their early years. (Freud, quoted by Strachey, 1955, p. 4)

Even though he appeared to recant his original seduction theory that proposed an environmental causation of neuroses, and affirmed that this had been based on unquestionable clinical evidence, he still recorded a number of clinical observations that attributed the child's responses to actual parental behaviour. One such instance appeared in the *Three Essays on the Theory of Sexuality* (1905d), where he wrote,

> If there are quarrels between the parents or if their marriage is unhappy, the ground will be prepared in their children for the severest predisposition *to* a disturbance of sexual development or to a neurotic illness. (p. 228)

A more forceful exposition of this idea is to be found in the *Introductory Lectures on Psychoanalysis* (1916–1917), which says as follows:

> Incidentally, *children often react in their Oedipus attitude to a stimulus coming from their parents*, who are frequently led in their preferences by difference of sex, so that the father will choose his daughter and the mother her son as a favourite, or, in case of a cooling-off in the marriage, as a substitute for a love-object that has lost its value. (p. 207, my italics)

Later in the book, in a more extensive discussion of the Oedipus complex, he repeats his observation, but now with a caveat:

> We must not omit to add that *the parents themselves often exercise a determining influence on the awakening of a child's Oedipus attitude* by themselves obeying the pull of sexual attraction, and that where there are several children the father will give the plainest evidence of his greater affection for his little daughter and the mother for her son.[4]

But then he adds:

> *But the spontaneous nature of the Oedipus complex in children cannot be seriously shaken even by this factor.* (p. 333, my italics)

Obviously, no one can accuse Freud of ignoring the vital importance of the parents' contribution to the child's emotional problems, but he clearly felt that he should qualify his clinical observations on this matter, in order to avoid any temptation to abandon or dilute the tenets of the theories of instinctual drives and the universality of the Oedipus complex. But it is a fact that both metapsychology and psychoanalytical practice have had, from the very beginning, a place for extra-psychic reality, which has to be acknowledged and taken into account by mental processes, which necessarily have to adapt to it, as he clearly demonstrates in "Two principles of mental functioning", which he considered to be only a "few remarks on the psychical consequences of adaptation to the reality principle" (1911b, p. 226).

But all this requires a further probing into the concept of "reality", which Freud takes for granted and leaves undefined—obviously under the assumption that we all know what reality is.

What is real, anyway?

The point of departure of psychoanalytic inquiry was the ordinary and socially shared conception of things, from which psychoanalysis was bound to depart. Consequently, consciousness was taken for granted as a given, intuitively known, since the unconscious was the real mystery to be untangled, the dark continent to be explored.

Similarly, the concept of reality, usually identified with our sense perception of the material world, was taken for granted, since the focus of interest lay in the radically new concept of *psychic reality*, which derived from Freud's discovery that unconscious fantasies could be the determining factor of neurotic symptoms. Nonetheless, just as we know today that consciousness is a much more complex phenomenon than what we used to believe and deserves deep and ample research (Ornstein, 1972), we should also inquire into the nature of reality itself, starting by questioning what we actually mean when using the term "real".

"Real" is whatever exists independently from our will, wishes, or thought, and that resists our attempts to modify it, thus requiring work and effort in order to introduce any changes in it, and sometimes proves to be impossible to change, in spite of our efforts.[5] In this sense, the material world is real: a brick wall is real because we cannot go through it as we may wish, but need instead to break through it with a pick or somehow wander about in order to find an opening. But not only material objects are real, but also other human beings, groups, institutions, and society. So are emotions, which in ordinary thought are usually considered "unreal". However, they have an existence of their own, we cannot create or destroy them,[6] and we can only control or modify them by means of an effort, which necessarily includes striving to name and understand them. All this is what makes them real.

Other instances of the real, which are not usually thought of as such, are symbolic systems, such as languages, laws, and theories. It is a fact that these exist in their own dimension—what Karl Richard Popper (1972) called the "third world", as opposed to the first world of material events and the second world of subjective experiences. They determine us and understanding and apprehending them is hard work, as anyone who has ever tried to study law, learn a language, or comprehend a mathematical theorem well knows.

Fantasy, on the other hand is usually considered something false and unreal. But it was precisely Freud who discovered the enormous power held by unconscious fantasy over the life, thought, behaviour, and relations of human beings. Later, Melanie Klein showed us how fantasy draws its strength from deep emotional strivings (Klein et al., 1952).

Unconscious fantasy is, therefore, fully real, since it exists independently from our will, imposes on and resists us, and we can only understand, control, channel, or modify it, albeit only partially, by means of an expenditure of work. This reality of fantasy stems from various sources. First, it is based on and expresses emotions, which, as we have seen, are always real. Then, there is the fact that fantasy constitutes a complex symbolic system, with its own organisation, which is as determinant and resistant to change as the grammar of a language, the logic of a legal code, a tradition, or a dressing code. In this, Jacques Lacan's (1966) work, based on the structuralism of Claude Lévy-Strauss, represents a major contribution.

There is yet another driving force of fantasy, which is the relational and social experiences and processes, and here we are bound to face some major problems, since this has always generated controversy in the history of psychoanalysis. Freud's concept of "instinctual drives" (*Triebe*) derived from his perception that the symptoms he was inquiring were being driven by an impersonal current that stemmed from the demands of bodily life and entered into a sharp conflict with the patients' persona, which he called "the I" (*das Ich*, usually translated as "the ego"). It was indeed tempting, if we consider his positivistic and physicalist upbringing, to compare it with the concept of "energy" in the Newtonian model of the universe, and to conceive it as the material cause of symptoms (and later of all human experience and behaviour). It is this quasi-physical aspect of Freudian theory that has become the target of much criticism by the various relational and culturalist theories, which discarded the causal theory of drives and emphasised instead the concrete experiences of relating to other human beings and participating in social systems.

Nonetheless, as I have noted in a previous paper (Tubert-Oklander, 2015), this seems to be a case of throwing away the baby together with the dirty bathwater. There is no doubt that the personal aspects of human existence play an essential part in the dynamics of our experience, thinking, feeling, and behaviour, as pointed out by object-relational, interpersonal, and self-psychological theories, but we still have to account for the impersonal side of our existence discovered by Freud. Although a major part of our wishes are highly personal, as acknowledged by psychoanalytical theory since "Mourning and melancholia" (Freud, 1917e), there is certainly an impersonal dimension of sexual and aggressive wishes, which Freud (1915c) strived to explain by means of his hypothesis that the object "is what is most variable about an instinct and is not originally connected with it, but becomes assigned to it only in consequence of being peculiarly fitted to make satisfaction possible" (p. 122).

Human beings are certainly also driven by mighty impersonal currents that clearly transcend the limits of their personal identities. An essential part of these currents stem from bodily existence and its unrelenting demands, but there is still another impersonal current that drives and orients us, and this is the pressure of the community we belong to, which also extends in time (as in transgenerational transmission and the history of families and peoples) and space (as in the case of the impact of institutions, culture, and politics) far beyond the apparent limits of personal existence (Tubert-Oklander, 2013, 2014). Such issues were addressed by Freud in *Totem and Taboo* (1912–1913) and *Moses and Monotheism* (1939a).

Such social processes surround, go through, and determine us, exist independently of our thought and will, and can only be changed partially by means of a collective effort and long-time work. This makes them real enough. Consequently, it should be expected that they have an inscription in the unconscious, no less than the bodily processes traditionally acknowledged by psychoanalytical theory. Unconscious fantasy should then be considered to reflect *the whole of reality*—material, mental, and symbolic—albeit in terms of the language of unconscious mentation—the primary process—which is in sharp contrast with that of verbal consciousness and communication, the secondary process. Hence, our daily work of making conscious the unconscious should include a painstaking exploration of all the various dimensions of reality, and contrast it with wishful thinking, as Freud's seminal paper indicates. But this is where trouble begins, as we shall readily see.

Real for whom?

The key concept here is that social currents and their impact on individual and group thinking, feeling, and acting are mainly unconscious. Hence, it is only natural that they differ from and contradict the conscious image that society and its members have of themselves, just as the individual's inner truth contrasts with that carefully censored and idealised image of him- or herself that Freud called "the I". This phenomenon, which resembles our well-known mechanism of rationalisation, was studied by Marx and Engels (1932), in socio-political terms, under the name of "ideology".

Ideology, in this sense, is the false image of a society and its nature that its members have of it, both individually and collectively, and should be clearly differentiated from the dire reality it conceals. One can certainly take exception at some unilateral uses of this concept, but the fact remains that the true human motives are, more often than not, unknown by the subject—as our discipline has shown over and over again—and that there is no reason to assume that this should be any different in the case of social issues. Both individuals and groups are likely to define what is real for them, in terms of their own experiences, persuasions, and interests, and not be aware of the fact that they are actually constructing their reality through this definition (Berger & Luckmann, 1967). This is as true for patients as it is for analysts, politicians, psychoanalytical theorists, and ordinary citizens.

One should expect a psychoanalytical treatment to explore these issues, but the fact is that all our theory and practice has tended to omit them. We have, therefore, to face the problem of who is to define what is real and what is not. We usually leave this task to the analyst, but we should ask ourselves whether this is fair and, especially, if it works and how.

In this, the question of material reality is not usually an issue, but it certainly becomes one when we have to deal with other aspects of reality, unless analyst and patient fully share—as they frequently do—a same conception of the world (Hernández de Tubert, 2009). But when there are cultural, religious, or political differences between the two parties, these issues come to the fore, unless they are swept under the carpet by a categorical statement that the patient is "out of touch with reality". And if this seems too strong a judgement of analysts' rationalisations, we should well remember the many occasions in which a theoretical difference was summarily dismissed by a whole group of analysts on the grounds that the dissenter "was psychotic" or "lacked sufficient analysis".[7]

There is no way in which a psychoanalyst could carry out her or his interpretative activity without starting from a whole set of assumptions and prejudices, derived from personal experience, upbringing, the social context, training, theory, and the psychoanalytical tradition of which he or she is a part.[8] The patient also bases all her perceptions, thoughts, feelings, and expressions on a similar set of assumptions. The analytic dialogue confronts, identifies, verbalises, and inquires these assumptions and the similarities and differences between them. From such shared inquiry, a certain agreement may emerge, which is the basis of the parties' conviction about their findings.

What just will not do is the common practice of assuming *a priori* that the way in which the analyst conceives things is the reliable version of reality, and that the patient's view is, when it differs from the former, "unreal". Such an approach would be tantamount to turning the analysis into a form of indoctrination, instead of an open inquiry that brings about liberation and freedom of thought.

We have by now reviewed the various kinds of reality, thus showing this concept to be much more complex than it initially appeared to be. We have also seen that our conception of the real is by no means straightforward, that it brings about divergence and conflict, and that this requires a shared inquiry, discussion, and negotiation between patient and analyst, in order to reach the partial and temporary agreements that lead to a moderate conviction about the findings of an analysis.

Taking all this into consideration, we may well ask ourselves why we should deal with reality at all. Would it not be better for us to focus only on *meaning*, as some postmodern versions of psychoanalysis would have it (Civitarese et al., 2015)? Does reality matter at all for psychoanalysis? The answer is that it certainly does, as a consequence of the fact that our discipline has always focused on the search for truth, as we shall see in the next section.

The search for truth

Most psychoanalysts would agree that our practice involves such a search, but they would probably differ in the meaning they assign to the word. This is not only a problem for psychoanalysis, since philosophy has also had to deal, throughout history, with various concepts of truth. We shall presently see a brief review of what I consider to be the main ones (Tubert-Oklander, 2008).

The first one is *semantic truth*, also called "truth by correspondence", that is, the concordance between a thought or statement—a logical proposition—and a state of affairs that is independent of the subject. This is the usual scientific meaning of truth.

The second is *syntactical* or *logical truth*. In a symbolic system based on axioms and rules for combination, it is possible to infer certain consequences that are necessarily true, on account of their consistency with the rest of the system. This is the type of truth to be found in logic and mathematics.

The third kind is *pragmatic truth*, which identifies truth, following William James, Dilthey, and Peirce, with what is useful. This implies that the validity of ideas depends on their capacity to orient our actions vis-à-vis the world we inhabit. Such a stance, which has been heartily endorsed by postmodernist thinkers, has the advantage of taking into account the impact of relation and context, and the disadvantage of forsaking the search for wider truths.

The fourth one is *consensual* or *social truth*, which represents the general agreements, which are mainly unconscious, that the members of a certain community have about what is and what is not, what is possible, and what should be. This includes the customs, beliefs, and values that compound a *Weltanschauung* or conception of the world. The fact that this is largely unconscious makes it a valid object for psychoanalytic inquiry, but it also generates many blind spots, as it is quite likely to be shared by analyst and patient alike (Hernández de Tubert, 2009; Tubert-Oklander & Hernández de Tubert, 2004).

The fifth possible sense is that of *expressive truth*, which is the concept of truth in the arts. This is based on the harmonious consistency between the expressed message, which creates an aesthetic impact, and its capacity to evoke and induce in the receiver emotional states akin to those that the emitter wanted to convey.

One last sense, which is clearly related to the previous one, is that of *narrative truth*. Here it is the consistency of discourse that generates the power of conviction of the narrative. In literature, this moves and makes the reader think, but in the humanistic sciences it also requires verisimilitude, which turns the reader into an active participant and convinces him of the validity of the story that has been told. In the particular case of *historical truth*, the narrative should also be based on established facts, derived from documents, testimonies, and evidences, without omitting any that might be relevant for the matter at hand.

All these forms of truth are characterised by their *power of conviction*, that is, that we are dealing with a message (statement, interpretation, construction) that convinces both the emitter and the receptor of its validity. The experience of truth always gives us certainty, which may not be absolute, but good-enough—that is, adequate and sufficient—for a given context.[9] As Wilfred Bion (1962c, 1970) suggests, this corresponds to a basic and primary need of the human spirit, which is to have at its disposal certain ideas that can be considered valid, at least for the time being, as a basis for thinking, relating, and acting. Although he emphasised emotional truth, this being the very gist of psychoanalytic inquiry, this need also includes the relational, social, political, and moral aspects of truth.

And what is the case of *psychoanalytic truth?* Sigmund Freud conceived it as a semantic truth, in other words, as a precise, complete, and reliable description of a state of affairs that took place independently of the observer's intentions and mental processes. In other words, it was for him an instance and expression of the reality principle, which clearly corresponds to the ethos of natural science. Nonetheless, in the actual practice of the treatment method he created, both he and the many generations of analysts that came after him, up to our present days, have relied on a highly complex admixture of all the above-mentioned forms of truth.

There is certainly a dimension of semantic truth whenever we give a name to a patient's feelings or to a shared emotional experience in the transference–countertransference field. But there is also a space for syntactic truth, not in the absolute sense of the formal sciences of logic and mathematics, but in our understanding of the inner coherence of the symbolic systems, starting with language, that determine our mentation, experience, and action, in the context of the analytic relation and dialogue. Besides, these very systems and their influence become an object for the analytic inquiry, as a part of the consensual truth that both allows patient and analyst to understand each other and then becomes an obstacle for further insights, unless they are themselves analysed.[10] Thus, the analytic dialogue, in which there is a confluence of thinking, feeling, and relating, generates a new kind of consensual truth, based on the shared analytic experience, an agreement that is fully convincing for both parties (Tubert-Oklander, 2013).

And what about pragmatic truth? An interpretation is much more than a valid hypothesis: it is a verbal action, intended to produce a certain effect in both the receptor and the emitter. As Madeleine and Willy Baranger (2009) have suggested, insight is not an intrapersonal event, but a field phenomenon. A valid insight represents a reorganisation of the analytic field, and this is the validity of interpretations, in pragmatic terms.

Expressive truth represents the capacity of the patient's and the analyst's utterances and other forms of expression to somehow convey and share the emotional experiences that generated them. When this effort is successful, it generates an aesthetic experience.

Finally, narrative truth has always been basic for the analytic endeavour. Thus Freud (1895d) remarked, in the case of Elizabeth von R., that he found it strange that his case histories "should read like short stories" and they lacked "the serious stamp of science". But he consoled himself "with the reflection that the nature of the subject is evidently responsible for this, rather than any preference of my own" (p. 160). In other words, the results of an analysis should take the form of a good story, this being an essential part of their value of conviction, and this is not a mere adornment, but a basic requirement of the analytic inquiry.

But the very fact that the subject matter of our investigation determines the form of our interpretations and the findings of the analytic dialogue and relation, imply that there is not a complete freedom for our thoughts and our agreements, but that they necessarily have to take into account *something* that exists independently from us, and this takes us back to the problem of reality.

In sum

What Freud's (1911b) great article taught us is one of the main findings of his clinical research: that the human being is torn between a basic need for truth, and a desire to conceal it from himself and others and replace it with a bowdlerised version that eschews the more distasteful aspects of human existence—individual, relational, and social. Since such aspects exist in spite of our will, wishes, and beliefs, they are clearly a part of what we call "reality". But there are other aspects of reality that are not concealed, but merely unknown, and yet remain unconscious unless they be inquired, interpreted, and constructed by the analytic dialogue. And yet this task must also overcome a resistance, which in this case is not fuelled by the effort to deny an unsavoury truth, but by the rejection of new ideas that would require a replacement or reformulation of old and well-known systems of mentation and relation. Such restructuring is painful and laborious, and therefore avoided unless imposed by the dire need to overcome a greater discomfort or suffering. This is perhaps the reason why psychoanalysis was discovered by a psychopathologist who was striving to alleviate neurotic suffering.

Consequently, the opposition and dialectic between the reality principle and the pleasure principle may be understood in terms of the contrast between truthfulness, on the one hand, and mendacity, self-deception, and laziness, on the other. Freud strove to explain this in terms of his grandiose project of constructing a metapsychology that was to go beyond his psychological discoveries to the material bases—which he believed to be biological—of all mental processes (Letter from Freud to Fliess, March 10, 1898, in Masson, 1985, p. 301). Although nowadays many psychoanalysts do not share this project, and even sternly criticise it, none can ignore the momentous import of the discoveries that he put forward in these few fundamental pages.

Notes

1   I am using the non-standard term "minding" as a neologism to refer to the processes of mind-building. This implies a conception of mind as a set of evolving processes for the construction of mental contents (what Freud, 1900a, called "presentations"), processes that are steered by one or the other of the principles introduced by Freud (1911b) in the article we are now discussing. Nonetheless, I shall not discuss it further on this occasion.

2.   Indeed, Freud does not speak of "learning from experience", this being a term borrowed from Bion (1962c). Nonetheless, I believe this to be a valid introduction in this context, since learning from experience can only happen as a result of the operation of the reality principle.

3.   There has also been much discussion about whether the newborn is really so out of touch with reality as this theory affirms, and this has led some authors to suggest that the reality principle is active from the very beginning, albeit in a primitive form, but good-enough for the baby to recognise the breast when in meets it (Fairbairn, 1952; Rycroft, 1962). Such a revision would bring about a theory of a life-long dialectic and complementarity of the reality and the pleasure principles (Rycroft, 1968) that I do not intend to discuss on this occasion.

4.   This is probably the inspiration of Jean Laplanche's (1997) theory that the real basis of the original fantasies of seduction is the unconscious impact of adult sexuality on the baby. According to him, "the breast transmits to the child a message and . . . this message is sexual . . . [since] the breast is firstly sexual for the mother, . . . [and] it forms part of her sexual life as an erogenous zone" (p. 660). But this would be a universal phenomenon, quite different from the effect of family dynamics that Freud was describing.

5.   This is, of course, my own definition of reality in terms of the resistance we find in it ("an object is something that objects"), but it is consistent

with Freud's description, in which the reality principle that rules the secondary process is contrasted with the hallucinatory wish-fulfilment of the primary process, which meets no resistance (Freud, 1900a, 1911b).

6. Of course, a material object can be destroyed, albeit with an effort, but emotions cannot; they can only be ignored, misnamed, or deviated, but they will still be there. This is indeed a difference between their kind of reality and that of the material world.

7. Such was the case of the analytic group's reaction to Ferenczi's (1949) last paper. Various letters of the time qualify him as "paranoid" and "psychotic", on the sole basis that he actually believed his patients' memories of child abuse and that he dared disagree with Freud (Masson, 1984).

8. Hans-Georg Gadamer (1960) has shown this to be the case for all sorts of interpretation, in his major theory of hermeneutics.

9. This concept of a partial, contextual, and temporary, but sufficient, truth is taken from *analogical hermeneutics* (Tubert-Oklander & Beuchot Puente, 2008).

10. This is indeed crucial: any new piece of insight that opens new ways of understanding things, later becomes an obstacle, when it becomes an established knowledge, and requires to be questioned and inquired again, in a process akin to Hegelian dialectics. I believe this to be the meaning conveyed by Bion's (1967b) puzzling statement that "What is 'known' about the patient is of no further consequence: it is either false or irrelevant. If it is 'known' by patient and analyst, it is obsolete. . . . The one point of importance in any session is the unknown. Nothing must be allowed to distract from intuiting that" (p. 272).

Editors' introduction to Chapter Ten

Heenen-Wolff invites us to reflect on Freud's "Two principles" by inquiring if psychoanalysis can conceive freedom beyond relief from symptoms. She puts forward the idea that if this is the case, psychoanalysis has the potential to have a liberating impact enabling patients to tolerate increased displeasure yet be more able to acknowledge reality.

Before developing her argument, the author links the "Two principles" paper to other works of Freud, for example *Beyond the Pleasure Principle* and *The Ego and the Id*. Freud's conceptualisations of psychic functioning became more complex with the ideas put forward in these two other papers. The concept of the pleasure principle was founded on the theory of drives: the sexual instincts, and after 1920, the death drive. And with the way he conceptualised the ego in *The Ego and the Id* so Freud added that there was no human behaviour that was not in some way determined by unconscious wishes or unconscious prohibitions.

Taking into consideration the over-determined nature of psychic life, Heenen-Wolff then proposes that psychoanalysis has much to offer in increasing the patient's freedom. She suggests three avenues for this to happen.

The first is related to the analytic setting that provides freedom to speak. Heenen-Wolff elaborates the different ways in which the analytic setting introduces the conditions to express oneself in the freest way possible. She also points out, however, a paradox: the basic rule invites unparalleled freedom of expression, but the setting imposes at the same time a set of non-negotiable rules. This paradoxical reality allows for regression and the transference neurosis to emerge, the analysis of which will enable the patient to be aware of the extent to which his psychic conflicts are an attempt to avoid displeasure. Awareness in this sense, leads to a new acquired freedom.

The second way in which psychoanalysis can contribute to greater freedom is related to the phenomenon of afterwardness (*après-coup*) according to which present experiences can have an effect on how past experiences are remembered. The transference analysis can impact the patient's experience of the past in a retroactive manner, allowing as a consequence a new economic organisation that has the potential to bring freedom to the patient vis-à-vis his or her own history. In a particularly poignant statement Heenen-Wolff summarises this point as follows: "The past is responsible for what we have become; but conversely, what we are today is also responsible for what we believe we were; the present shapes and transforms the past, our own internal understanding, and perception of our past" (p. 210, this volume).

Heenen-Wolff then moves to the third way in which she thinks psychoanalysis can contribute to increase psychic freedom in an individual. In this third argument she makes more direct connections to the "Two principles" paper. She highlights the tension resulting from unconscious and conscious thinking, that is, between the two principles of mental functioning and suggests that it is within this tension that the capacity to think can emerge, and gradually become stronger and enriched. The ability to reflect in the midst of an experience of desire and lack of satisfaction has the potential to provide the freedom to ponder: the wish can now be thought, transformed, and perhaps lead into an action. In other words, "the ability to maintain a tension between pleasure-ego and reality-ego, undoubtedly implies a sphere of freedom" (p. 215, this volume). The author makes connections with Bion's theory of thinking. She concludes that analysis contributes to improving the ability to think freely to allow thinking to circulate between the drive desires, liberating the psychic work from the dominance of the pleasure principle, thus making the associative thought process possible.

Heenen-Wolff generously presents two clinical vignettes as well as a personal experience to illustrate her ideas about mental freedom and psychoanalytic work.

10

Mental functioning and free thinking

Susann Heenen-Wolff

People consult an analyst because they want to *free* themselves from their symptoms, from inhibitions, from particular representations and conceptions, from compulsions. They do not usually formulate their concerns in so many words. Initially, they are mostly unaware that their quest for "healing" can be thought of as a search for greater freedom, particularly in regards to the more or less obvious repetition compulsion.

As psychoanalysts, how can we think about the individual's freedom that would transcend the mere freedom from symptoms? With Freud, we know only too well the over-determination[1] of unconscious and conscious human thought, of behaviour and of mental functioning altogether.

It strikes me as interesting to reflect on Freud's paper on "Formulations on the two principles of mental functioning" by asking how we can conceive freedom of man beyond—relative—relief from symptoms or new or rediscovered creativity.[2] Does the psychoanalytical experience help us to acquire *new spaces of freedom*? If so, psychoanalysis would have an emancipatory impact that enables the subject to tolerate increased unpleasure that allows him to acknowledge reality, to be able to think more rationally, and to attain more reason.

Initially, the Freudian discoveries in regards to mental functioning left us rather at a loss as to how one might imagine "freedom" of the individual, especially the freedom to command one's capacity for perception and thinking. Freud reduced this idea to the handy formula that "the Ego is not master in its own house" (1917a, p. 143). The unconscious processes and the drives as well as the constraints imposed by civilisation and society are responsible for men's inability to experience himself as "free". Contrary to his original conviction, Freud proposed that unconscious representation has an influence on thoughts and actions, even if the individual believes that his thoughts and actions are the result of conscious thought and volition.

Freud goes further still, to the point of questioning the objectivity of perception. In his view we never deal with "mere" perception. We always deal with perception, which has already gone through various layers within the psychic apparatus before the perception reaches consciousness. In particular, the ineluctable need to avoid unpleasure is responsible for distorted perception.

Overall one can say that Freud spoke more about the forces governed by the pleasure principle inherent in mankind, as opposed to reason and reality-oriented thinking. Repression inhibits thoughts that threaten to produce unpleasure, and as Freud said "This is the weak spot in our psychical organization" (Freud, 1911b, p. 223). The reality principle and pleasure principle do not face each other on equal terms, do not cancel out each other. They do not negotiate compromises; rather, the reality principle serves to enable a certain amount of pleasure discharge: this is the reality principle "in the service of the pleasure principle" (1923b, p. 44). And if reality does not allow itself to be modified according to our desires, we may then find escape from reality, flight into neurosis, which implies the misrepresentation of reality, escape into psychosis, which creates a new "reality", escape into collective delusion. All this in an attempt to avoid unpleasure.

Freud assumes that the genetic constitution and the individual's history structure the fate determined by an individual's drives, that is her fantasy world and repetition compulsion. Mankind is viewed by Freud as being subject to multiple determinants, which elude both her consciousness and her will. During the 1920s, Freud conceptualised mankind as being a slave to primary erogenous masochism (1924c) and to repetition compulsion (*Beyond the Pleasure*

Principle, 1920g). At this point in Freud's thinking the urge for repetition no longer represented just the search for drive satisfaction; it was considered as being at the service of the death drive.

As a consequence, the discovery of the repetition compulsion of unpleasant past experiences inherent in human functioning only apparently seemed to question a vision of the psyche that highlighted its vitality as Freud had viewed it in 1911. For we now (1920) find Freud's concept of unpleasure and avoidance, as the core of the concept of pleasure principle, on another, more complex level. This time, the concept of the pleasure principle was founded on the theory of drives: Eros in the service of the death drive.

By means of analytical therapy, we attempt to liberate the analysand at least to some extent from her tendency to avoid unpleasure and from repetition compulsion. The patient acquires a mental functioning characterised by a freer circulation between the drive desires and the demands of reality, between pleasure and unpleasure. At the beginning of his conceptualisation, Freud had hoped that analytic therapy would strengthen the ego and, as a consequence, unconscious forces would less affect the patient. With the help of psychoanalysis and the concomitant ego-strengthening, the individual would become aware of its neurotic "irrationalism". However, in *The Ego and the Id* (1923b) Freud established that the ego is itself preoccupied with drive derivatives. And he then came to consider that "The ego is after all only a piece of the id, a piece purposefully modified by its proximity to the dangers of reality" (Freud, 1933a, p. 76).

For its part, the superego, to which the ego is accountable, is unconscious as well. So, we can see that according to Freud's conception, there was no hope that man would be able to think, make decisions, and commit acts without them being over determined by unconscious wishes or unconscious prohibitions.

Spheres of freedom

Psychoanalytical theory certainly emphasises the over-determination of psychic functioning, but it also allows us to think of man's spheres of freedom and attempt to expand them in analytical practice. In a clinical example I will present later, I shall show how painful it can be to obtain greater freedom of imagination and thought, and not to succumb to the temptation referred to by Freud to "bring back under the dominance of the pleasure principle thought-processes which had already become rational" (Freud, 1911b, p. 223).

If psychoanalysis has anything to offer in regards to increasing the patient's freedom, one may think particularly of: 1) analytical treatment as the place of a unique freedom to speak; 2) the concept of *afterwardness, après-coup* according to which present events can have an effect on past experiences; 3) the tension between unconscious and conscious thinking, as portrayed by Freud in the text on the "Two principles of mental functioning". I shall develop these points hereafter.

The setting of analysis—free speaking

Freud's first original clinical invention was undoubtedly to institute what Anna O. called the "talking cure". This involved a change of approach, since free speaking replaced hypnosis and the famous pressure technique. Hypnosis tries to achieve maximum subject compliance. By bypassing the patient's free will and waking consciousness, the hypnotist tries to make the patient focus on his or her symptoms. By abandoning hypnosis, Freud not only relinquished having power over the patient but in addition, he created a research paradigm where the research subject—the patient—was now in a similar position to the researcher—the analyst. In other words, the analyst would be just as dependent on his patient as the patient was on him. By encouraging the patient (simply) to say everything that occurred to her—demanding the analyst to *follow* her in her associations—Freud opened up a field of a new way of talking freely: it was now a matter of speaking without a precise goal and without conscious censorship.

Making oneself dependent on the subject's free associations represented a significant shift in the scientific approach. It implied relinquishing the principle of research that was dominant at that time, which focused on an attempt at *mastering* illness and, as a consequence, mastering the neurotic patient. Freud now takes into consideration and works with his patients' fantasies without aiming to control them or direct them according to his own volition. In spite of his attachment to the values of enlightenment and his search for general "truth", Freud discovers a new truth/reality: psychic reality.

Freud ascertains that in the realm of fantasy there are no lies. He attributed more importance to psychic reality than to "objective" reality. The discovery of mental reality prompted Freud to abandon the seduction theory.

At this time, Freud was no longer interested in the question of how things have "really" come about, but instead what the subject experiences in his inside world. In this way, a new sphere of freedom opened up in regard to taking into account the reality of fantasy and its free circulation. In a radical manner, the subject became the sole centre of interest. Moreover, Freud's self-analysis showed that the laws of the unconscious were operative in every individual.

With the invention of psychoanalysis, Freud took a fundamental distance from his colleagues' conventional approach, which was based on a hierarchical vision of a doctor–patient relationship. Moreover, Freud's new vision did not include a clear differentiation between "normal" and "abnormal".[3]

However, just like hypnosis, psychoanalytical procedure is not free of restrictions and direct impacts: the analytical framework—the couch, the regular sessions, the free association, the analyst's neutrality, and the payment—offers the security to support the analytic process but may also engender the transference neurosis in all its intensity. In hypnosis the subject is at the mercy of suggestion by the hypnotist; in psychoanalysis the subject surrenders to the force of his or her own transference. During the session, the appearance of the analytical transference, teaches us that the analysand is considerably more "neurotic" in his consulting room functioning than he is in his everyday life! And if the intensity of the transference neurosis is not forthcoming, we as analysts frequently have the impression of experiencing an analytical process that lacks depth!

With regards to the question of the individual's freedom in the analytical situation, we can ascertain a paradox: the basic rule permits unparalleled freedom to talk about anything that comes to mind, ideally with no guidance from the analyst. But, the analytical situation grounds on a different set of rules that the analysand must accept without negotiation. Paradoxically, the analysand can use and benefit from his freedom only within the conditions imposed on him by the analyst (the setting). The transference neurosis and accompanying regression are brought about and supported by this disparity of forces.

However, this conception of the analytical space is no longer followed by all analysts (Ogden, 1993), and one may wonder whether unpleasure avoidance is actually in action here! In contemporary psychoanalysis the relational aspects between analyst and analysand are increasingly being stressed, as well as the implication of the analyst as subject or even the understanding of the analytical situation as an exchange of mutual projective identifications.

Other authors (Ferro, 2015) highlight the importance of narrative processes to the detriment of free association. In my view, this emphasis on "reciprocity" shifts the actual transference neurosis and its meaning into the background and instead favours the patient's "mental growth" based on the analyst's reparative functions. In general we observe a certain informality with regard to the classic analytical framework and a return to a face to face psychotherapeutic relationship, a less asymmetrical relationship, which might, in my opinion, allow avoiding unpleasure in respect of analytical abstinence.

Does this therapeutic strategy, with less restrictions and conditions, bring with it more freedom for the analysand? This question can be answered in the affirmative if the transference neurosis triggered by the classic analytical situation is viewed as a phenomenon psychically opposed to freedom; but I think the analysis of the transference neurosis alone can very much be thought to enable the subject to gauge the extent to which her psychic conflicts take her to avoid unpleasure and lead her to the repetition compulsion.

Après-coup—freedom from the determining forces of past events

Within the framework of the analytical transference relationship, interpretation initially enables the analysand to take up a modified position within the transference. Ideally, the classic analyst, who rejects a reciprocal "relationship" as well as the mutual recognition that goes hand in hand with it, never takes the analysand's accounts of his past experiences as being "real". The (past) reality is only considered to the extent that events have a current impact at the subject's fantasy level. In the context of the transference experience, the analysand's associations, wishes, fantasies, and dreams emerging during analysis can impact on his subjective experience of the past *retroactively*, permitting a new economic organisation, a recasting of the imagoes and thus of the analysand's inner world in general too. In this *retroactive* action it is possible to have access to a real sphere of freedom that extends across a developmental process and also involves what Winnicott, understood by the term *creativity*: a freedom of the subject vis-à-vis his or her own history and its determining force.

It is the great merit of Lacan, first, then Laplanche and Pontalis (1967), to have drawn attention to the Freudian concept of *afterwardsness*, (*après-coup*) which as Green (2000b) describes it, "explodes" linear time. In Freud's thinking, the notion of retroactive (*après-coup*) involves:

(a) What comes later.
(b) What at a second event enlivens something previously merely "lodged" in the psyche as a perceptual trace. In the case of Freud this second moment can trigger a formerly traumatic unrepresented event to appear. Adopting this view, there is no event "per se" in the psyche.
(c) In the publication *From the History of an Infantile Neurosis* (1918b) Freud finally develops the third modality of afterwardness (*après-coup*): all infantile experiences leave behind perceptual traces, which will be re-interpreted anew later on.

As a child of one and a half, the Wolf Man had observed sexual intercourse between his parents and, in so doing, had at best been disconcerted. At the age of four, as Freud explained, the Wolf Man had already acquired an age appropriate capacity to construct a fantasy of the primal scene, in which the previous sheer perception could now be inserted and then reworked in the form of a dream. In the history of this infantile neurosis, as Freud shows, a dream triggers the Wolf Man's phobia; Freud explains the phobia as an *après coup* response to the first event ". . . the dream brings the witnessing of coitus at 1½ years to bear retroactively" (1918b, p. 109).

The past is responsible for what we have become; but conversely, what we are today is also responsible for what we believe we were; the present shapes and transforms the past, our own internal understanding, and perception of our past.

The concept of afterwardness (*après-coup*) questions in a fundamental manner the representation of man on his own, his relationship with the world at large and his relationships with others, "blowing up" (Green, 2000b) the concept of causality. Not only is the individual incapable of attributing his actions to his conscious will, but in addition he is continually disappointed since—in spite of his achievements—there will always be an insatiable eternal craving. But also: man can never explain the present through the past. That which happened before is never really the past, it is always present, yet still impalpable and forever having to be processed.

In Freud's example of the Wolf Man, he explains the concept of afterwardness twice. The first is when the child witnesses the parental intercourse. The second is when the memory trace of this event becomes traumatic because of a purely psychical event: the dream. But we can now know that such afterwardness is in no way restricted to two events. Retroactive recasting can be multiple. Afterwardness could be seen as a general psychical movement, which is not limited to the recasting of traumatic experiences. On the contrary, one could even presume that, just as the wish is the basis of the quest for the object, the psyche's libidinal need to bind, can be thought of as being at the base of an *après coup* movement.

Let us try to think the analytical situation keeping this hypothesis in mind: A drive desire is the engine of analysis on which analytical work, and above all, transference emerges. This desire is primarily the wish to find—hallucinatory—satisfaction in regards to primal object. This desire, of course, first manifests itself in a disguised form through the repetition compulsion. I think that it is, in fact, this drive desire—universal according to Freud—which is the condition *sine quo non* of the analytic transference and also the conditions that allows analytic *après-coup* to occur.

According to Freud, the universal drive desire is the foundation of analytical transference and of retroactive analytical movements, roughly a retroactive formation of representation in terms of dissociated experiences. The phenomena involved in the movement of analytical afterwardness involve reactivations of that which has not been integrated, thus permitting dissociated events to either be resignified or, perhaps, to be represented for the first time.

A clinical example

How can one conceive the psychic transformation in Mr M, a thirty-five-year-old man, who reaches out to me for analysis? He has no success in establishing a stable relationship with a woman. His erotic experiences, which used to be gratifying, give him no satisfaction any more. For several years now his wish has been to start a family.

During his analysis, Mr M gave the picture of a mother intensively occupied with herself, completely constrained psychologically by traumatic events of her own childhood. Even as a small child, the analysand was more inclined to spend time with his father who was more readily available. Since his pre-adolescence he was very involved in sports activities with his father. Mr M continued to practise sports in his leisure time in his adult life but—without apparent reason and without regret—Mr M stopped all sports activities soon after the beginning of his analysis.

After the first two years of the analysis the transference–countertransference phenomena starts to acquire a structure. When he discovers his distress with regards to experiencing a mother who was mentally absent, he experiences me as a stabilising and supportive presence. Only on certain occasions—for example, holiday breaks—he occasionally sees me as a depressed, absent, and negligent mother.

What, may we wonder, has supported such a generally very positive coloured transference? It is very unlikely that the relationship with the mother, as he perceived it, was the basis for it. One may think that it was a father transference and that gratifying experiences with the father have most likely been brought back to life in the analysis. But the fact that he was so quick to stop his sports activities, which for a long time connected him to his father, may also have been an indication that he was in search of a sort of satisfaction, which extended beyond the relationship with his father. It might also be possible to understand this positive transference as I have done, as Mr M's unconscious wish—to find drive satisfaction vis-à-vis a mother-imago—a wish that had persisted despite the frustrating, indeed traumatising experiences with his mother.

At any rate, the interpretation of this wish in the transference has re-animated it, so that it came again to life between analysand and analyst: one day, during the fourth year of his analysis, he recounts the following dream. He sees the face of his mother, smiling at him affectionately. He associates that his mother has never smiled at him in this way and he has missed this terribly. He becomes sad and starts to cry. Later on in the session, he continues to associate and tells me how pleased he is that his dream depicts the image of his mother looking at him lovingly, which makes him happy.

This dream can be understood as an expression of a new drive derivative, rooted in his desire for satisfaction within his relationship with the mother-imago. A drive derivative rediscovered, created, reinforced, represented, and experienced through, and in, the transference and transference interpretations.

This is not about reconciliation with an image of the mother, which until then had been portrayed as hostile; nor is it a case of gratitude resulting from a working through of feelings of envy. It is about the creation of a new mother-imago by means of a dream—whereby the dream gives form to the unconscious wish—an imago that has surfaced within the framework of a precise transference constellation and as a result of the interpretation of the underlying unconscious desire that ultimately leads to its working-through. Mr M's new truth is that the affectionate image of his mother makes him happy. As André Green says with regard to these retroactive new formations:

> Conversely, however, one must accept the paradox of a truth that does not "discover" itself in the true sense but rather remains mere conjecture, unverifiable, which, construed consistently, nevertheless has an unambivalent effect for mental change (Green, 2000b, p. 45). In actual fact, Mr M—as a result of analytic work—was able to enjoy new experiences in his relationships with women. He has been able to establish an ongoing steady relationship with a woman who is now pregnant. Mr M is pleased with the couple's pregnancy. The analysand has translated the dream-image of the mother–wife smiling at him into a new relationship reality! The interpretations of the transference wish to find satisfaction in the object relationship with the mother–wife, the analyst has intensified this repressed or dissociated libidinous longing. In this way the analysand has been able to create something really new in a *retroactive* movement, to invent the image of a mother–wife who responds to his longing!

Understanding the paradox of temporality allows us to appreciate the extent to which mankind has access to potential spheres of freedom with regard to his past. Analytical experience can trigger *retroactive* movements. As Cournut expresses it: "To be an analyst is to promise *afterwardness*" (Cournut, 1991, p. 123).

The capacity for (free) thinking

I would now like to address the question: "How to conceive freedom in psychoanalysis?" How can we imagine man's capacity to think of his own condition and that of others consciously and rationally if the unconscious avoidance of unpleasure is taken as a determining force? Can the subject deliberate, formulate arguments, work things with his thinking capacities without being condemned "to find" that everything he thinks is in fact always predetermined by his unconscious desire?

To start with, Freud (as he well explains in his paper "Formulations of the two principles of mental functioning", 1911b) conceptualises thinking as a representational activity (of the absent breast/mother). This representational activity extends and integrates impressions from the object relationship with the mother. This paves the way for the transformation of "the thing" into word presentations; from the primary to the secondary thought process; to the establishment of preconscious, and ultimately conscious functions.

But the primary and the secondary thought process are never entirely disentangled, hence the difficult question: can conscious thinking, reflection, be different from rationalisation of the original unconscious wish?

As a way of addressing this question I will use an example by way of illustration:

> My country is occupied by a dangerous assailant. I am convinced that it would be only right and proper to join the resistance groups, accepting all the perils that come along in this context. But at the last minute, I decide that my relatives, my husband, my children, my friends need me (what luck!). I then think that I do not have the right to jeopardise them by siding with a group that carries the risk of being eliminated by the aggressor. Conversely, we can take the other possibility: after all the reasoning, the toing and froing, despite family life and my inner conflicts, I decide to join the resistance groups!

In the first case, the narcissistic—all too understandable—longing to stay alive with the family may be assumed to have been stronger than the conviction that it would be right to join the resistance. In the second case, one might think that rational thought had greater weight than emotional ties to the family—what emotional poverty!—Another way of looking at this is to think that an unconscious longing to leave husband and children has taken this "opportunity" to carve out a path for itself! My little example, of course, takes me back to the "Formulation on the two principles of mental functioning", as described by Freud in 1911: one of these principles conforms to the reality principle, the other to the pleasure principle. These two principles of mental functioning are omnipresent in every human being, and consequently Freud divided the ego into "pleasure-ego" and "reality-ego".

The tension, the relation between these two principles of mental functioning is the mulch on which thought can originate, structure itself, nourish, and enrich. This functioning involves an exclusively human ability: the capacity to reflect—based on the experience of desire and of the lack of satisfaction of it and under the influence of the ego reality—and ponder the pros and cons that will reach a compromise between the unconscious wish and the capacity to think.

This ability, that is, the ability to maintain a tension between pleasure-ego and reality-ego, undoubtedly implies a sphere of freedom! Once again, I return to my example: even if I decide to stay with my family and not join the resistance, I was able to weigh up the pros and cons, and in particular I can still keep my conviction that from a political perspective, resistance is the right way to go, even though that is not the case for me personally, not at this point in my life. I was therefore able to make a decision determined neither exclusively by unconscious wishing—or thinking under the exclusive influence of the pleasure-ego—nor solely by thinking under the influence of the reality-ego while disregarding the original—unconscious—wish. But if this decision is only the expression of a compromise: can it be regarded as "free"?

The tension between thinking under the influence of pleasure principle and reality principle must be insisted upon, thereby emphasising that it is not just a compromise, but we are referring here to a qualitative leap: a wish that can be thought of, can then be transformed and perhaps lead to an action.

I can wish that the car driver in front of me lost his or her driving licence for life because he does not pull away from the traffic lights swiftly. I can wish that my neighbour be struck down by lightening because he is mowing his lawn at lunchtime. But this wishing does not necessarily lead to an action. The superego, the ego ideal, and the reality-ego also have a point of view and thus open the way for thought-*work*. The individual's ability to think can take place in this field of tension. In this way thinking permits one not to succumb to purely energetic inner movements. As Freud stated in his 1911 paper, thinking fulfils that function previously occupied by motor discharge in the sense of unpleasure avoidance—namely that of liberating the psyche from an increase in stimulation and excitation. The thinking process is essentially an "experimental kind of acting, accompanied by displacement of relatively small quantities of cathexis together with less expenditure (discharge) of them" (Freud, 1911b, p. 221).

The question can also be addressed in a more specifically analytical manner, by considering the psychopathology of conscious thinking. We know that any "change in mental equilibrium can impact on the level of intellectual functioning—this delicate machinery which can so rapidly derail" (Flagey, 1972, p. 5). This applies equally to the thinking of the adult as well as that of the child, which is in process of developing.

As Freud already said, the search for knowledge is the seed of infantile sexual curiosity. In this sense various psychoanalytical schools have put the emphasis into different aspects that can play a part in learning. Experientially, acquiring knowledge can be roughly equated with incorporating the breast; fractional arithmetic can mean fragmenting or dismembering the mother's body; passing an examination can assume the meaning of usurping the paternal phallus, and so on. The superego quickly appears on the scene to inhibit such inquisitiveness, even when it has moved away from its original source and has achieved sublimation. One can be stupid in order to maintain a regressive connection with the mother and in order not to have to tackle the fear and guilt associated with the desire to see and understand. Intellectual inhibition can stem from avoiding rivalry with peers or kindred spirits. Failing examinations is often connected with castration anxiety, which is ascribable to the sexualisation of learning processes.

Critical philosophy has taught us that the integration of new knowledge or information can pose a hazard for narcissism, the intellectual functioning can then be questioned and create an experience of unpleasure. Thus, as a way of resisting the narcissistic injury, a type of thinking can be formed, which the Frankfurt School has designated as "false consciousness" ("false" because accessible knowledge is not taken into account).

Freud had already shown which neurotic manifestations have a negative impact on thinking and intelligence. We only need to think, for instance, of *verbal decathexis* in the context of a forbidden or alarming representation: a signifier seems to be on the tip of the tongue, but with the best will in the world does not have access to consciousness. Such a decathexis, especially if it generalises into neurosis, can considerably handicap the thought process. The repression due to proscriptions on the part of the superego can cripple intelligence, since insufficient space is left for the capacity for conscious judgement. We also observe the shortcomings in the thinking process in conjunction with splitting processes in the ego if parts of reality are repudiated.

Bion (1962c) has shown how the destructive urge can be so overpowering that it leads to a dismemberment of the personality, which entails the destruction of the verbal capacity for thought. The thinking apparatus itself is attacked and ousted together with the "bad objects". In place of a thought-thinking apparatus, an apparatus then develops that has as a goal to rid the psyche of internal objects, which simultaneously entails the evacuation of thinking.

In our everyday clinical situation we work with people with such pathologies of thinking. We see patients who appear to be developing not in a world of thought enhanced by affects and fantasies, but a world populated by mere things, or thing presentations; by beta elements, as Bion would say. The thinking is then not synthetic, but at best can compress or juxtapose unconnectedly. Instead of coming to terms with failure and the unpleasure associated with it, the infant evacuates this and hence at the same time parts of its self and its capacity for thought. The curiosity for knowledge, the longing to learn and to acknowledge, the K—knowledge—connection, is severely impaired by this.

Now: the ideal from the classic analytical situation is to have the analysand associate freely From the outset of the analytical work, we challenge her, although we know that free association is an utopia, something that can never be achieved completely. If we challenge the analysand to associate freely, we simultaneously challenge her to think freely! If, in the analytical process, she now sees herself confronted with her relative incapacity for free association, she will simultaneously come face-to-face with her difficulties in thinking clearly and her inhibitions to follow her own thoughts. Usually the analysand's capacity for free association often improves only towards the end of analysis, and for the most part this is then experienced very consciously and expressed correspondingly.

So we might say: analysis contributes to improving the ability to think freely: that is, the ability to allow thinking to circulate between drive desires, the existing relations with others, and with reality in general, between pleasure-ego and reality-ego. In this sense the goal of the analytical process does lend itself to being redefined: it is not about detecting the *ultima ratio* of an unconscious motive. Rather, it is about liberating the psychical work from the dominance of the pleasure principle at the detriment of the reality principle—thus making the associative thought process possible. From the id to the ego: for Freud this imperative was the equivalent of draining the Zuider Zee (1933a, p. 79), a "cultural project", realisable only in the form of a collective endeavour, a service to be performed by society. As Freud said: fall ill or make progress in culture ("a flight into neurotic illness", Freud, 1930a, p. 84).

The unpleasure experience of thinking one's own condition

In concluding this chapter, I present a clinical example to illustrate how painful it can be to gain the freedom that allows thoughts, representations, and affects to circulate more freely between the pleasure-ego and reality-ego, and to think about one's own condition. This example can also give some pointers to aspects of resistance to psychoanalysis in general.

In her early childhood an analysand experienced long-lasting separations from her mother, a hypochondriac depressive woman with no capacity for empathy, who failed to engage with her little daughter's needs. She fed her newborn child on a timetable and never during the night, despite the cries of the hungry infant.

The analysand consults me in connection with an operation and radiotherapy for skin cancer. According to her own words during our initial conversation, she expresses the hope that analysis might save her from a relapse. During the early years of her analysis she speaks—rarely—about her cancer as if talking about a "nasty flu" she had weathered. Over the course of analysis, she reconstructs the following family history: the depressive mother had entrusted her daughter, just several months old, to her own elder sister where the analysand lived for at least two years—in a family with more children, where she was spoilt and became the much-loved "baby of the family". The mother demanded to have her little daughter returned to her when she was about two and a half years old. Both for the little girl and for the "adoptive family", the separation was very painful.

In resonance to her mother's inability to look after her as a daughter the analysand grew up being incapable of looking after herself. When she was undergoing cancer treatment she overdid things in a highly responsible manner despite her cancer, despite the radiotherapy. Not having integrated mentally a reassuring maternal attitude she was unable to avoid and protect herself against the ubiquitous stress. It was therefore impossible for her to interpret her own physical needs, and she was constantly susceptible to over excitation. The only means of dealing with this excitation was the quest for physical exhaustion. It took many years of intense analysis until she became more responsive to her own inner experiences. Above all, the analytical work centred on her experience of weekends and holidays separations. Her fears of dying of cancer and her traumatic separation experiences during childhood could be understood and worked through. The analysand subsequently developed clearer transference movements: she began to endow me with more specific aspects of her inner objects. In parallel with this, her relationships intensified in her everyday life. She felt more alive, more capable of feeling emotions and of having fantasies and daydreams. She was, without any doubt, better able to contemplate and understand more fully the clear connections between her own mental functioning and what befell her in day-to-day life, and her way of reacting to it. These changes allowed her to have a more satisfying life, which she attributed to the analytic experience.

When—sadly—she suffered a recurrence of cancer, she could no longer succeed, by dissociation, in evacuating the overpowering idea of the finality of her own life. She could no longer believe that it is a case of "flu". What suffering! The defence mechanisms of splitting and denial that she was able use before, were not as "radically" effective in keeping the representation of death at bay, and she shivered during many sessions, terrified of dying for weeks and months.

What a paradox we see again as regards to the question of healing in analysis! Has this analysand been "healed"? If we say she has been healed from a mental functioning based on splitting and denial, assuredly! But with it this "healing" brings very much stronger suffering. Analysis does not necessarily lead to less suffering! It would be more appropriate to say that psychoanalysis does not lead to healing; that, rather, it allows the subject to experience his or her suffering at another psychical level and to process, as well as to think, more freely.

Notes

1. *Over* determination, when symptoms, fantasies, dreams each have *several* determinants (Freud, 1895d).

2. In contemporary psychoanalytical theory, along with Winnicott we talk about "creativity", which as a result of an analysis can be regained or developed. "Creativity" undoubtedly involves a way of functioning, which contrasts with repetition compulsion and can be regarded as *one* facet of the way freedom is able to express itself.

3. One may wonder whether the tendency in the psychoanalysis of the time to regard those patients who present to the analyst as always being pathological is not also an—unconscious—attempt to reintroduce the old pre-Freudian distinction between "normal" and "abnormal", this time between the "neurotics" (of which there are hardly any, apparently, any longer) and the "borderline cases" with their "inability" to cultivate transference neurosis.

11

Concluding thoughts

Lawrence J. Brown and Gabriela Legorreta

In the concluding paragraph of "Two principles", Freud (2011b) states

> The deficiencies of this short paper, which is preparatory rather than expository, will perhaps be excused only in small part if I plead that they are unavoidable. (p. 226)

His humility seems unwarranted when we considered the richness of psychoanalytic ideas that owe their lineage, in part, to this brief "preparatory" paper. David Bell (Chapter Two, this volume) commented that the ideas developed in "Two principles" are present in most of Freud's other writings and we have seen the immense heuristic value of these concepts in the rich assortment of papers gathered together in this volume. The richness of the contributions in this volume is a testimony to the paramount importance of Freud's paper in the development of psychoanalytic theory and practice. Indeed, Civitarese maintains that Freud understood the importance of this brief article when he stated:

> But I hope it will not escape the notice of the benevolent reader how in these pages too the dominance of the reality principle is beginning. (p. 226)

Several of our contributors paid attention to the importance of contextualising the "Two principles" within the oeuvre of Freud's life and writings, as Aguayo (this volume) does this in his Introduction. Strachey notes in his preface to "Two principle"s that this paper was written while Freud simultaneously worked on the Schreber case; thus the question of how the psychotic (Schreber) and the neurotic (discussed in "Two principles") dealt with reality was obviously on his mind. Aguayo also views the Freud–Jung conflict as a backdrop to the paper: having "co-starred" in the highly successful visit to America in 1909 and with Jung seemingly anointed to assume the mantle of psychoanalysis, by 1911 they had become adversaries. In regards to the context of Freud's paper, Civitarese brings to our attention a 1910 letter from Freud to Jung in which he said he was working on a paper that would be taking to task Jung's different stance regarding sexuality. Freud said the tentative title of that paper was "The two principles of psychic action and education", which subsequently became the "Two principles". Though Jung is not mentioned in this ("Two principles") paper, Civitarese offers convincing evidence that his presence is nevertheless felt. Mauger, on the other hand, highlights the socio-cultural reality at the time when Freud wrote the "Two principles" in Austria. He does this not only out of historical interest. Mauger wants to emphasise how, at that time in Austria and elsewhere, the pace of human life had been increasing with rapid cultural changes for several decades.

The authors of different chapters in this book bring up many insights and new developments in regards to what Freud envisioned at as the scope of "Two principles": "the task of investigating the development of the relation of neurotics and of mankind in general to reality" (p. 218). Aguayo, for instance, asserts that Freud's focus on the neurotic is partly due to the split with Jung; thus, classical psychoanalysis tended to focus more on the *neurotic's relationship to reality* while Jung took up the study of psychosis more. Consequently the investigation of psychosis in Freudian analysis was back-burnered and returned to years later in the work of Klein and her collaborators. Aguayo ties Freud's original idea that the psychotic hates reality with Bion's later assertion that it is the *awareness* of reality he loathes. Furthermore, Bion effectively brought together Freud's and Klein's views on the nature of psychosis which he discussed in his (1957) paper, "Differentiation of the psychotic from non-psychotic personality". In addition, Bell reminds us of the importance that the death instinct holds in the Kleinian tradition that brings a "darker colour" to the pleasure principle We believe, therefore, that Freud's (1911b) comment in "Two principles" that "Neurotics turn away from reality because they find it unbearable" (p. 218) opened up the notion of how reality cannot be tolerated by many patients and, perhaps, it is a malady that afflicts "mankind in general", whether "normal", neurotic, or psychotic.

Tubert-Oklander invites us to revisit the question of the notion of "reality". His contribution addresses this issue with two questions: the first is what do we mean by "reality"? The second is who is to decide what is and what is not real? Tubert-Oklander traces the origins of these questions to the time at which Freud abandoned the seduction theory and, even though he continued to affirm that there was clinical evidence that events were also a cause for neurosis (e.g., the Wolf Man), he gave priority to the concept of psychic reality. Tubert-Oklander believes that ever since Freud's shift from actual reality to psychic reality there has been a tendency to reject the value of analytic exploration of real external events. This was in fact the source of rupture between Freud and Ferenczi.

Tubert-Oklander believes that the term "reality", which is usually identified with our sense perception of the material world, has been taken for granted. He puts forward a definition of "real" as being,

> whatever exists independently from our will, wishes, or thought, and that resists our attempts to modify it, thus requiring work and effort in order to introduce any changes in it, and sometimes proves to be impossible to change, in spite of our efforts. But also human being, institutions, groups and society as well as emotions are real. (Tubert-Oklander, p. 191, this volume)

So for Tubert-Oklander, social currents and their impact are mainly unconscious.

Tubert-Oklander also discusses the links between what is real and the truth. He proposes different kinds of truths: semantic, syntactical or logical; pragmatic; consensual or social; expressive and narrative. They are all characterised by their power of conviction. He emphasises that the analyst is neither in a position to define what is real nor can he consider himself the bearer of the truth.

> This requires a shared inquiry, discussion, and negotiation between patient and analyst, in order to reach the partial and temporary agreements that lead to a moderate conviction about the findings of an analysis. (p. 195, this volume)

Therefore, the analytic exchange and experience creates a new form of consensual truth that is convincing for both the analyst and patient.

Still related to the notion of "reality", some authors also question what is meant by the *reality* that may be felt as unbearable. Bell opines that one aspect of reality is the awareness of other minds that think independently of the subject. This may motivate the patient to attack the analyst's thinking capacity since it is the analyst's mind that is bringing awareness of painful realities to the patient. Regarding the death instinct as expressed in the destruction of the capacity for thought, Bell (Chapter Two, this volume) says, "There is in some cases a peculiar kind of ultimate pleasure associated with this destruction of the capacity to think, felt as a hated burden—it is perhaps one of deadliest of pleasures." In addition, contemporary Kleinian thinking ties the analyst's relationship with his own mind to early oedipal configurations in that the analyst communing with his capacity for thought may be experienced by more disturbed patients as a painful exclusion from a primitively organised oedipal couple. Indeed, as Aguayo points out, in Bion's (1958) paper, "On arrogance", he refers to the realisation of the oedipal complex as equivalent to coming into contact with reality; however, his emphasis is not so much on the sexual dimension but rather on Oedipus' drive to know the *truth*, regardless of the destruction that may follow from that discovery. For Bion, therefore, it was Oedipus' arrogant search for the *truth* (the answer to the Sphinx's riddle) that led to his ruin more than the incestuous theme. Needless to say, as noted by Cassorla, positive experiences in the oedipal situation also promote important changes in the capacity for knowing reality:

> The capacity to symbolise is connected to the patient's ability to observe himself and to realise his separateness from others; including his independence of the parental couple. (Cassorla, p. 89, this volume)

On the same topic of the reality felt as unbearable, Levine, in his theorising about the *metapsychology of the representation of reality*, and also inspired by Bion, stresses the importance of frustration tolerance in the development of thought and mind. In the process of representing reality, the role of the object is paramount. In the absence of the object, the individual not only experiences frustration, but also creates an opportunity where an internal representation of the absent object may be inscribed. It is the capacity to tolerate and withstand the frustration of a desire in the face of the absence of the object that initiates the process of thinking and therefore of representation of reality. Following this line of thought, the incapacity to tolerate frustration will lead to the destruction of the capacity to think. This ensues in an experience of hate for psychic reality that leads to projective identification that leaves the individual more subject to frustration because, not having a representation of reality, the individual cannot act in a way that diminishes frustration. This compromises both the sense of reality and, as a consequence, the capacity for psychic growth. Levine moves to elaborate on the notion of no-thing, negative hallucination. If reality is not represented in the mind, the psychic emotional space becomes infinite or incomprehensible, time is annihilated and patients lose a coherent sense of self, reality, and/or narrative continuity.

Elaborating on the notion of reality being at times unbearable, Ferro develops the idea that defensive activities can be thought of as lies; they provide humans with "shock absorbers" (Ferro, p. 143, this volume). The truth, both internal and external is often unbearable. Internal experiences such as rage, terror, envy, homicidal feelings, etc., can be so unbearable that they may lead to the renunciation of the internal truth in favour of a truth that is more tolerable and allows thinking. For instance projecting feelings of homicidal rage on to someone, can both compromise the recognition of internal truth while still preserving the contact with it in the outside. In this manner, lying can be paradoxically considered a capacity, the capacity to preserve the pleasure principle yet at the same time preserving contact with reality. Ferro states that,

> The capacity to lie must therefore be considered one of the markers of having reached psychic maturity . . . The ability to tolerate this defence mechanism with elegance is a sign of psychic maturity, both in the patient and in the analyst, or in the analytic field. (p. 143, this volume)

Another interesting subject that was questioned and updated by some authors was the notion of "the pleasure principle". Levine helps the reader clarify, based on the work of Schur, some of the difficulties that one may encounter with the "Two principles" paper. One example of this is that Freud did not use the notion of the pleasure principle in a linear fashion. Freud also used this concept in two different and apparently contradictory ways: pleasure seeking *vs.* pain avoidance. One needs to make a distinction between,

> the trajectory of the unpleasure principle (avoidance of that which is unpleasurable) is towards withdrawal or decathexis, while that of the pleasure principle (seeking out that which is pleasurable) is towards approach and re-cathexis, although both share an ultimate goal of tension reduction within the psychic apparatus. (p. 156, this volume)

Prior to introducing the concept of the *pleasure principle* in "Two principles", Freud (1900a) had only spoken of an *unpleasure principle*, which he had coined in *The Interpretation of Dreams*. The pleasure principle was linked with the primary process that characterised unconscious processes; thus, the pleasure principle, the primary process, and the unconscious were joined and "These processes strive towards gaining pleasure; psychical activity draws back from any event which might arouse unpleasure" (Freud, 1911b, p. 219). Busch (Chapter Three, this volume) up-dates this view and states that the equation of primary process with the unconscious and the secondary process with conscious thinking is too simplistic; consequently, he writes that "by the time Freud (1923b) wrote *The Ego and the Id*, the concepts of primary and secondary processes all but disappeared" (p. 84). Bell, too, observes that these equations lack the necessary distinctions between the concepts and are too simplistic. Busch notes that Freud (1915e) spoke of the seeming paradox of the *preconscious* that has been formed in the unconscious, yet has all the characteristics of secondary process thinking. Furthermore, in *The Ego and the Id*, Freud's (1923b) growing understanding of the nature of resistance led him to realise an unconscious component of the ego and Freud (1933a) himself later said (quoted in Busch, 2013a)

> It is a fact that ego and conscious, repressed and unconscious, do not coincide. We feel a need to make a fundamental revision of our attitude to the problem of conscious-unconscious. (p. 70)

From a more clinical perspective Heenen-Wolff suggests that analytic work allows for a more fluid interchange between the primary and secondary processes. She thinks psychoanalysis can contribute to increase psychic freedom in an individual. She highlights the tension resulting from unconscious and conscious thinking, that is, between the two principles of mental functioning and suggests that it is within this tension that the capacity to think can emerge, and gradually become stronger and enriched. The ability to reflect in the midst of an experience of desire and lack of satisfaction has the potential to provide the freedom to ponder: the wish can now be thought, transformed, and perhaps lead into an action. In other words, "the ability to maintain a tension between pleasure-ego and reality-ego, undoubtedly implies a sphere of freedom" (Heenen-Wolff, p. 215, this volume). Heenen-Wolff states that analysis contributes to improving the ability to think freely to allow thinking to circulate between the drive desires, liberating the psychic work from the dominance of the pleasure principle, thus making the associative thought process possible.

Another subject of discussion and elaboration in this book is that of adaptation related to Freud's statement that the development of the reality principle was a "momentous step" (1911b, p. 219) that placed new demands on the *psychical apparatus* for adaptation to the external world: sense organs and the *consciousness* connected to them were now of greater importance; the function of *attention* to search the data accrued from the external world; a system of *notation* that "lay down the results of this periodical activity of consciousness" (pp. 220–221), that is part of *memory*. These factors allowed for an *impartial passing of judgment* to decide whether something perceived was true or false, thereby enhancing one's contact with reality.

The inception of the structural theory, according to Busch, furthered our understanding of the kinds of "new adaptations" demanded of the psychical apparatus now seen through the lens of the tripartite theory: "Originally, of course, everything was id; the ego was developed out of the id by the continual influence of the external world" (Freud, 1940a[1938], p. 43) (quoted by Busch, p. 69, this volume). Taken from another perspective, Civitarese draws our attention to the influence of Freud's proposal of these new adaptations (attention, notation, etc.) on Bion's concept of the grid in which the focus is on functions instead of content.

Within the framework of ego psychology, there has been some controversy about when these new adaptations develop, now viewed as constituents of the ego, and what factors account for their development. Do these functions emerge from the clash between the pleasure principle and the need for adaptation to reality as Freud suggests in "Two principles"? Busch quotes an observation by Freud (1937c) in "Analysis terminable and interminable": "before the ego exists, its subsequent lines of development, tendencies, and reactions are already determined" (p. 242), which Hartmann took as positing an origin of the ego independent of the demands placed on the psyche by coming into contact with reality. Hartman believed that the ego and id were at first an undifferentiated state and that the ego had its own line of separate development and did not emerge solely out of the need to adapt to reality. However, later ego psychologists even doubted the existence of an undifferentiated stage and instead saw an ego present at birth. Busch (Busch, p. 72, this volume) concludes that, "I would suggest that very rudimentary ego functions are in existence from the beginning of life . . . [and that] the infant is dependent on the external world to serve as an auxiliary ego." This notion of an "auxiliary ego" opens a much larger discussion of the object relational aspects that account for the nurturing required for inchoate ego functions to mature.

From a very different perspective on the notion of new demands placed on the psychic apparatus to adaptation to the reality principle, Cassorla (p. 88, this volume) makes an important contribution in saying "When Freud (1911b) describes the necessary modifications in order for the mental apparatus to deal with reality, he does not refer directly to dreaming." Freud used *dream-work* to describe the process by which an unconscious instinctual wish is disguised in order to be "smuggled" past the censor and achieve partial drive satisfaction; a view of dreaming *in the service of the pleasure principle*. But Bion (1992), expanding the functions of dreaming, suggested that dream-work also functions while we are awake and *in the service of the reality principle* by giving meaning to awareness of emotional experience (see also Brown, 2012). With respect to the clinical relevance of this view of dream-work, Cassorla reminds us of Bion's statement that "the analyst dreams the session" (Bion, 1992) and he (Cassorla) broadens this statement into an intersubjective viewpoint that the patient and analyst dream the session together: "As the analytical process develops itself the dreams of both members of the analytical dyad constitute a complex, dreams-for-two, in which is not always possible to differentiate the contribution of each one" (Cassorla, p. 90, this volume).

In continuity with Cassorla's ideas, Ferro's reading of Freud's "Two principles" paper highlights that the concept of the alpha function has its origins in Freud's notion of the recognition by the conscious mind of sensory qualities. The alpha function will then become the "great elaborator of sensoriality, and whose significant factors will be attention, notation, and memory, alongside many other that are unknown" (Ferro, p. 134, this volume). The theory of container–contained has its origins in Freud's ideas about the passage from the motor discharge to action to thought processes, which open the possibility "for the mental apparatus to tolerate an increased tension of stimulus while the process of discharge was postponed" (Freud, 1911b, p. 221).

With these advances in post-Bionian theory, the notion of a reality principle from Ferro's perspective is no longer a question of relinquishing the pleasure principle and using thinking as a way of affecting reality. Reality is something that "must be dreamed in order to become thinkable and digestible". For Ferro, this has important implications in the analytic work: "a very meaningful and painful mourning process must be undergone by the analyst, who must mourn the reality of the patient's communications" (Ferro, p. 136, this volume).

We want to return to the important question regarding the object relational factors that are midwives to the birth of the reality principle. In an important footnote Freud, (Freud, 1911b, footnote 4, p. 220) in discussing the "fiction" that an infant can develop on its own like a bird in its self-enclosed egg, casually states "provided one includes with it the care it receives from its mother", and then adds that

> The dominance of the pleasure principle can really come to an end only when a child has achieved complete psychical detachment from its parents.

These brief comments beg expansion and a more in-depth consideration about the role of the parents, especially the mother, in fostering the movement to the reality principle. Bell links this development to the transition from the paranoid–schizoid to the depressive position as an evolution from reliance on wish-fulfilment to a beginning acceptance of reality. Furthermore, Bell considers the role played by the epistemophilic instinct that drives the urge to know and that

> When the depressive position is more established the drive to know has a more secure foundation derived from the capacity to bear frustration (the frustration brought by not-knowing), essential to the process of finding out about the world and oneself. (p. 50, this volume)

In contrast, the epistemophilic instinct in the paranoid–schizoid position is more in the service of a sadistic effort to occupy and dominate the object which, when projected, becomes a terror of being known; in contrast, in the depressive position knowing the other and appreciating the reality of their separate existences can lead to empathically based reparative gestures to an object accurately perceived as injured.

Civitarese discusses this footnote and Freud's hypothetical "fiction" that the psychic system is a closed one, like a (autistic-like) bird developing only with warmth from the mother. Civitarese's point is that this footnote anticipates later developments, as in Winnicott, in last half of the twentieth century that address the central role of the mother in the growth, though this notion is barely there in the footnote. Civitarese (p. 114, this volume) says,

> The metaphor of the bird in the egg is the quintessential illustration of Freud's conception of man as an isolated subject endowed with consciousness, a solipsistic entity: and, besides, it matches the psychological and philosophical dogma of his time.

Regarding an aspect of the mother's role in fostering the emergence of the reality principle, Busch quotes Brown's (2009) opinion of Bion's view of the "ego" and how the mother brings meaning to the infant's experience. Busch (Busch, p. 73, this volume) also says

> Brown highlights Bion's addition of a previously unspecified function, an alpha function, as a "superordinate ego function responsible for ascribing emotional meaning to experience".

Emphasising that Bion's notion of alpha function entails an intersubjective connection between the mother and infant, Aguayo (p. 31, this volume) notes, "In Freud's terms, the reality principle now operated at the intersection between a subjectively attuned mother to a subjectively receptive infant." Civitarese similarly underscores the importance of mother's alpha function as a factor in the appearance of the reality principle.

On the importance of the role of the mother, Levine also reminds us that Freud did not develop in depth the way in which an individual is able to acquire the reality principle. Winnicott and Bion developed this idea by taking into account the role of external objects, and a facilitating environment. Levine states that in the process of representing reality, the role of the object is paramount. In the absence of the object, the individual not only experiences frustration, but also creates an opportunity where an internal representation of the absent object may be inscribed. It is the capacity to tolerate and withstand the frustration of a desire in the face of the absence of the object that initiates the process of thinking and therefore of representation of reality.

Another important subject that was developed by some contributors to this book is the question examined by Freud regarding the shifting role of "motor discharge" as the psyche matured from the pleasure principle to the reality principle: in the former, motor discharge "served as a means of unburdening the mental apparatus of accretions of stimuli" (1911b, p. 221) while in the latter motor discharge "was now employed in the appropriate alteration of reality; it was converted into *action*" (p. 221). In Bell's view, Bion offers a "clinical reference" to Freud's theoretical statement about the psyche unburdening itself of excess stimuli. Though projective identification was not discussed by our authors, we believe that Klein's (1946) original concept was based on "unburdening the mental apparatus" of painful mental content (affects and internal objects), while Bion's (1959) emphasis on the communicative aspects of projective identification is *an action that alters the emotional reality of the recipient* and therefore aids adaptation by allowing the receiver to understand the needs of the sender more fully. Coming at the question of how the psyche manages the "accretions of stimuli" from the angle of Bion's theory of dreaming, Cassorla considers these as "raw elements" that have yet to be "dreamed", that is, transformed into thinkable thoughts, which may be projected into the analyst thereby "attacking his capacity of dreaming and thinking" (Cassorla, p. 85, this volume). Additionally, Cassorla states that when the analyst's and/or the patient's capacity for thinking is attacked, the mental apparatus in each is rendered incapable of perceiving and *representing* their respective experiences, thereby diminishing their capacity to know reality.

Continuing with the theme of restraining motor discharge, Freud posited that this restraint ". . . was developed from the presentation of ideas" (1911b, p. 221). Thinking was endowed with characteristics that made it possible for the mental apparatus to tolerate an increased tension of stimulus while the process of discharge was postponed. "It is essentially an experimental kind of acting . . ." (p. 221). The idea that thinking aims to foster motor restraint has been expanded by our authors. Aguayo sees Bion's introduction of alpha function as a concept that enhances our understanding of how thinking develops. Alpha function has its roots in an intersubjective exchange between mother and infant in which communicative projective identification and maternal *reverie* play significant roles. Bion's theory of alpha function, by which emotional experience is *represented*, grew out of his elaboration of Freud's dream-work as occurring while we are awake and asleep (Bion, 1992; Brown, 2012, 2013). Cassorla discusses the importance of developing representations of reality through a process of dreaming as underlying the capacity to think. Where Freud would say that mature thinking abilities develop when the infant "understands" hallucinatory wish-fulfilment is unsatisfying, Cassorla stresses the importance of (Cassorla, p. 86, this volume), "Symbols [that] make the absent reality present, representing and expressing it, initially for ourselves . . . [and that] When the function of the mental apparatus is not adequate the reality cannot be sufficiently symbolised" resulting in impaired reality testing. And, finally, Cassorla notes that "Bion (1962a,b, 1992) links Freud's ideas about thinking in "Two principles" with his concept of *alpha-function*" (Cassorla, p. 87, this volume). Levine also underlines this hypothesis in developing his idea of a *metapsychology of the representation of reality* and, inspired by Bion, stresses the importance of frustration tolerance in the development of thought and mind. In the process of representing reality, the role of the object is paramount. In the absence of the object, the individual not only experiences frustration, but also creates an opportunity where an internal representation of the absent object may be inscribed.

Bell (p. 51, this volume) emphasises Bion's idea that absence of the object is an important factor is the development of a thought. There must be an *at* of the absence of the objects that once brought satisfaction that Bion terms the "no-breast". This "no-breast" may become a thought if the mother can transform it through her alpha function into a *representation* of that which is no longer present. If the maternal alpha function is disturbed or even lacking, then the "no-breast" experience does not become a thought and is rather felt to be a malignant object—Freud's "accretions of stimuli"—to be off-loaded from the psyche through projective processes. Levine expresses a very similar idea when he states that the hatred of psychic reality may lead to the projective identification of early registrations of reality, thus leaving the individual more subject to frustration because, not having a representation of reality, the individual cannot act in a way that diminishes frustration. This compromises both the sense of reality and as a consequence, the capacity for psychic growth. Levine moves to elaborate on the notion of no-thing, negative hallucination. If reality is not represented in the mind, the psychic emotional space becomes infinite or incomprehensible, time is annihilated and patients lose a coherent sense of self, reality, and/or narrative continuity.

With respect to the clinical implications of these ideas, Bell (Bell, p. 56, this volume) speaking of enactments states

> So, the enactments within the transference have a double valency. From one perspective, they provide the possibility for the development of thought, from the other they aim in exactly the opposite direction; it would be hard indeed to imagine how thought can develop when there is no capacity for this foundational differentiation between inner from outer.

There is a somewhat enigmatic and speculative comment that Freud makes about the nature of "thinking" in its original unconscious state that few authors discuss:

> It is probable that thinking was originally unconscious, in so far as it went beyond mere ideational presentations and was directed to the relations between impressions of objects, and that it did not acquire further qualities, perceptible to consciousness, until it became connected with verbal residues. (1911b, p. 221)

This is a prescient statement that seems to anticipate current analytic work on the nature of *unrepresented states*, that is, "ideational presentations" not yet linked to words. Furthermore, in our view, the comment about "relations between impressions of objects" appears to address interactions between unconscious internal objects as a sort of preliminary type of thinking or, put in Bionian (1970) terms, "thoughts without a thinker". Cassorla describes earlier modes of experience that are not yet consigned to the unconscious because the unconscious must be formed. This is achieved through a first registration of emotional experience that Barros (2000) terms *affective pictograms*, which are sensory-perceptual in nature. We believe that when Freud (above) speaks of "relations between impressions of objects" he may have in mind a process akin to what Cassorla and Barros refer to as the formation of *symbolic networks* composed of imagistic registrations of experience connected by affective linkages. These phenomena, therefore, are the psyche's early attempts to make contact with reality through the formation of affective pictograms.

Another aspect of Freud's thinking in "Two principles" that our authors found thought provoking was his comment that phantasy is a "species" of thinking that remains apart from reality testing and continued to operate under the auspices of the pleasure principle alone: it begins in children's play and is also in evidence in day dreaming. Bell cites the need to differentiate between play, day dreaming, and the Kleinian notion of unconscious phantasy. Furthermore, he argues that

> there can be no phantasy free state. After all it is the penetration of phantasy into our real perceptions of the world that gives those perceptions resonance and meaning—a life severed from this connection would be deprived of all the qualities we naturally think of a being part of what it is to be human. (Bell, p. 46, this volume)

Cassorla, along similar lines, states that we should consider *reverie* as another "species of thought" and discusses the clinical use of reverie as well as the importance of the analyst's receptivity. He also underscores the intersubjective aspect of reverie and that "Through his reverie capacity, the analyst comes into contact with the dreams and non-dreams of his patient" (Cassorla, p. 94, this volume). Along the same lines suggested by Bell and Cassorla, while Ferro does not specifically refer to the activity of phantasy, he refers to mental functions that are capable of transforming the sensory data into alpha elements that can be used for thinking states: "the waking dream function is thus a positive operation of the alpha function and leads to the capacity, during waking hours as well, to create visual images as a consequence of sensory stimulation—in some way *to dream what happens to us*" (Ferro, p. 132, this volume, Editors' italic). This perspective transforms the way in which we think about dreams: as a psychic activity that serves to continuously transform sensory data into thinking and into narrations of reality.

Referring to Freud's (1925h) paper, "Negation", Bell importantly says that the capacity for judgment, based on the most sophisticated level of mental activity, owes its origin to processes that are rooted in the body. For example, he asserts that accepting something as true is connected to swallowing (taking it in) and that rejecting something as false is a mental activity akin to spitting it out. Thus, Bell, by referencing Freud's "Negation", deepens our understanding of the origin of the reality principle, that "momentous step" in the development of the human psyche, in "their original bodily inscription" (Bell, p. 47, this volume). Bell also relates the concept of negation and the death drive to the pleasure principle in which pleasure arises from the total negation of desire.

The following statement from Freud also prompted some interesting reflections from our authors:

> Actually the substitution of the reality principle for the pleasure principle implies no deposing of the pleasure principle, but only a *safe guarding of it*. A momentary pleasure, uncertain in its results, is given up, but only in order to gain along the new path and assured pleasure at a later time. (p. 223, Editors' italics)

Aguayo reads this quote as a statement suggesting an interaction between the reality principle and the pleasure principle, which he regards as an analogue to Bion's exploration of the relationship between the psychotic and non-psychotics segments of the personality, "namely the neurotic islands that existed inside the psychotic" (Aguayo, p. 27, this volume). Bell avers that we should not take too literally Freud's comment that the pleasure principle substitutes for the reality principle because this view would imply "a rather static stage-like theory" (Bell, p. 42, this volume), which seems at odds with the tenor of Freud's thinking. Civitarese, too, underscores the relationship between the pleasure and reality principles when he characterises Bion's view of dreaming, "that dream thoughts are a rough draft of thought" (Civitarese, p. 116, this volume), that is, that dreaming is also in the service of reality (also discussed in more detail above).

Somewhat later in "Two principles", Freud himself clarifies the issue of whether the reality principle replaces the pleasure principle or instead sees them as interacting. In this connection, he views *education* as the "conquest of the pleasure principle" (1911b, p. 224) by the reality principle while *art* involves a "reconciliation" between these two principles. The artist is at first someone who cannot renounce instinctual satisfaction but who

> finds the way back to reality, however, from this world of phantasy by making use of special gifts to mold his phantasies into truths of a new kind, which are valued by men as precious reflections of reality. (p. 224)

Mauger's contribution extensively elaborates on the activity of art; one of the four civilising attempts described by Freud to transcend the pleasure principle, the others being religion, science, and education. He highlights the crucial difference between art and the other attempts; Mauger develops the argument that artistic creation becomes part of the culture that both simultaneously expresses and contains a collective hostility to reality.

As a way of illustrating this argument, Mauger describes the evolution of dance from court dances to the Viennese Waltz, which sought to maintain the illusion of harmony in the wake of political forces that led to the disintegration of the system, to Ravel's *La Valse*, which expressed the despair and destructivity of that age. Ravel's *La valse* is a new "precious reflexion" that leaves the listener with the impression of an overwhelming intensity in the pace of life and a disintegration of the political world. Mauger's title "time is short" attempts to capture this sense of overwhelming intensity with its urgent quality.

Continuing this line of thought, Bell refers to Freud's (1933a) description of the mind's complexities that cannot be explained "by means of linear contours . . . but we need rather the areas of colour shading off into one another that are to be found in modern pictures" (p. 105). This observation, though written many years after "Two principles", seems to suggest Freud's on-going reflections on the nature of the mind that can no longer be explained in terms of binary opposites (e.g., pleasure and reality principles, conscious and unconscious) but instead as comprised by interconnected elements that "shade off into one another".

Freud closes "Two principles" by relating a dream of patricidal wishes that Civitarese examines through an intertextual analysis by comparing this with the two well-known dreams ("father don't you see I'm burning" and "you are requested to close the/an eye(s)") from *The Interpretation of Dreams* in which patricidal and filicidal themes predominate. Civitarese's analysis brings us back to Bion's (1958) comment (above) that awareness of the oedipal situation equates with coming into contact with reality; but Civitarese elaborates the inherent danger:

> Freud tells us that if we truly want to be realists we must open our eyes also with respect to the most inadmissible desires inspired by the pleasure principle. As he writes elsewhere, the child desires to possess the mother entirely for himself and for this reason would like to kill the father. (Civitarese, p. 112, this volume)

Therefore, the "momentous step" that the reality principle represents in mankind's evolution is also a precipitously dangerous one since contact with reality also entails awareness of our own darkness.

From a different angle, Mauger also refers to the dangers inherent in the tension between the pleasure and the reality principle in psychic life. He makes a link between Freud's "Two principles" and the *Beyond the Pleasure Principle* paper. He suggests that the ideas presented in "Two principles" where later transformed and expressed differently in *Beyond the Pleasure Principle* and in *Civilization and its Discontents*. In *Beyond the Pleasure Principle*, reflecting on the First World War, Freud would come to grips with the magnitude of human destructiveness. It is at this point that Freud realised what he had proposed in his previous work could no longer explain psychic functioning. Mauger explains: "He proposed to take into consideration a *beyond*, a compulsion to repeat at the heart of any drive pressure, a *beyond* without principles, or better, a new radicalism at the heart of the two principles already established: a death-compulsion" (Mauger, p. 172, this volume). Mauger links these two papers with

Civilization and its Discontents. He refers to the time of "our" civilisation with its pressing qualities and its lack of consideration for the need to take time to wait for development, that is, to wait for things to come about. He claims there is a collective propensity for the "present" time, which seeks to reduce the experience of time to its simplest expression (we think about the virtual time of information technology). Following this argument, Mauger reminds us that in *Civilization and its Discontents* Freud (1930a) was deeply concerned about man's need to gain control over the forces of nature. He cites Freud "Men have gained control over the forces of nature to such an extent that with their help they would have no difficulty in exterminating one another to the last man. They know this, and hence comes a large part of their current unrest, their unhappiness and their mood of anxiety" (1930a, p. 145).

REFERENCES

Abensour, L. (2013). *The Psychotic Temptation*. Hove: Routledge.
Adorno, T. (1951). Freudian theory and the nature of fascist propaganda. In: *The Culture industry*. London: Routledge Classic, 1991.
Aguayo, J. (2009). On understanding projective identification in the treatment of psychotic states of mind: the publishing cohort of H. Rosenfeld, H. Segal and W. Bion. *International Journal of Psychoanalysis*, 90(1): 69–92.
Aguayo, J. (2013). Freud, Jung, Sabina Spielrein and the Countertransference: David Cronenberg's "A Dangerous Method". *International Journal of Psychoanalysis*, 94: 169–178.
Allen, W. (Ed. & Dir.) (1983). *Zelig* (film).
Arendt, H. (1954). *Between Past and Future*. London: Penguin.
Arendt, H. (1978). *The Life of the Mind Part One: Thinking*. New York: Harcourt Brace Jovanovich.
Baranger, M. (1963). Mala Fé Identidad y Omnipotencia. *Revista Uruguaya de Psicoanalisis*, 5: 199–229.
Baranger, M., & Baranger, W. (2009). *The Work of Confluence: Listening and Interpreting in the Psychoanalytic Field*, L. Glocer Fiorini (Ed.). London: Karnac.
Baranger, M., Baranger, W., & Mom, J. (1983). Process and non-process in analytic work. *International Journal of Psychoanalyisis*, 64: 1–15.

Barros, E. M. R. (2000). Affect and pictographic image: the constitution of meaning in mental life. *International Journal of Psychoanalysis*, *81*: 1087–1099.

Barros, E. M. R., & Barros, E. L. R. (2011). Reflections on the clinical implications of symbolism. *International Journal of Psychoanalysis*, *92*: 879–901.

Barros, E. M. R., & Barros, E. L. R. (2014). The function of evocation in the working-through of the countertransference: projective identification, reverie and the expressive function of the mind. In: H. B. Levine & G. Civitarese (Eds.), *The W. R. Bion Tradition. Lines of Development—Evolution of Theory and Practice over the Decades*. London: Karnac.

Bell, D. (2009). Is truth an illusion? Psychoanalysis and postmodernism. *International Journal of Psychoanalysis*, *90*: 331–345.

Bell, D. (2011). Bion the phenomenologist of loss. In: C. Mawson (Ed.), *Bion Today* (pp. 81–101). London: Routledge.

Bell, D. (2015). The death drive: phenomenological perspectives in contemporary Kleinian theory. *International Journal of Psychoanalysis*, *96*: 411–423.

Berger, P. L., & Luckmann, T. (1967). *The Social Construction of Reality*. New York: Anchor.

Bion, W. R. (1954). Notes on a theory of schizophrenia. *International Journal of Psychoanalysis*, *35*: 113–118 [reprinted in *Second Thoughts* (pp. 23–35). New York: Basic Books, 1967].

Bion, W. R. (1955). Language and the schizophrenic. In: M, Klein., P. Heimann, & R. Money-Kyrle (Eds.), *New Directions in Psycho-Analysis* (pp. 220–239). London: Tavistock.

Bion, W. R. (1956). Development of schizophrenic thought. *International Journal of Psychoanalysis*, *37*: 344–346 [reprinted in *Second Thoughts* (pp. 36–42). New York: Basic Books, 1967].

Bion, W. R. (1957). Differentiation of the psychotic from non-psychotic personalities. *International Journal of Psychoanalysis*, *38*: 266–275 [reprinted in *Second Thoughts* (pp. 43–64). New York: Basic Books, 1967].

Bion, W. R. (1958). On arrogance. *International Journal of Psychoanalysis*, *39*: 144–146.

Bion, W. R. (1959). Attacks on linking. *International Journal of Psychoanalysis*, *40*: 308–315.

Bion, W. R. (1962a). The psychoanalytic theory of thinking. *International Journal of Psychoanalysis*, *43*: 306–310.

Bion, W. R. (1962b). A theory of thinking. In: *Second Thoughts—Selected Papers on Psycho-Analysis* (pp. 110–119). London: Heinemann, 1967.

Bion, W. R. (1962c). *Learning from Experience*. London: Heinemann [reprinted London: Maresfield Reprints, Karnac, 1984].
Bion, W. R. (1963). *Elements of Psycho-Analysis*. London: Heinemann.
Bion, W. R. (1963–1977). *Taming Wild Thoughts*. London: Karnac.
Bion, W. R. (1965). *Transformations*. London: Heinemann.
Bion, W. R. (1967a). *Second Thoughts*. New York: Basic Books.
Bion, W. R. (1967b). Notes on memory and desire. *Psychoanalytic Forum*, 2: 272–273 [reprinted in E. Bott Spillius (Ed.), *Melanie Klein Today—Vol. 2: Mainly Practice* (pp. 17–21). London: Routledge, 1988].
Bion, W. R. (1970). *Attention and Interpretation*. London: Heinemann.
Bion W. R. (1977). *Two Papers: The Grid and the Caesura*. London: Karnac.
Bion, W. R. (1992). *Cogitations*. London: Karnac.
Bion W. R. (1997). The grid. In: *Taming Wild Thoughts*, F. Bion (Ed.). London: Karnac.
Bion, W. R. (2005). *The Tavistock Seminars*. London: Karnac.
Bion, W. R. (2013). *Wilfred Bion's Los Angeles Seminars and Supervision*, J. Aguayo & B. Malin (Eds.). London: Karnac.
Blum, H. P. (2004). Beneath and beyond the "Formulations on the two principles of mental functioning". *Psychoanalytic Study of the Child*, 59: 240–257.
Bolognini, S. (2010). *Secret Passages*. London: Routledge.
Botella, C., & Botella, S. (2013). Psychic figurability and unrepresented states. In: H. B. Levine, G. Reed, & D. Scarfone (Eds.), *Unrepresented States and the Construction of Meaning* (pp. 95–121). London: Karnac/IPA.
Britton, R. (2007). The baby and the bathwater. Unpublished paper.
Brown, L. J. (2007). On dreaming one's patient: reflections on an aspect of countertransference dreams. *Psychoanalytic Quarterly*, 76: 835–861.
Brown, L. J. (2009). Bion's ego psychology: implications for an intersubjective view of psychic structure. *Psychoanalytic Quarterly*, 78(1): 27–55.
Brown, L. J. (2011). *Intersubjective Processes and the Unconscious: An Integration of Freudian, Kleinian and Bionian Perspectives*. London: Routledge.
Brown, L. J. (2012). Bion's discovery of alpha function: thinking under fire in the battlefield and in the consulting room. *International Journal of Psychoanalysis*, 93: 1191–1214.
Brown, L. J. (2013). Bion at a threshold: Commentary on papers by Britton, Cassorla, Ferro and Zimmer. *Psychoanalytical Quarterly*, 82: 413–433.

Busch, F. (1993). "In the neighborhood": aspects of a good interpretation and a "developmental lag" in ego psychology. *Journal of the American Psychoanalytic Association, 41*: 151–177.

Busch, F. (1995). Do actions speak louder than words? A query into an enigma in analytic theory and technique. *Journal of the American Psychoanalytic Association, 43*: 61–82.

Busch, F. (1999). *Rethinking Clinical Technique*. Northvale, NJ: Jason Aronson.

Busch, F. (2006). A shadow concept. *International Journal of Psychoanalysis, 87*(6): 1471–1485.

Busch, F. (2009). Can you push a camel through the eye of a needle? *International Journal of Psychoanalysis, 90*: 53–68.

Busch, F. (2013a). *Creating a Psychoanalytic Mind: A Psychoanalytic Method and Theory*. Routledge: London.

Busch, F. (2013b). Changing views of what is curative in 3 psychoanalytic methods and the emerging, surpriing common ground. *The Scandinavian Psychoanalytic Review, 31*: 27–34.

Calderón de la Barca, P. (1635) *Life Is a Dream*. Nick Hern Books, 1998.

Caper, R. (1999). *A Mind of One's Own: A Kleinian View of Self and Object*. London: Routledge.

Cassorla, R. M. S. (2005). From bastion to enactment: The "non-dream" in the theatre of analysis. *International Journal of Psychoanalysis, 86*: 699–719.

Cassorla, R. M. S. (2008). The analyst's implicit alpha-function, trauma and enactment in the analysis of borderline patients. *International Journal of Psychoanalysis, 89*(1): 161–180.

Cassorla, R. M. S. (2012). What happens before and after acute enactment? An exercise in clinical validation and broadening of hypothesis. *International Journal of Psychoanalysis, 93*: 53–80.

Cassorla, R. M. S. (2013a). Considerations on non-dreams-for-two, enactment and the analyst's implicit alpha-function. In: H. B. Levine & L. J. Brown (Eds.), *Growth and Turbulence in the Container and Contained* (pp. 151–176). Boston: Routledge.

Cassorla, R. M. S. (2013b). In search of symbolization: the analyst task of dreaming. In: H. B. Levine; G. S. Reed, & D. Scarfone (Eds.), *Unrepresented States and the Construction of Meaning* (pp. 202–219). London: Karnac.

Cassorla, R. M. S. (2013c). When the analyst becomes stupid: an attempt to understand enactment using Bion's theory of thinking. *Psychoanalytical Quarterly, 82*: 323–360.

Cassorla, R. M. S. (2014). Commentary to case Ellen: the silent movies. *International Journal of Psychoanalysis*, 95: 93–102.
Chekhov, A. (1886). *The Exclamation Mark*. London: Hesperus Press Ltd, 2008.
Civitarese, G. (2008). "Caesura" as Bion's discourse on method. *International Journal of Psychoanalysis*, 89: 1123–1143.
Civitarese, G. (2011). Exploring core concepts: sexuality, dreams and the unconscious. *Inernational Journal of Psychoanalysis*, 92: 277–280.
Civitarese, G. (2013a). The grid and the truth drive. *The Italian Psychoanalytic Annuals*, 7: 91–114.
Civitarese, G. (2013b). *The Necessary Dream: New Theories and Techniques of Interpretation in Psychoanalysis*. London: Karnac.
Civitarese, G. (2013c). The inaccessible unconsciouos and reverie as path of figurability. In: H. B. Levine, G. S. Reed, & D. Scarfone (Eds.), *Unrepresented States and the Construction of Meaning* (pp. 220–239). London: Karnac.
Civitarese, G. (2014). Bion and the sublime: roots of an aesthetic paradigm. *International Journal of Psychoanalysis*, 95(6): 1059–1086.
Civitarese, G., Katz, M., & Tubert-Oklander, J. (Eds.) (2015). *Postmodernism and Psychoanalysis*. Thematic issue of *Psychoanalytic Inquiry*, 35(6): 559–662.
Cournut, J. (1991). *L'ordinaire de la passion*. Paris: PUF.
Dante, A. (1321). *The Divine Comedy*. Penguin Classics, 2012.
De Filippo, E. (1951). *Filumena Marturano*. Einaudi, 1975.
De Marchi, E. (1890). *Demetrio Pianelli*. Guanda, Biblioteca di scrittori italiani, 2000.
Derrida, J. (1978). *The Truth in Painting*. Chicago: University of Chicago Press.
Dumas, A. (1822). *The Three Musketeers*. Vintage Classics, 2014.
Eagleton, T. (1996). *The Illusions of Postmodernism*. Blackwell: Oxford.
Escalona, S. (1953). Emotional development in the first year of life. In: M. See (Ed.), *Problems of Infancy and Childhood*. New York: Josiah Macey Foundation.
Faimberg, H. (1996). Listening to listening. *International Journal of Psychoanalysis*, 77: 667–677.
Fairbairn, W. R. D. (1952). *Psychoanalytic Studies of the Personality*. London: Tavistock [reprinted, London: Routledge, 1992].
Feldman, M. (1994). Projective identification in phantasy and enactment. *Psychoanalytic Inquiry*, 14: 423–440.
Ferenczi, S. (1933). Confusion of the tongues between the adults and the child—(*The language of tenderness and of passion*). *International*

Journal of Psychoanalysis, *30*: 225–230. Also in *Contemporary Psychoanalysis*, 1998, *24*: 196–206.

Ferré, L. (1970). "Avec le temps" (song).

Ferro, A. (2005a). *Seeds of Illness, Seeds of Recovery*. New York: Brunner-Routledge.

Ferro, A. (2005b). Which reality in the psychoanalytic session? *Psychoanalytic Quarterly*, *74*(2): 421–442.

Ferro, A. (2006). *Psychoanalysis as Therapy and Story Telling*. London: Routledge.

Ferro, A. (2009a). *Mind Works: Technique and Creativity in Psychoanalysis*, P. Slotkin (Trans.). Hove: Routledge.

Ferro, A. (2009b). Transformations in dreaming and characters in the psychoanalytic field. *International Journal of Psychoanalysis*, *90*: 209–230.

Ferro, A, (2011). *Avoiding Emotions, Living Emotions*, I. Harvey (Trans.). Hove: Routledge.

Ferro, A. (2015). *The Analytic Field and its Transformations*. London: Karnac.

Fisher, J. V. (2009). The emotional experience of the container-in-K. Unpublished paper from the "Bion in Boston" Conference, July 2009.

Flagey, D. (1972). *Points de vue psychanalytiques sur l'inhibition intellectuelle*. Paris: PUF.

Flaubert, G. (1857). *Madame Bovary*, F. Steegmuller (Trans.). New York: Vintage Books, 1992.

Freud, A. (1945). Indications for child analysis. *Psychoanalytic Study of the Child*, *1*: 127–149.

Freud, A. (1963). The concept of developmental lines. *Psychoanalytic Study of the Child*, *18*: 245–265.

Freud, A., Nagera, H., & Freud, W. E. (1965). Metapsychological assessment of the adult personality—the adult profile. *Psychoanalytic Study of the Child*, *20*: 9–41.

Freud, S. (1890a). Psychical (or mental) treatment *S.E.*, 7: 283–302. London: Hogarth.

Freud, S. (1891). *On Aphasia*. New York: International Universities Press, 1953.

Freud, S. (1894a). The neuro-psychoses of defence. *S.E.*, *3*: 43–70. London: Hogarth.

Freud, S. (1895a). A project for a scientific psychology. *S.E.*, *1*: 283–397. London: Hogarth.

Freud, S. (1895d). *Studies on Hysteria* (with J. Breuer). *S.E.*, *2*. London: Hogarth.

References

Freud, S. (1898). *Letter #82. The Origins of Psychoanalysis*. New York: Basic Books, 1954.
Freud, S. (1900a). *The Interpretation of Dreams*. S.E., *4–5*: ix–627. London: Hogarth.
Freud, S. (1901a). On dreams. S.E., *6*: 629–686. London: Hogarth.
Freud, S. (1905d). *Three Essays on the Theory of Sexuality*. S.E., *7*: 123–246. London: Hogarth.
Freud, S. (1910k). "Wild" psycho-analysis. S.E., *11*. London: Hogarth.
Freud, S. (1911b). Formulations on the two principles of mental functioning. S.E., *12*: 213–226. London: Hogarth.
Freud, S. (1911c). *Psycho-analytic Notes on an Autobiographical Account of a Case of Paranoia* (*dementia paranoides*). S.E., *12*: 1–82. London: Hogarth.
Freud, S. (1912e). Recommendations to physicians practising psycho-analysis. S.E., *12*: 109–120. London: Hogarth.
Freud, S. (1912–1913). *Totem and Taboo*. S.E., *13*. London: Hogarth.
Freud, S. (1913c). On beginning the treatment. S.E., *12*: 123–144. London: Hogarth.
Freud, S. (1914c). On narcissism: an introduction. S.E., *14*. London: Hogarth.
Freud, S. (1914g). Remembering, repeating and working-through. S.E., *12*: 145–156. London: Hogarth.
Freud, S. (1915b). Thoughts for the times on war and death. S.E., *14*: 273–300. London: Hogarth.
Freud, S. (1915c). Instincts and their vicissitudes. S.E., *14*: 109–140. London: Hogarth.
Freud, S. (1915e). The unconscious. S.E., *14*: 159–215. London: Hogarth.
Freud, S. (1916–1917). *Introductory Lectures on Psycho-Analysis*. S.E. *15–16*. London: Hogarth.
Freud, S. (1917). Eine Schwierigkeit der Psychoanalyse [A difficulty in the path of psycho-analysis]. G.W., *12*: 3–12.
Freud, S. (1917d). A metapsychological supplement to the theory of dreams. S.E., *14*: 217–235. London: Hogarth.
Freud, S. (1917e). Mourning and melancholia. S.E., *14*: 237–258. London: Hogarth.
Freud, S. (1918b). *From the History of an Infantile Neurosis*. S.E. *17*: 1–124. London: Hogarth.
Freud, S. (1920g). *Beyond the Pleasure Principle*. S.E., *18*: 3–64. London: Hogarth.
Freud, S. (1921c). *Group Psychology and the Analysis of the Ego*. S.E., *18*: 67–143. London: Hogarth.

Freud, S. (1923b). *The Ego and The Id*. S.E., *19*: 1–66. London: Hogarth.
Freud, S. (1924a). Neurosis and psychosis. S.E., *19*: 149–156. London: Hogarth.
Freud, S. (1924b). Neurosis and psychosis. S.E., *19*: 147–153. London: Hogarth.
Freud, S. (1924c). The economic problem of masochism. S.E., *19*: 155–170. London: Hogarth.
Freud, S. (1924e). The loss of reality in neurosis and psychosis. S.E., *19*: 183–190. London: Hogarth.
Freud, S. (1925h). Negation. S.E., *19*: London: Hogarth.
Freud, S. (1926d). *Inhibitions, Symptoms and Anxiety*. S.E., *20*: 77–174. London: Hogarth.
Freud, S. (1927c). *The Future of an Illusion*. S.E., *21*. London: Hogarth.
Freud, S. (1930). Letter from Sigmund Freud to Arnold Zweig. *The International Psycho-Analytical Library*, *84*: 21–22.
Freud, S. (1930a). *Civilization and its Discontents*. S.E., *21*: 57–146. London: Hogarth.
Freud, S. (1932). Die Zerlegung der psychischen Persönlichkeit [The dissection of the psychical personality]. G.W., *15*: 62–86.
Freud, S. (1933a). *New Introductory Lectures on Psycho-analysis*. S.E., *22*: 1–182. London: Hogarth.
Freud, S. (1937c). Analysis terminable and interminable. S.E., *23*: 209–254. London: Hogarth.
Freud, S. (1937d). Constructions in analysis. S.E., *23*: 255–270. London: Hogarth.
Freud, S. (1939a). *Moses and Monotheism*. S.E., *23*: 1–138. London: Hogarth.
Freud, S. (1940a[1938]). An outline of psycho-analysis. S.E., *23*: 204. London: Hogarth.
Freud, S. (1940e[1938]). The splitting of the ego in the process of defence. S.E., *23*: 271–278. London: Hogarth.
Freud, S. (1950a[1895]). *Project for a Scientific Psychology*. S.E., *1*: 281–391. London: Hogarth.
Freud, S., & Jung, C. G. (1974). *The Freud/Jung Letters: The Correspondence Between Sigmund Freud and C. G. Jung*, W. McGuire (Ed.). Princeton, NJ: Princeton University Press.
Gabbard, G. O. (1995). Countertransference: the emerging common ground. *International Journal of Psychoanalysis*, *76*: 475–485.
Gadamer, H.-G. (1960). *Truth and Method* (2nd edn), W. Glen-Doepel (Trans.), revised by J. Weinsheimer & D. G. Marshall. London: Continuum, 2004.

Gariepy-Boutin, C. (2012). Review of A. Fayek *The Crisis in Psychoanalysis*. *International Journal of Psychoanalysis*, *91*: 547–550.
Genette, G. (1982). *Palimpsests: Literature in the Second Degree*. Lincoln, NE: University of Nebraska Press.
Genette, G. (1987). *Paratexts: Thresholds of Interpretation (Literature, Culture, Theory)*. Cambridge: Cambridge University Press.
Ginzburg, C. (1979). Clues: roots of an evidential paradigm. In: *Clues, Myths and the Historical Method* (pp. 96–125). Baltimore, MD: John Hopkins University Press.
Goethe, J. W. (1832). *Faust*. CreateSpace Independent Publishing Platform, 2014.
Gray, P. (1982). "Developmental lag" in the evolution of technique for psychoanalysis of neurotic conflict. *Journal of the American Psychoanalytic Association*, *30*: 621–655.
Green, A. (1990). *La folie privée. Psychanalyse des cas-limites*. Paris: Gallimard.
Green, A. (1998). The primordial mind and the work of the negative. *International Journal of Psychoanalysis*, *79*: 649–665.
Green, A. (2000a). Illusion and disillusion in an attempt to present a more reasonable theory of mind. In: M. Bergmann (Ed.), *The Hartmann Era*. New York: Other Books.
Green, A. (2000b). *Le temps éclaté*. Paris: Les Editions de Minuit.
Green, A. (2002). *Idées directrices pour une psychanalyse contemporaine*. Paris: PUF.
Greenberg, J. (2001). The analyst's participation. *Journal of the American Psychoanalytic Association*, *49*: 359–381.
Grinberg, L. (1979). Countertransference and projective counter-identification. *Contemporary Psycho-Analysis*, *15*: 226–247.
Grinberg, L., Sor, D., & Tabak de Bianchedi, E. (1977). *Introduction to the Work of Bion*. New York: Jason Aronson.
Grotstein, J. (2000). *Who is the Dreamer Who Dreams the Dream? A Study of Psychic Presences*. Hillsdale: Analytic Press.
Grotstein, J. (2007). *A Beam of Intense Darkness: Wilfred Bion's Legacy to Psychoanalysis*. London: Karnac.
Grotstein, J. (2009). *But at the Same Time and on Another Level: Psychoanalytic Theory and Technique in the Kleinian/Bionian Mode, Vol. 1*. London: Karnac.
Guntrip, H. (1965). Book review of *Learning from Experience* by W. Bion. *International Journal of Psychoanalysis*, *46*: 381–385.
Hartmann, H. (1939). *Ego Psychology and the Problem of Adaptation*. New York: International Universities Press.

Hartmann, H. (1950). *Essays on Ego Psychology*. New York: International Universities Press, 1964.
Hartmann, H. (1964). *Essays on Ego Psychology*. New York: International Universities Press.
Harvey, D. (1990). *The Condition of Postmodernity*. Oxford: Blackwell.
Heidegger, M. (1927). *Being and Time*. Albany, NY: State University of New York Press.
Heidegger, M. (1983). *The Fundamental Concepts of Metaphysics*: *World, Finitude, Solitude*. Bloomington, IN: Indiana University Press.
Heimann, P. (1950). On countertransference. *International Journal of Psychoanalysis*, *31*: 81–84.
Hernández de Tubert, R. (2009). Inconsciente y concepción del mundo. Implicaciones filosóficas y psicoanalíticas [The unconscious and the *Weltanschauung*: philosophic and psychoanalytic implications]. In: R. Blanco Beledo (Ed.), *Filosofía ¿y? psicoanálisis* [Philosophy (and?) psychoanalysis] (pp. 79–103). Mexico City: Universidad Nacional Autónoma de México.
Homer (between 675 and 725 BC). *The Odyssey* (rev. edn). Penguin Classics, 2003.
Hugo, V. (1862). *Les Miserables*. Penguin Classics, 1982.
Imbeault, J. (2006). Réalité et conformité. *Penser/Rêver*, *10*: 95-105. Lonrai (Orne): Éditions de l'Olivier.
Isaacs, S. (1948a). The nature and function of phantasy. *International Journal of Psycho-Analysis*, *29*: 73–97.
Isaacs, S. (1948b). The nature and function of phantasy. In: J. Riviere (Ed.), *Developments in Psycho-analysis* (pp. 67–201). London: Hogarth, 1952.
Jones, E. (1953). *Sigmund Freud Life and Work, Volume One*: *The Young Freud 1856–1900*. London: Hogarth, 1972.
Jones, E. (1957). *The Life and Work of Sigmund Freud, Vol. 3*. New York: Basic Books.
Joseph, B. (1985). Transference: the total situation. *International Journal of Psychoanalysis*, *66*: 447–454.
Klein, É. (2005). *Chronos*: *How Time Shapes Our Universe*. New York: Thunder's Mouth.
Klein, M. (1930). The importance of symbol-formation in the development of the ego. *International Journal of Psychoanalysis*, *11*: 24–39.
Klein, M. (1946). Notes on some schizoid mechanisms. *International Journal of Psychoanalysis*, *27*: 99–110.
Klein, M. (1952a). Some theoretical conclusions regarding the emotional life of the infant. In: *Developments in Psycho-analysis* (pp. 198–236). London: Hogarth.

Klein, M. (1952b). The origins of transference. *International Journal of Psychoanalysis*, *33*: 433–438.

Klein, M., Heimann, P., Isaacs, S., & Rivière, J. (1952). *Developments in Psycho-Analysis*. London: Hogarth [reprinted, London: Karnac, 2002].

Kris, E. (1952). *Psychoanalytic Explorations of Art*. New York: International Universities Press.

Kristeva, J. (1980). *Desire in Language: A Semiotic Approach to Literature and Art*. New York: Columbia University Press.

Lacan, J. (1966). *Écrits: The First Complete Edition in English*, B. Fink (Trans.). New York: Norton, 2006 [original French publication: *Écrits*. Paris: Seuil].

Laplanche, J. (1976). *Life and Death in Psychoanalysis*, J. Mehlman (Trans.). Baltimore, MD: Johns Hopkins University Press.

Laplanche, J. (1997). The theory of seduction and the problem of the other. *International Journal of Psychoanalysis*, *78*: 653–666.

Laplanche, J, & Pontalis, J.-B. (1967). *The Language of Psycho-Analysis*. London: Karnac, 1988.

Laplanche, J., & Pontalis, J.-B. (1973). *The Language of Psychoanalysis*. London: Hogarth and the Institute of Psycho-Analysis.

Levine, H. B. (2010). The consolation which is drawn from truth: the analysis of a patient unable to suffer experience. In: C. Mawson (Ed.), *Bion Today* (pp. 188–211). London: Routledge.

Levine, H. B. (2011). Construction then and now. In: S. Lewkowicz & T. Bokanowski, with G. Pragier (Eds.), *On Freud's Constructions in Analysis* (pp. 87–100). London: Karnac.

Levine, H. B. (2012). The colourless canvas: representation, therapeutic action and the creation of mind. *International Journal of Psychoanalysis*, *93*: 607–629.

Levine, H. B. (2013). The colourless canvas: representation, therapeutic action and the creation of mind. In: H. B. Levine, G. S. Reed & D. Scarfone (Eds.), *Unrepresented States and the Construction of Meaning* (pp. 43–71). London: Karnac.

Levine, H. B., Reed, G., & Scarfone, D. (Eds) (2013). *Unrepresented States and the Construction of Meaning*. London: Karnac/IPA.

Levy, R. (2012). From symbolizing to non-symbolizing within the scope of a link: from dreams to shouts of terror caused by an absent presence. *International Journal of Psychoanalysis*, *94*: 837–862.

Lewkowicz, S., & Flechner, S. (Eds.) (2005). *Truth, Reality, and the Psychoanalyst: Latin American Contributions to Psychoanalysis*. London: International Psychoanalytical Association.

Makari, G. (2008). *Revolution in Mind: The Creation of Psychoanalysis*. New York: Harpers.
Mann, H. (1905). *The Blue Angel*. Howard Fertig, 2009.
Marucco, N. (2007). Between memory and destiny: repetition. *International Journal of Psychoanalysis*, *88*: 309–328.
Marx, K. (1976). *Capital, Vol. 1*, B. Fowkes (Trans.). Harmondsworth: Penguin.
Marx, K., & Engels, F. (1932). *The German Ideology*. Eastford, CT: Martino, 2011.
Masson, J. M. (1984). *The Assault on Truth*. London: Fontana, 1992.
Masson, J. M. (1985). *The Complete Letters of Sigmund Freud to Wilhelm Fliess, 1887–1904*. Cambridge: Belknap Press of Harvard University Press.
Meltzer, D. (1983). *Dream-life: Re-examination of the Psycho-analytical Theory and Techniques*. Strath Tay: Clunie.
Meltzer, D. (2005). Creativity and countertransference. In: M. H. Williams (Ed.), *The Value of the Soulmaking: The Post-Kleinein Model of the Mind* (pp. 175–182). London: Karnac.
Miller, A. (1967). *Death of a Salesman*. New York: Viking Press.
Molière (1673). *The Hypochondriac*. Nick Hern Books, 1994.
Money-Kyrle, R. (1956). Normal countertransference and some of its deviations. In: *The Collected Papers of Roger Money-Kyrle* (pp. 220–342). Perth: Clunie.
Nagera, H. (1963). The developmental profile: notes on some practical considerations regarding its use. *Psychoanalytic Study of the Child*, *18*: 511–540.
Ogden, T. (1993). *The Matrix of the Mind: Object Relations and the Psychoanalytic Dialogue*. Lanham: Rowman & Littlefield.
Ogden, T. (1994). The analytical third: working with intersubjective facts. *International Journal of Psychoanalysis*, *75*: 3–19.
Ogden, T. (1997). *Reverie and Interpretation: Sensing Something Human*. New York: Jason Aronson.
Ogden, T. H. (2005). *This Art of Psychoanalysis: Dreaming Undreamt Dreams and Interrupted Cries*. Hove: Routledge.
Ogden, T. H. (2012). *Creative Readings: Essays on Seminal Analytic Works*. London: Routledge.
Orenstein, A. (2003). *A Ravel Reader: Correspondence, Articles, Interviews*. New York: Dover Publications.
Ornstein, R. E. (1972). *The Psychology of Consciousness* (4th revised & enlarged edn). New York: Penguin, 1986.
O'Shaughnessy, E. (1981). A commemorative essay on W. R Bion's theory of thinking. *Journal of Child Psychotherapy*, *7*: 181–192.

Paniagua, C. (2001). The attraction of topographical technique. *International Journal of Psychoanalysis*, *82*(4): 671–684.
Paniagua, C. (2008). Id analysis and technical approaches. *Psychoanalytic Quarterly*, *77*(1): 219–250.
Peterfreund, E. (1978). Some critical comments on psychoanalytic conceptualizations of infancy. *International Journal of Psychoanalysis*, *59*: 427–441.
Piaget, J. (1926). *The Language and Thought of the Child*. New York: Harcourt Brace.
Piaget, J., & Inhelder, B. (1959). *The Psychology of the Child*. New York: Basic Books.
Pine, F. (1981). In the beginning: contributions to a psychoanalytic developmental psychology. *International Review of Psycho-Analysis*, *8*: 15–33.
Pinker, S. (1994). *The Language Instinct*. New York: William Morrow.
Pirandello, L. (1917). *Right You Are If You Think You Are*. Players Press, 2002.
Popper, K. R. (1972). *Objective Knowledge: An Evolutionary Approach* (revised edn). Oxford: University Press, 1979.
Potter, D. (1978). *Pennies From Heaven*. BBC Television Drama.
Racker, H. (1957). The meanings and uses of countertransference. *Psychoanalytic Quarterly*, *26*: 303–357.
Reed, G. S. (2013). An empty mirror: reflections on nonrepresentation. In: H. B. Levine, G. S. Reed, & D. Scarfone (Eds.), *Unrepresented States and the Construction of Meaning* (pp. 18–41). London: Karnac.
Reitani, L. (2003). Poetiche della caducità. In: Schiller (1793), *Del sublime* (pp. 109–139). Milano: Abscondita.
Renik, O. (1998). The analyst's subjectivity and the analyst's objectivity. *International Journal of Psychoanalysis*, *79*: 487–497.
Rosen, Ch. (1975). *Schoenberg*. London: University of Chicago Press.
Rosenfeld, H. (1987). *Impasse and Interpretation*. London: Tavistock.
Rycroft, C. (1962). Beyond the reality principle. *International Journal of Psychoanalysis*, *43*: 388–394 [reprinted in *Imagination amd Reality* (pp. 102–113), 1968].
Rycroft, C. (1968). *Imagination and Reality*. New York: International Universities Press.
Sander, L. W. (1977). Regulation of exchange in the infant–caretaker system: a viewpoint on the ontogeny of "structures". In: N. Freedman & S. Grand (Eds.), *Communicative Structures and Psychic Structures* (pp. 13–34). New York: Plenum.
Sandler, A. (1975). Comments on the significance of Piaget's work for psychoanalysis. *International Review of Psychoanalysis*, *2*: 365–377.

Sandler, J. (1976a). Dreams, unconscious fantasies and "identity of perception". *International Review of Psychoanalysis*, *3*: 33–42.

Sandler, J. (1976b). Countertransference and role-responsiveness. *International Review of Psychoanalysis*, *3*: 43–47.

Sandler, P. C. (2005). *The Language of Bion*. London: Karnac.

Sapisochin, G. (2013). Second thoughts on Agieren: listening to the enacted. *International Journal of Psychoanalysis*, *94*: 967–991.

Scarfone, D. (2013). From traces to signs; presenting and representing. In: H. B. Levine; G. S. Reed, & D. Scarfone (Eds.), *Unrepresented States and the Construction of Meaning* (pp. 75–94). London: Karnac.

Scarfone, D. (2014). L'impassé, acutalité de l'inconscient. *Revue Française de Psychanalyse*, *78*(5). Presses Universitaires de France, Spécial Congrès.

Schafer, R. (1995). In the wake of Heinz Hartmann. *International Journal of Psychoanalysis*, *76*: 224–235.

Schur, M. (1966). *The Id and the Principles of Regulatory Functioning*. New York: International Universities Press.

Segal, H. (1956). Depression in the schizophrenic. *International Journal of Psychoanalysis*, *37*: 339–343.

Segal, H. (1957). Notes on symbol formation. *International Journal of Psychoanalysis*, *38*: 391–397.

Shakespeare, W. (1600). *Henry IV*. New York: Washington Square Press, 1994.

Shakespeare, W. (1611). *The Tempest*. London: Simon & Schuster, 2004.

Silverman, M. A. (1971). The growth of logical thinking: Piaget's contribution to ego psychology. *Psychoanalytic Quarterly*, *40*(2): 317–341.

Sodré, I. (1998). Death by daydreaming. In: *Psychoanalysis and Culture: A Kleinian Perspective*, D. Bell (Ed.). Tavistock/Duckworth: Tavistock Clinic Series, 1998, reprinted Karnac, 2004.

Spillius, E. B. (1988). *Melanie Klein Today, Vol. 1 (Mainly Theory)*. London: Routledge.

Spitz, R. A. (1945). Hospitalism: an inquiry into the genesis of psychiatric conditions in early childhood. *Psychoanalytic Study of the Child*, *1*: 53–74.

Stanton, A. (Dir.) (2008). *WALL-E*. Walt Disney Pictures, Pixar.

Sterba, R. (1934). The fate of the ego in analytic therapy. *International Journal of Psychoanalysis*, *15*: 117–126.

Stern, D. (1991). *The Interpersonal World of the Infant*. New York: Basic Books.
Strachey, J. (1955). Editor's Note. *From the History of an Infantile Neurosis. S.E., 17*: 3–6. London: Hogarth.
Strachey, J. (1958). Editor's Note to "Formulations on the two principles of mental functioning". *S.E., 12*: 215–217. London: Hogarth.
Symington, J., & Symington, N. (1996). *The Clinical Thinking of Wilfred Bion*. London: International Universities Press.
Tronick, E. Z. (2002). A model of infant mood states and Sandarian affective waves. *Psychoanalytic Dialogues, 12*(1): 73–99.
Tubert-Oklander, J. (2006). The individual, the group, and society: their psychoanalytic inquiry. *International Forum of Psychoanalysis, 15*: 151–156.
Tubert-Oklander, J. (2008). ¿De qué verdad hablamos? [What is the truth we are talking about?]. In: Pastor, M. (Ed.), *Testigos y testimonios. El problema de la verdad* [*Witnesses and testimonies: the problem of truth*] (pp. 47–71). Mexico City: Universidad Nacional Autónoma de México.
Tubert-Oklander, J. (2013). *Theory of Psychoanalytical Practice: A Relational Process Approach*. London: IPA/Karnac.
Tubert-Oklander, J. (2014). *The One and the Many: Relational Psychoanalysis and Group Analysis*. London: Karnac.
Tubert-Oklander, J. (2015). The wind and the tide: on personal acts and impersonal currents. *Canadian Journal of Psychoanalysis, 23*: 187–194.
Tubert-Oklander, J., & Beuchot Puente, M. (2008). *Ciencia mestiza. Psicoanálisis y hermenéutica analógica* [*Hybrid science: psychoanalysis and analogical hermeneutics*]. Mexico City: Torres.
Tubert-Oklander, J., & Hernández de Tubert, R. (2004). *Operative Groups: The Latin-American Approach to Group Analysis*. London: Jessica Kingsley.
Tuckett, D. (2011). *Minding the Markets: An Emotional Finance View of Financial Instability*. London: Palgrave Macmillan.
Vitale, S. (2005). *La dimore della lontanaza. Saggi sull'esperienza nello spazio intermedio*. Firenze: Clinamen.
Vozza, M. (2014). *Il nuovo infinito di Nietzsche. La futura obiettività tra arte e scienza*. Roma: Castelvecchi.
Winnicott, D. W. (1965). *The Maturational Process and the Facilitating Environment: Studies in the Theory of Emotional Development*. New York: International Universities Press.

Wollheim, R. (1969). The mind and the mind's image of itself. *International Journal of Psychoanalysis*, 50: 209–220.
Wollheim, R. (1971). *Freud*. London: Fontana.
Wollheim, R. (1984). *The Thread of Life*. Cambridge, MA: Harvard University Press.

INDEX

Abensour, L., 162
Abraham, K., 18, 22
adaptation, 8, 14, 21, 37, 81, 86, 107, 153, 157, 190, 227–228, 231
Adler, A., 21, 119
Adorno, T., 59
affect(ive), 77, 86–87, 110, 141, 153, 155, 206, 217–218, 231
   colouring, 73
   dangerous, 77
   disturbing, 77
   linkages, 234
   manifestations of, 9
   neurotic, 20
   pictograms, 87, 234
   powerful, 88
   states, 26
   tolerance, 157
   unnamed, 96
aggression, 23, 31, 180, 183, 192, 214
Agieren (acting out), 91

Aguayo, J., 21–22, 24, 222, 224, 230–232, 235
Allen, W., 80, 144
alpha, 160–161
   deficient, 160
   elements, 74, 76–77, 81, 87, 89, 126, 131, 140, 149, 153, 235
   function, 47, 66, 73–76, 81, 87, 92, 94, 103, 127, 129, 131–135, 137, 149, 154, 157–159, 229–230, 232–233, 235
   maternal, 116, 231
   super-, 132
   transformative, 74, 126
anger, 75, 78, 96, 136, 146
Anna Freud Centre, 73
anxiety, 55, 77, 101, 137, 162, 174, 176
   annihilation, 163
   castration, 216
   catastrophic, 34
   human, 176

intolerable, 49
   mood of, 167, 180, 238
apparatus, 87
   analytical, 178
   for thinking, 18, 66, 87, 217
   mechanical, 81
   mental, 9–10, 24, 41, 51, 86–88, 93, 124, 127, 134, 155, 228–229, 231–232
   of awareness, 26
   psychic(al), 7–8, 20, 51, 71, 86, 116, 130, 148, 153–154, 156, 175, 205, 226–228
   symbolisation, 87
après coup, 111, 124, 179, 202, 207, 209–211
Arendt, H., 62, 64, 179
auto-erotism, 10–12
autonomy, 71, 79, 139, 143–144, 158, 163

Baranger, M., 102, 143, 197
Baranger, W., 102, 197
Barros, E. L. R., 87, 91, 103, 234
behaviour(al), 34, 71, 78, 80, 82, 141, 144, 183, 191–192, 204
   human, 201
   parental, 189
   risky, 99
   uncontainable, 145
Bell, D., 62–64, 221, 223–224, 226, 229–231, 233–236
Berger, P. L., 194
beta elements, 74–75, 77, 81, 87, 89, 126, 131–132, 140, 149, 153, 217
Beuchot Puente, M., 200
Bion, W. R. (*passim*)
   cited works
      A theory of thinking, 29–30, 86–87, 95
      Attacks on linking, 28, 31, 91, 231
      Attention and Interpretation, 95, 100, 103, 132, 153–154, 157–160, 163, 196, 234

Cogitations, 87, 89, 93, 99, 116, 151, 154, 161, 228, 232
      Development of schizophrenic thought, 24, 26
      Differentiation of the psychotic from non-psychotic personalities, 25–27, 222
      Elements of Psycho-Analysis, 32
      Language and the schizophrenic, 25, 31
      Learning from Experience, 30, 47, 51–52, 74–76, 81, 103, 153–154, 157–158, 161, 196, 199, 217
      Notes on a theory of schizophrenia, 24
      Notes on memory and desire, 93, 100, 200
      On arrogance, 28–29, 224, 237
      Second Thoughts, 24, 26, 28–29, 33, 116
      Taming Wild Thoughts, 135
      The grid, 115
      The psychoanalytic theory of thinking, 29, 52, 87, 89, 232
      The Tavistock Seminars, 161
      Transformations, 46, 90
      Two Papers: The Grid and the Caesura, 115
      Wilfred Bion's Los Angeles Seminars and Supervision, 23
   K, 140, 217
   –K, 52
   O, 133, 139–141, 143, 145
Bleuler, E., 8, 21–22
Blum, H. P., 119
Bolognini, S., 79
Botella, C., 103, 164
Botella, S., 103, 164
Britton, R., 31
Brown, L. J., 32, 66, 72–74, 78–79, 91, 104, 124, 157, 228, 230, 232

Burghölzi Clinic, 21
Busch, F., 70, 75–76, 80–82,
    226–228, 230

caesura, 116–118, 125
Calderón de la Barca, P., 139
Caper, R., 89
Cassorla, R. M. S., 90, 94–95,
    102–103, 224, 228–229,
    231–232, 234
Chekhov, A., 135–136
Civitarese, G., 91, 115–116, 124–125,
    130, 195, 221–222, 227,
    230–231, 236–237
clinical vignettes
  Anna O, 207
  F, 33–35
  Jeff, 77–78
  John, 95–99, 104
  K, 49
  Manuela, 140
  Marco, 137–138
  Maristella, 138–139
  Mr A, 56
  Mr G, 53
  Mr M, 211–213
  Ms H, 44
  Sally, 79
  Stefano, 145–146
  Wolf Man, 111, 182, 189, 210–211,
    223
Conan Doyle, A., 109
conscious(ness) (*passim*) *see also*:
    unconscious
  activity of, 9–10, 20
  altered state of, 93
  awareness, 24, 82, 162
  censorship, 207
  connections, 88
  demand, 178
  dream, 95
    waking, 99
  elements, 81
  event, 41
  experience, 93

  false, 217
  fantasies, 89
  functions, 214
  image, 193
  impact, 199
  judgement, 217
  life, 126, 131
  meaning, 93
  mind, 127, 134, 229
  perceptions, 87, 175
  phantasies, 63
  pre-, 68, 76–78, 82, 152, 214,
    226
  psychology of, 81
  thinking, 67, 100, 202, 204–205,
    207, 214, 216, 226–227
  verbal, 88
  verbal, 193
  waking, 207
  will, 211
Controversial Discussions, 22
countertransference, 23, 35, 75, 84,
    89, 91–92, 197, 212 *see also*:
    transference
  dreams, 102, 104
  feelings, 75
  reaction, 75, 77
Cournut, J., 213
culture, 40, 166, 170–172, 176–177,
    179, 183, 193, 218, 236
  celebrity, 57
  crisis of, 171
  human, 40, 57
  psychoanalytic, 79
  religious, 176

Dante, A., 139
De Filippo, E., 139
De Marchi, E., 147
death
  -compulsion, 165, 172, 237
  drive, 40, 47–48, 55, 63, 171, 201,
    206
  instinct, 25, 36, 38, 57, 63,
    223–224, 235

mass, 172
noble, 42
paternal, 105, 111, 121
representation of, 219
wish, 14, 42, 112
depression, 33–34, 138, 188, 212, 218
   manic-, 22
   mother, 219
   position, 27–28, 38, 48, 50, 89, 100, 103, 146, 230
Derrida, J., 109
desire, 12, 48, 53, 58, 93, 95, 101, 103, 112, 116, 118, 122, 124–125, 131, 160, 163, 198, 202, 205, 211, 213, 216, 225, 237
   drive, 202, 206, 211, 218, 227
   experience of, 215, 227
   filicidal, 122
   forbidden, 88
   frustration of, 149, 231
   human, 178
   immediacy of, 178
   inadmissible, 106, 112, 237
   negation of, 235
   object of, 51, 157
   prohibited, 116
   realisation of, 86, 132
   repressed, 112, 130
   satisfaction of, 116
   unconscious, 213–214
destruction, 52–53, 60, 99, 149, 161, 217, 224–225
   active, 52
   instinct of, 52
   literal, 82
   self-, 40, 180
   runaway, 170
development(al), 10, 12–13, 25, 67, 76, 101–102, 114–115, 153, 166, 177, 228, 230, 238
   cultural, 180
   derailments, 20
   delayed, 81

ego, 12, 70–73, 81, 228
emotional, 160
human, 37
infantile, 64, 73
intellectual, 82
interferences, 72
mental, 51, 70, 126, 131, 135
normal, 31
of culture, 176
of object relations, 73
of secondary process thinking, 69
of the personality, 161
of the psyche, 157, 235
of the reality
   principle, 17, 154, 227
   testing, 66, 71
of thought, 50, 56, 72, 74, 86, 91, 137, 149, 157, 225, 232–233
of understanding, 55
pathological, 31
personal, 102
phase, 7, 130
process, 12, 210
psychic(al), 10, 31, 149, 152–153, 158, 161
psychological, 51
sexual, 10, 189
theoretical, 65
view, 65, 71
displacement, 9, 20, 76, 88, 92, 131, 157, 216
dream (*passim*)
   asleep, 89
   awake, 89
   book, 186
   capacity, 90 102, 231
   collective, 139
   counter-, 101
   day-, 10, 37, 41–43, 54, 87, 89, 91–92, 98, 219, 234
   diurnal, 102
   false, 95
   -for-two, 84, 90, 92, 229
      non-, 84, 90, 94
   image, 88, 213

manifest, 88–89, 95
meaningful, 94
meta-psychology of, 4
nature of, 106
night, 20, 91
nocturnal, 131, 135
non-, 88, 90–91, 93–96, 99–101, 103, 234
  psychotic, 102
-sensical, 13
-pictures, 161
positivist, 110
process, 84
theatre, 112
theory, 32, 154, 231
thoughts, 7, 13, 88, 93, 116–117, 236
  unconscious, 88–89, 92
traumatic
  non-, 88
un-, 84, 139
unconscious, 88–89, 97, 99
waking, 92, 99–100, 126, 132, 235
-work, 92, 154, 228, 232
drive(s), 48, 50, 81, 127, 133, 155–156, 179, 192, 205, 230
  aggressive, 183
  death, 40, 47–48, 55, 63, 171, 201, 206, 235
  derivatives, 153, 206, 213
  desires, 202, 206, 211, 218, 227
  ego, 117
  energy, 126, 131
  epistemophilic, 50, 52
  for knowledge, 50, 53
  for projection, 60
  individual, 205
  instinctual, 70, 72, 182, 190, 192
  life, 54
  need, 158
  of the psyche, 48
  parricidal, 121
  pressure, 165, 172, 237
  representations of, 89
  satisfaction, 156, 206, 212, 228
  sexual, 50, 130, 135, 171
  tension, 156
  theory, 48, 182–183, 192, 201, 206
Dumas, A., 142
dyad, 94, 102
  analytical, 90–92, 99, 229

Eagleton, T., 61
ego, 12, 23, 26, 28, 47, 49, 53, 65–66, 68–72, 74–77, 79–81, 115, 117, 129, 172, 176, 192, 201, 206, 215, 217–218, 226–228, 230
  auxiliary, 72, 228
  bodily, 47
  capacity, 158
  defence, 70
  development, 12, 73, 81
  drives, 117
  early, 71
  elaboration of the, 73
  empowering of the, 113
  functions, 25, 71–73, 81, 228
    inchoate, 228
    mature, 72
    superordinate, 230
  gratifications, 157
  human, 170
  ideal, 216
  individual, 124
  -instincts, 10, 21
  limitations of the, 72
  limitedness, 113
  mechanism, 66
  narcissistic, 64
  pleasure-, 11–12, 164, 171, 202, 215, 218, 227
  psychologists, 65–66, 79, 81–82, 228
  psychology, 70, 72, 77, 79, 81, 228
  psychotic's, 27
  reality-, 11–12, 164, 202, 215–216, 218, 227

reinforcement of the, 169
resistance, 70
-sphere, 124
splitting of, 62
-strengthening, 206
super-, 65–66, 69, 81, 102, 141, 162, 206, 216–217
susceptibility, 72
unconscious, 66, 70, 76–77
  defence, 76, 80
  resistance, 77
elements
  alpha, 74, 76–77, 81, 87, 89, 126, 131, 140, 149, 153, 235
  beta, 74–75, 77, 81, 87, 89, 126, 131–132, 140, 149, 153, 217
  distanced, 124
  essential, 36
  interconnected, 237
  K, 140
  mental, 162
  non-thought, 85
  of genuine contact, 35
  of totalitarianism, 64
  raw, 231
  sensorial, 131
  somato-sensory, 87
  textual, 108
    para-, 119, 121
  unconscious, 81
  undifferentiated, 144
Engels, F., 193
envy, 23, 27, 31, 53, 128, 141–142, 144, 213, 225
epistemophilic, 31
  drive, 50, 52
  instinct, 18, 28, 38, 230
  passion, 122
Eros, 103, 206
Escalona, S., 73
Eurydice, 110

Faimberg, H., 102
Fairbairn, W. R. D., 199

fantasy, ix, 37, 43–44, 63, 77, 88, 92, 103, 144, 146, 156, 162, 187–188, 191–192, 210
  activity, 92, 117
  default, 44
  level, 209
  life of, 92, 117
  primitive, 77
  reality of, 191, 208
  realm of, 208
  unconscious, 91, 191, 193
  world, 205
Feldman, M., 64
Ferenczi, S., 109, 175, 182, 188, 200, 223
Ferré, L., 176, 181
Ferro, A., 66, 74, 76–77, 103, 127–128, 132–133, 140, 209, 225, 229, 234–235
Fisher, J. V., 25
Flagey, D., 216
Flaubert, G., 54
Flechner, S., 143
free association, 163, 174, 207–209, 217–218
Freud, A., 73, 81
Freud, S. (*passim*)
  cited works
    A metapsychological supplement to the theory of dreams, 4, 154
    A project for a scientific psychology, 45, 62
    An outline of psycho-analysis, 48, 69, 155, 176, 227
    Analysis terminable and interminable, 69, 228
    Beyond the Pleasure Principle, 36, 40, 57, 62, 155, 164–165, 172, 206
    Civilization and its Discontents, 24, 40, 48, 167, 180–181, 218, 238
    Constructions in analysis, 91, 93

Index	261

Die Zerlegung der psychischen Persönlichkeit (The dissection of the psychical personality), 37
Eine Schwierigkeit der Psychoanalyse (A difficulty in the path of psycho-analysis), 205
Formulations on the two principles of mental functioning, 20, 30, 42, 51, 71, 81, 83, 85, 87–88, 92–93, 99, 107, 111–113, 116–117, 122, 124, 127, 129–130, 134, 148, 151–152, 155, 157, 159, 164, 166, 169–172, 179, 185–186, 190, 198–200, 205, 207, 214, 216, 223, 226–229, 231–233, 236
From the History of an Infantile Neurosis, 111, 189, 210
Group Psychology and the Analysis of the Ego, 59
Inhibitions, Symptoms and Anxiety, 155
Instincts and their vicissitudes, 11, 64, 192
Introductory Lectures on Psycho-Analysis, 189
Letter #82. The Origins of Psychoanalysis, 57, 199
Letter from Sigmund Freud to Arnold Zweig, 169
Moses and Monotheism, 193
Mourning and melancholia, 192
Negation, 9, 47, 52, 235
Neurosis and psychosis, 26–27, 50, 155–156
New Introductory Lectures on Psycho-analysis, 43, 65, 68–70, 81, 206, 218, 226, 236
On Aphasia, 164

On beginning the treatment, 90
On dreams, 109
On narcissism: an introduction, 39
Project for a Scientific Psychology, 4, 185
Psychical (or mental) treatment, 174
Psycho-analytic Notes on an Autobiographical Account of a Case of Paranoia (dementia paranoides), 3, 18–19
Recommendations to physicians practising psychoanalysis, 90, 93
Remembering, repeating and working-through, 81, 91
Studies on Hysteria, 63, 198, 220
The economic problem of masochism, 205
The Ego and The Id, 42, 47, 68–69, 103, 153, 155, 205–206, 226
The Freud/Jung Letters: The Correspondence Between Sigmund Freud and C. G. Jung, 19, 119
The Future of an Illusion, 40
The Interpretation of Dreams, 4, 6, 14, 50, 56, 62, 86, 88, 111, 154–155, 169–170, 185–186, 199–200, 226
The loss of reality in neurosis and psychosis, 162
The neuro-psychoses of defence, 6, 152
The splitting of the ego in the process of defence, 63
The unconscious, 9, 24, 68, 153, 155, 164, 226
Thoughts for the times on war and death, 171, 180
Three Essays on the Theory of Sexuality, 189

Totem and Taboo, 40, 193
"Wild" psycho-analysis, 52, 82
Freud, W. E., 73
function
  alpha, 30–32, 47, 66, 73–76,
    81, 87, 92, 94, 103, 116,
    126–127, 129, 131–135, 137,
    149, 154, 157–159, 229–233,
    235
  analyst's, 28
  cognitive, 47
  conscious, 214
  ego, 25, 71–73, 81, 228, 230
  expressive, 103
  fundamental, 160
  human, 206
  intellectual, 216
  mathematical, 30
  mental, 7, 20, 26, 44, 48, 51, 85,
    87, 91, 126, 129, 131,
    134–135, 144, 186, 202,
    204–206, 215, 219–220, 227,
    235
  neurotic, 94
  nocturnal dream, 135
  of attention, 8
  of dreaming, 228
  of *parergon*, 111
  of phantasy, 46
  of reality, 6
  of the psyche, 115
  of thought, 164
  oneiric, 132
  pathological, 139
  primordial, 94
  psychic, 54, 106, 115, 152,
    154–155, 165, 172, 181, 201,
    206, 237
  psychotic, 95
  reality, 119
  reparative, 209
  thinking, 30
  unconscious, ix
  unspecified, 73
  waking dream, 126, 132, 235

Gabbard, G. O., 91
Gadamer, H.-G., 200
Gardner, S., 46
Gariepy-Boutin, C., 82
Genette, G., 109, 111, 124
Ginzburg, C., 109
Goethe, J. W., 52, 139
Gray, P., 70
Green, A., 72, 76, 100, 103, 161–162,
  210–211, 213
Greenberg, J., 80
Grinberg, L., 91, 157
Grotstein, J., 88, 132, 140, 145
Guntrip, H., 31

hallucination, 7–8, 20, 41, 45, 51, 57,
  71, 88, 90, 93, 106, 112,
  116–117, 132, 156–157, 159,
  178, 211
  images, 114
  manner, 7
  negative, 150, 162–163, 225,
    233
  psychosis, 6, 20
  realisation, 86
  route, 116
  satisfaction, 116
  wish-fulfilment, 20, 43, 66, 178,
    200, 232
  world, 117
Hampstead Clinic, 73, 81
Hartmann, H., 65–66, 70–73, 81,
  228
Harvey, D., 61
Heidegger, M., 114, 124
Heimann, P., 23, 91, 191, 222
Hernández de Tubert, R., 194,
  196
Homer, 101, 143
Hugo, V., 143
hypnosis, 207–208
hypothesis, 95, 112, 157, 175, 192,
  197, 211, 232
  audacious, 188
  frustration, 65–66, 71

id, 27, 69–70, 72, 76, 81, 206, 218, 227–228
identity, 61
　analytical, 98
　enhanced, 137
　non-, 53
　perceptual, 56–57, 156–157
illusion, 39–40, 56–57, 62, 123, 166, 168–169, 172, 176, 180, 236
Imbeault, J., 171
Inhelder, B., 72
instinct(ual), 22, 72, 146, 192
　death, 25, 36, 38, 57, 63, 223–224
　demands, 31
　drive, 70, 190, 192
　　theory, 182
　ego, 10, 21
　epistemophilic, 18, 28, 38, 230
　life, 25, 63
　of aggression, 180
　of destruction, 52
　satisfaction, 236
　sexual, 10–12, 18, 21, 43, 63, 81, 117, 201
　source, 169
　strength of the, 72
　taming of, 79
　wishes, 20, 228
International Psychoanalytical Association, 21
intervention, 74, 90, 98, 138, 163, 186
　analyst's, 82
　complicated, 98
introjection, 103, 116, 125, 134, 160
Isaacs, S., 43, 86, 191, 222

Janet, P., 6, 115, 119, 122
Janus, 40, 80
jealousy, 119, 136, 141–142, 144
Jones, E., 3, 63, 67, 185, 187
Joseph, B., 55, 76, 89
Jung, C. G., 18–19, 21–22, 24, 109, 119–122, 222

Katz, M., 195
Klein, É., 173
Klein, M., 18, 22–26, 30–32, 40, 48–50, 76, 83, 85, 159, 223–224
　cited works, 22, 30, 47, 55, 86–87, 89, 191, 222, 231
　death of, 29
　Dick, 47
　epistemophilic instinct, 18, 28, 31, 38, 52
　formulations, 31
　implicit assumptions, 35
　infant's phantasmic relationship, 31
　key concepts, 31
　notion of unconscious phantasy, 234
　on fantasy, 191
　on the nature of psychosis, 222
　pathological view of the infant, 31
Kris, E., 79
Kristeva, J., 111

Lacan, J., 178, 191, 210
Laplanche, J., 43, 63, 199, 210
Levine, H. B., 103, 148–150, 157, 163, 224–225, 231–233
Levy, R., 103
Lévy-Strauss, C., 191
Lewkowicz, S., 143
life (*passim*)
　adult, 212
　after-, 11, 117
　beginnings of, 50, 69, 71–72, 228
　bodily, 192
　boring, 54
　civilised, 125
　communal, 180
　conscious, 126, 131
　daily, 139
　day-to-day, 219
　drive, 54
　earliest, 72
　emotional, 94
　eternal, 176

everyday, 57, 145, 178, 208, 219
experience, 157
family, 214
fantasy, 92, 117
human, 165, 222
individual, 131
instinct, 25
internal, 113
mental, 7, 20, 23, 40, 53, 56, 160
nature of, 132
pace of, 166, 171
personal, 118
phantasy, 12
psychic, 201, 237
real, 6, 19, 130
realities of, 40
satisfying, 219
-saving defence, 55
sexual, 63, 199
socioeconomic, 59
-style, 143
success in, 45
waking, 117
work, 67
Luckmann, T., 194

Makari, G., 21
Mann, H., 132, 139
Marucco, N., 103
Marx, K., 57, 59, 64, 193
Masson, J. M., 187–188, 199–200
maternal, 31–32, 116, 233
    approaches, 73
    attitudes, 219
    body, 31
    provision, 22
    response, 157
    reverie, 31, 232
    warmth, 114
Meltzer, D., 88, 94, 101
Miller, A., 54
Molière, 139
Mom, J., 102
Money-Kyrle, R., 91

mourning, 106, 122–123, 128, 133, 136, 229

Nagera, H., 73
narcissism, 4, 45, 151–153, 171, 214, 216
    ego, 64
    infantile, 39
    injury, 139, 216
    primary, 30
neurosis, 6, 11–12, 115, 122, 130, 152, 162, 182, 202, 205, 208–210, 217, 220, 223
notation, 8, 20, 29, 32, 127, 134, 149–150, 152–154, 163, 227, 229
not-knowing, 50, 93, 95, 100–101, 230

object(ive) (*passim*)
    absent, 52, 123, 149, 158, 225, 231–233
    bad, 52, 64, 217
    bizarre, 24, 27, 87
    cultural, 57
    desired, 51, 157
    external, 63–64, 149, 156, 158, 231
    facilitating, 158
    facts, 43
    fantastic, 59
    feared, 124
    frustrating, 159
    good, 50
    gratifying, 156
    impressions of, 233–234
    inanimate, 71
    internal, 133, 217, 219, 231, 234
    love, 12, 103, 189
    malign, 52, 233
    material, 191, 200
    part, 101
    persecutory, 159
    presentation, 164
    primal, 211

psychoanalytic, 163
real, 10, 42, 92
reality, 43, 208
relations, 23, 31, 48, 49, 55, 66,
    73, 86, 91, 153, 182, 186, 192,
    213–214, 228–229
sexual, 11
social, 64
transferential, 89
valid, 196
wished for, 45
objectivity, 43, 61
of perception, 205
richer, 113
oedipal, 89
complex, 224
configurations, 224
couple, 224
situation, 224, 237
stage, 89
theme, 111
triangulation, 89–90
Oedipus, 28, 121, 224
attitude, 189
complex, 28, 189–190
drive, 224
situation, 28
Ogden, T., 88, 90–91, 110, 139, 209
Orenstein, A., 170
Ornstein, R. E., 190
Orpheus, 110
O'Shaughnessy, E., 48–49

Paniagua, C., 79
paranoid, 200
dread, 50
psychosis, 152
–schizoid position, 23, 49–50, 59,
    100, 103, 146, 203
parergon, 109, 111, 119
perception, 45–46, 85–86, 91,
    116–117, 152, 155, 157, 162,
    186, 192, 194, 202, 205, 210,
    234
conscious, 87, 175

distortion of, 56, 205
identity of, 56–57
mis-, 23, 34
real, 46, 234
sense, 183, 190, 223
Peterfreund, E., 71
phantasy, 10–12, 42–46, 63–64, 92,
    234, 236
activity, 43, 235
concept of, 54
structures, 64
unconscious, 37, 43, 234
wishful, 50
Piaget, J., 72, 81–82
Pine, F., 71
Pinker, S., 72
Pirandello, L., 139
Pontalis, J.-B., 43, 63, 210
Popper, K. R., 191
posteriority (*Nachträglichkeit*), 108,
    110–111, 124
Potter, D., 64
principle (*passim*)
anti-thought, 48
economic, 10
fiction, 123
Mephistophelian, 52
methodological, 108
of mental functioning, 7, 20, 48,
    51, 215, 227
of non-contradiction, 122, 141
of research, 207
pleasure, 4, 7–13, 17–18, 20–21,
    25–26, 30, 32, 36–37, 40–42,
    44, 47–50, 67, 81, 86, 92, 103,
    106, 110, 112, 115–117, 122,
    124, 127–130, 144, 148, 151,
    155–156, 166, 169–170, 176,
    186, 199, 201, 203, 205–207,
    215, 218, 223, 225–229, 231,
    234–237
–unpleasure, 7, 20, 40, 151, 155
reality, 4, 7, 10–12, 14, 17–18,
    20–21, 24–28, 30–32, 36–37,
    40, 42, 46–47, 51, 67, 92, 103,

106–107, 110, 112–113,
115–118, 122–123, 125,
127–130, 144, 149, 152, 154,
156, 160, 164, 166, 169–171,
178, 186, 190, 197, 199–200,
205, 215, 218, 221, 227–231,
235–237
  regulatory, 149, 155, 156, 158
  unpleasure, 7, 148, 155–156, 226
projection, 49–50, 60, 128, 144, 225
  fantasised, 59
  mythical, 11
projective, 23
  discharges, 96
  evacuation, 26, 29
  identification, 23–24, 26, 31, 35,
    49, 64, 84, 87, 91, 103,
    133–134, 145, 149, 157,
    159–160, 225, 231, 233
    communicative, 232
    mutual, 209
    processes, 233
    regressive systems, 60

Racker, H., 91
rage, 79, 128, 138, 142, 144, 160,
  225
  homicidal, 128, 225
  seething, 136
Rapaport, D., 66, 81
Ravel, M., 166, 168–172, 236
Reed, G. S., 103, 163
regulation, 125, 155–156, 186
  mutual, 73
  principles, 4, 67, 149, 151,
    155–156, 158
  self-, 71–72
Reitani, L., 118
Renik, O., 61
repression, 6–9, 11, 13, 20, 42–43,
  52, 65, 69, 74, 87, 92, 102, 114,
  124, 131, 162–163, 178, 205,
  213, 217, 226
  aspects, 87
  continuance of, 52

desire, 112, 130
  of pleasure, 124
  psychical structures, 13
  unconscious, 36, 40, 69, 90, 103,
    126, 173
reverie, 77, 84, 87, 91–94, 96, 100,
  103, 133, 135, 149, 154, 234
  capacity, 91–94, 99, 160, 234
  images, 92
  maternal, 31, 134, 232
  state, 93, 95, 163
revision, 6, 28, 79, 199
  fundamental, 69, 226
  secondary, 88, 92
Rivière, J., 191, 222
Rosen, Ch., 171
Rosenfeld, H., 22, 91
Rossini, G., 117
Rycroft, C., 199

Salome, A., 100
Sander, L. W., 71
Sandler, A., 81
Sandler, J., 49, 55, 64
Sandler, P. C., 115
Sapisochin, G., 103
Scarfone, D., 103, 163, 175–176
Schafer, R., 81
schizophrenia, 25–27, 53, 61
  mechanisms, 22, 30
  thinking, 24
Schur, M., 154–156, 164, 226
Segal, H., 22, 27, 47, 60, 64, 86, 103
self, 26, 40, 48, 50, 143, 155, 217
  -accusation, 121
  -analysis, 187, 208
  -constructed, 64
  -contempt, 34
  -contradiction, 68
  -deception, 40, 60, 62, 199
  -destruction, 180
  -devaluing, 34
  -discipline, 13, 112
  -enclosed, 229
  -knowledge, 102

-loathing, 34
-perpetuating, 161
-preservation, 71
-psychology, 183, 192
-reflection, 89
-regulating, 71–72
-reproach, 13
sense of, 150, 162–163, 225, 233
sexual(ly), 117, 199, 216
    abuse, 187
    attraction, 189
    curiosity, 216
    development, 10, 189
    dialect, 145
    dimension, 224
    drive, 50, 130, 135, 171, 183
    instincts, 10–12, 18, 21, 43, 81, 117, 201
        death, 63
        life, 63
    intercourse, 189, 210
    life, 199
    metaphor, 133
    narrative genre, 133
    nature, 130–131
    object, 11
    oriented, 28
    situations, 99
    theory of libido, 21
    wishes, 48, 192
sexuality, 121, 124–125, 127, 133, 222
    adult, 199
    bi-, 10
Shakespeare, W., 41, 103
Silverman, M. A., 81
Sodré, I., 54
Sor, D., 157
Spillius, E. B., 64
Spitz, R. A., 81
splitting, 10, 21, 26, 29, 42, 44, 49–50, 87, 92, 163, 188, 219–220
    processes, 217
    psychotic, 26
    vertical, 63

Stanton, A., 142
Stekel, W., 21
Sterba, R., 70
Stern, D., 71
Strachey, J., 67, 148, 151–152, 189, 222
subject(ive), 10, 88, 114–115, 125, 133, 178, 188, 193, 195, 198, 204, 207–210, 214, 220, 224
    attuned, 31, 231
    experience, 22, 191, 209
    inter-, 87, 90–91, 154
        aspect, 234
        connection, 230
        exchange, 232
        viewpoint, 228
    isolated, 114, 230
    receptive, 31, 231
    truth, 140
    weakened, 113
subjectivity
    established, 114
    inter-, 115
    proto-, 124–125
symbol(-ic), 47, 75, 83, 86–87, 97, 102–103, 114, 120, 125, 163, 193, 232
    apparatus, 87
    area, 102
    capacity, 85, 89–90, 125, 224
    emotional thoughts, 87
    equation, 24, 47, 103
    formation, 83
    imagetic, 88
    impaired, 91
    network, 86, 90–91, 94, 96–97, 102, 234
    order, 125
    process, 88
    representation, 86
    systems, 191, 195, 197
    transference, 76
    unconscious network, 88
    verbal, 88, 97

Symington, J., 160, 164
Symington, N., 160, 164

Tabak de Bianchedi, E., 157
Thanatos, 103
theory (*passim*)
  aetiological, 187–188
  Bionian, 115, 127, 157, 202, 229
  bodily, 47
  critical, 59
  developing, 39–40
  dream, 32
  drive, 48, 182–183, 192, 201, 206
  field, 105, 127, 134
  Freudian, 59, 114, 117, 131, 186, 192
  libido, 22
  meta-, 29–30
  object relations, 91
  of alpha function, 232
  of container–contained, 127, 229
  of dreams, 154, 231
  of hermeneutics, 200
  of infantile development, 64
  of intrapsychic agencies, 179
  of knowledge, 124
  of mind, 185
  of neuroses, 187
  of representation, 153, 158–159
  of schizophrenia, 24
  of thinking, 29–30, 100, 202
  psychoanalytic, 66, 114, 176, 192–193, 206, 220–221
  seduction, 182, 187, 189, 208, 223
  sexual, 21
  stage-like, 42
  structural, 65, 153, 227
  trauma, 111
  tripartite, 227
transference, 55–56, 76, 78, 89, 92, 175, 178, 197, 208–209, 211–213, 233 *see also*: countertransference
  analytic(al), 202, 208, 211
    relationship, 209
  constellation, 213
  enactment, 56
  experience, 209
  father, 212
  interpretations, 213
  movements, 219
  neurosis, 202, 208–209, 220
  positive, 212
  symbolic, 76
  wish, 213
transferential
  fantasies, 89
  object, 89
trauma(tic), 72, 85, 87–88, 90–91, 94, 102, 158, 176, 210–211
  childhood, 187
  effect, 187–188
  events, 188, 212
  experiences, 211–212
    separation, 219
  reality, 87, 172
  theory, 111, 187
  transformation, 103
Tronick, E. Z., 71
truth (*passim*)
  by correspondence, 195
  catastrophic, 133
  consensual/social, 118, 184, 196–197, 223–224
  disturbing, 61
  emotional, 145, 196
  existential, 137
  experience of, 196
  expressive, 184, 196–197, 223
  historical, 196
  illusion-, 62
  internal, 128, 193, 225
  narrative, 184, 196, 198, 223
  pragmatic, 184, 195, 197, 223
  psychic, 29, 141
  psychoanalytic, 197
  renunciation of, 144
  rhetorical, 118

scientific, 118, 195
semantic, 184, 195, 197, 223
subjective, 140
sublimated, 170
syntactical/logical, 184, 195, 197, 223
unsavoury, 198
Tubert-Oklander, J., 182–184, 188, 192–193, 195–197, 220, 223
Tuckett, D., 64

unconscious(ness) (*passim*) *see also*: conscious
   avoidance, 214
   communication, 77
   component, 226
   comprehension, 88
   connection, 88
   content, 74, 131
   creation of meaning, 66
   defences, 74
   denial, 121
   descriptive, 74
   desire, 213–214
   dream, 88–89, 99–100
      thoughts, 88–89, 92, 97
      waking, 92
   dynamic, 40
   ego, 66, 77
      defence, 76, 80
      resistances, 70, 77
   elements, 81
   event, 175
   exchanges, 84
   factors, 112
   fantasies, 86, 91, 190–191, 193
   forces, 206
   internal objects, 234
   longing, 215
   material, 84
   meaning, 93, 100
   mentation, 193
   motive, 218
   network, 88
   phantasies, 13, 37, 43, 63, 234
   processes, 13, 205, 226
      mental, 7
      psychic, 63, 116, 130
   prohibitions, 201, 206
   purpose, 74
   representation, 205
   repressed, 36, 69, 90, 103, 126, 163, 173
   roots, 181
   state, 233
   strength of the, 72
   thinking, 67, 79, 88, 202, 204, 207, 227
   wish, 88, 201, 206, 212–215
      death, 112
      instinctual, 228

vicissitudes, 94, 131, 133, 149, 158
   scientific, 118
Vienna Psycho-Analytical Society, 3
violence, 30, 48, 98, 102, 133, 141, 144–146, 187
   psychotic, 52
Vitale, S., 109
Vozza, M., 113

war, 59, 170–171, 180
   cold, 121
   First World, 165, 170–171, 179, 237
   post-, 172, 179
   Second World, 22
Winnicott, D. W., 114, 149, 157, 210, 220, 230–231
Wollheim, R., 45, 47, 63
world
   alternative, 54
   civilised, 174
   contemporary, 60
   external, 7–8, 12, 20, 25, 51, 64, 69, 71–72, 86, 90, 93, 116, 130, 153, 155, 227–228
   fantasy, 205
   -forming, 114
   imaginary, 54

in conflict, 179
inner, 37, 89, 112, 208, 210
invented, 54
material, 183, 190–191, 200, 223
non-existent, 137, 142
of hallucination, 106, 117
of nothingness, 48
of phantasy, 12, 236
of pleasure, 49
of shades, 110

omnipotent, 45
parallel, 143
pleasurable, 55
political, 166, 171, 236
psychical, 70
real, 171
solipsistic, 114
third, 191
uninhabitable, 142
view, 89